THE ORANGEBURG MASSACRE

THE
ORANGEBURG
MASSACRE

Jack Nelson and Jack Bass

THE WORLD PUBLISHING COMPANY
New York and Cleveland

Published by THE WORLD PUBLISHING COMPANY
2231 West 110th Street, Cleveland, Ohio 44102
Published simultaneously in Canada by
NELSON, FOSTER & SCOTT LTD.

First Printing—1970

COPYRIGHT © 1970 BY JACK NELSON AND JACK BASS

Library of Congress Catalog Card Number: 76–124283

PRINTED IN THE UNITED STATES OF AMERICA

WORLD PUBLISHING
TIMES MIRROR

". . . in pursuit of human dignity."

CONTENTS

ACKNOWLEDGMENTS

MANY PERSONS helped make possible our book, which essentially is a documentary. Professor Thomas F. Pettigrew of Harvard University, who wrote the foreword, first suggested that we write the book so that Orangeburg would "not be forgotten in the larger national context."

More than 100 persons were interviewed, some for several hours. We want to acknowledge by name a few who were especially helpful and generous of their time—former U.S. Attorney General Ramsey Clark; Stephen Pollak, former director of the Justice Department's civil rights division; Everett Waldo of the U.S. Commission on Civil Rights, and Dean of Men Oscar Butler of South Carolina State College.

Several South Carolina officials graciously provided information. They included Attorney General Daniel R. McLeod, Lt. Gov. John C. West, Highway Patrol Commander P. Frank Thompson, and National Guard General Robert L. McCready.

We are indebted to Howard Glickstein, director of the U.S.

Commission on Civil Rights, and to Jerris Leonard, Mr. Pollak's successor in the Justice Department, for the cooperation of their offices and for making available extensive files on Orangeburg. Other files were made available by the Southern Regional Council in Atlanta and by M. Hayes Mizell of the American Friends Service Committee in South Carolina. Dean Livingston, publisher of the *Times and Democrat* in Orangeburg, opened his newspaper files to us. Attorney Matthew Perry of Columbia permitted our use of his voluminous court transcripts.

For reading portions of the manuscript and for making helpful suggestions we thank author James McBride Dabbs of Mayesville, S.C.; Professor Robert J. Moore of Columbia College, Columbia, S.C.; Charles Morgan, Jr., southern director of the American Civil Liberties Union; and Bruce Galphin, Atlanta bureau chief of the *Washington Post*.

We are grateful for the understanding shown by the *Los Angeles Times* and *The Charlotte Observer* in permitting us to schedule our work time so that we would have time to write the book.

We owe a special thanks to President M. Maceo Nance, Jr., of South Carolina State College and to the college's faculty and students for their full cooperation.

FOREWORD

ON MARCH 21, 1960, a throng of unarmed, protesting Africans marched on a police station in Sharpeville, South Africa. The focus of their demonstration involved elementary justice, for it was aimed against the bitterly resented requirements for Africans to carry with them at all times identification and permission papers. Yet the tense government police began firing wildly into the crowd. In a matter of seconds, at least seventy-two Africans were killed and two hundred seriously hurt in the blood bath.

On February 8, 1968, a throng of angry, frustrated black-American students faced off heavily armed police on the grounds of their own college campus in Orangeburg, South Carolina. The focus of their demonstration also involved elementary justice, for it was aimed against the exclusion of blacks from a local bowling alley. Yet the tense police began firing wildly into the unarmed crowd. In a matter of seconds, there was an American blood bath.

The parallels between Sharpeville and Orangeburg are chilling and undeniable. But they break down in one major respect. The Sharpeville Massacre entered the annals of world infamy, and March 21, 1970, witnessed memorial observances around the globe a decade later. It was accurately and widely reported; and it was responded to in a manner befitting the event. Even the United States Department of State, not noted for its critical actions toward South Africa, issued an unprecedented statement of condemnation.

In sharp contrast, the Orangeburg Massacre, if it were heard about in the first place, is barely remembered by the world. It was generally either distorted or ignored by the mass media, and it was not responded to in any manner befitting the event. *Time* magazine didn't mention it, and the Associated Press never saw fit to correct its grossly incorrect initial reports of students exchanging gunfire with the police. Later assessments of the media's general failure specifically cited three outstanding exceptions to the poor coverage: The *Los Angeles Times, The Charlotte Observer*, and the National Broadcasting Company. The first two of these sources printed the real story of Orangeburg, because they were represented by the authors of this significant volume. Jack Nelson and Jack Bass are prize-winning young white southern journalists who believe passionately in the truth and in the interracial future of their native region. They are virtually the only reporters who could have written this book, and we are in their debt for their having done so.

Why is this accurate report of the Orangeburg Massacre so necessary? Why was the record not set straight in the initial reporting as with the Sharpeville Massacre? And why was America, indeed the world, so apathetic toward it? Surely, the fact that the number of casualties was much smaller is not an answer. Recall the intense interest in the triple civil rights murders near Philadelphia, Mississippi, a few years before. And recall, too, the worldwide attention paid to the Little Rock, Arkansas, school desegregation crisis back in 1957 in which no deaths occurred.

Nor can we account for the inattention to the Orangeburg "incident," as it came to be belittled, by the "persuasive" explanation of the event by the governor of South Carolina. Had the rest of the nation and the world grown accustomed to accepting the official versions of civil rights violence rendered by white southern politicians? Hardly. Was Governor George Wallace's explanation for the Selma bridge brutality in 1965 taken seriously? Or Governor Orval Faubus' slanted description of the Arkansas school crisis in 1957? Or Governor Ross Barnett's colorful propaganda about the Oxford, Mississippi confrontation over the entrance of James Meredith into the University of Mississippi in 1962? Why, then, was Governor Robert McNair's defensive version of the Orangeburg events in 1968 so immediately reported as the definitive interpretation and so readily accepted?

Nelson and Bass suggest a harsh answer. Unlike the earlier tragedies, Orangeburg followed a succession of race riots in major northern cities: First the Watts uprising in Los Angeles, then the spread of disturbances to cities ranging from Boston to San Francisco, and finally the culminating violence in Newark and Detroit. White America was frightened and its mood shifted. The Bull Connors and Sheriff Clarks who had served as the racial villains in the early 1960s were being replaced by the Rap Browns and the Panthers. Incorrectly described as a "backlash," the shift is best seen as a polarization of racial opinion fueled by fear and uncertainty. This mood heightened when eight weeks after Orangeburg, Dr. Martin Luther King, Jr., was murdered in Memphis, followed in ten weeks by the murder of Robert Kennedy in Los Angeles. And the climax to the grim year of 1968 came when the country elected a plurality president who ranked order over justice and openly ran his campaign on the basis of "a southern strategy." Add to this deteriorating situation the fact that it developed in the context of a costly and unpopular war, and one can hardly be surprised that the Orangeburg Massacre gained scant attention or concern throughout the nation.

In short, the media largely misrepresented the Orangeburg events of February 8, 1968, because these events were out of tune with the times. Had it occurred three or four years earlier, the Orangeburg Massacre would almost undoubtedly have achieved considerable notoriety and, perhaps, have led to constructive reforms. But in 1968 it was not "news." It was more in keeping with the national mood either to ignore the "incident" or to accept uncritically Governor McNair's strained explanation. With riots raging in northern streets, it was not difficult for many to believe that the students had been armed and had opened fire upon the police. Many probably still believe this version of the confrontation, and this book should prove enlightening in this respect.

But the value of this volume goes far beyond the function of simply setting the record straight, important as that is to its victims. By intensively exploring the development of this specific crisis, the actual confrontation as seen from "both sides," and the shabby events that followed, the authors present us with the raw data that pose hard questions for the future of American race relations. Their first-class reporting provides us with a front-row seat for viewing a drama that in the end involves us not as spectators but participants.

Carefully and tirelessly, Nelson and Bass accumulate the facts that enable us not only to understand the Orangeburg Massacre but also to grasp the depth of the factors which can always coalesce again to reproduce the tragedy. Their story answers why black college youth today are so singularly alienated from their country, why they find it almost impossible to believe that we shall in fact "overcome." And it implicates not only officials of South Carolina from local town authorities to the timid governor but also members of the Federal Bureau of Investigation as well. Yet it implicates far more—the media, the courts, and all of us who took the news so calmly.

Not a sensational exposé, *The Orangeburg Massacre* is a thoughtful and thorough exploration of a stained page in American history. Hopefully, the volume will ensure that the tragic episode is no longer ignored or distorted by thoughtful Americans. More important, the volume offers insight into the root causes of such events which must be attacked directly. Nelson and Bass wrote their important book not to generate still more white American guilt, an ineffective response at best, but to spur us to act to ensure that American citizens in search of their rights are never again shot down in the dark by "officers of the law."

THOMAS F. PETTIGREW
Professor of Social Psychology
Harvard University
April 1970

1 : PROLOGUE

Someone said Smitty was down there and I walked
back down to the field to see what was happening. When I
was walking down, people were hollering not to throw
anything because we didn't want to make them angry; all
we wanted was to see them put out the fire and see what
was happening . . . they opened up with gunfire without
warning. My first initial reaction was that they were
shooting blanks trying to frighten us. So I turned when
I heard the gunfire and then somebody next to me hollered,
"Oh, Lord, I'm hit." So immediately, I fell to the ground.
Upon falling, I felt a blow in the back of my leg which
felt like a piece of brick or something had been thrown
against it. So I stayed on the ground maybe a half-second
and got up and ran a step or two farther and was hit in the
hip. I got up and ran again . . . and was shot a third time
in the armpit . . . I hid behind a trash can.

Charles Hildebrand, a student at South Carolina State College in Orangeburg, was testifying about events on the night of February 8, 1968. Smitty was Henry Smith, who was typical of hundreds of activist black students throughout the South protesting discrimination and inferior facilities and rebelling against the conservatism of older southern Negroes. He was a major figure in the events of February 8, referred to politely as the "Orangeburg incident" in South Carolina and as the "Orangeburg Massacre" among civil-rights activists and the black community throughout America. Regardless of the label, the events shattered a record of racial peace that had made South Carolina unique in the Deep South.

These events occurred at a time when the nation was divided over the racial issues and its concern was increasing over how to react to growing black militancy. It was the winter after major riots in Detroit, Newark, and other cities caused damage in the millions of dollars and resulted in the death of scores of Negroes.

South Carolina had been making the painful transition from the old order to the new much more smoothly than the rest of the Deep South and without a single death attributed to civil-rights activity. The state's governor, forty-four-year-old Robert E. McNair, had followed and widened the path of moderate leadership shown by his predecessors.

When opposed by a Republican with a segregationist image in the 1966 campaign for governor, McNair used the state's record of racial peace to advantage and received 99 percent of the vote cast by Negroes. In his January 1967 inaugural address—with Alabama's George and Lurleen Wallace sitting on the platform—McNair said, "I intend to use all of the authority and influence at my command to see that the good name of our state is not tarnished." The events at Orangeburg not only tarnished the good name of the state, but accelerated as well as reflected the national mood of black militancy.

Orangeburg, a staunchly conservative, rural-oriented town of 20,000 located forty miles southeast of the state capital at Columbia, was the home of two predominantly Negro colleges, Claflin and South Carolina State.

Students at the two Negro colleges traditionally had little contact with downtown Orangeburg, but in the fall of 1967, the local newspaper, the *Times and Democrat*, sponsored a special fifty-six-page supplement on State College, loaded with institutional ads "welcoming" the college's 1,500 students. Mayor E. O. Pendarvis and publisher Dean Livingston were hosts at a luncheon on campus, by far the most attention official Orangeburg had ever shown the college.

Claflin University, with an enrollment of 800, was affiliated with the Methodist Church. Started after the Civil War, it was named for its founder, Boston philanthropist Lee Claflin, who also founded Boston University. The Orangeburg school received state support until 1896, when the state severed its interest in Claflin and created a separate industrial, agricultural, and mechanical college in Orangeburg for Negroes. It was the pattern of every state with a substantial Negro population to establish a separate Negro land-grant college after 1890 to meet the new federal requirement that states must either admit Negroes to their land-grant colleges or provide "separate but equal" colleges for them. The spacious, tree-studded State College campus adjoins that of Claflin.

At the same time, South Carolina established Clemson College as its land-grant college for whites on a site given by Thomas Clemson, son-in-law of John C. Calhoun. The official name of the college for Negroes was changed to South Carolina State College in 1954, and the white institution was subsequently renamed Clemson University.

There was never any pretense of equality.

South Carolina State College had some distinguished alumni, such as President Emeritus Benjamin Mays of Morehouse College in Atlanta—the alma mater of Martin Luther King, Jr., and of other civil-rights leaders—who was an inspiration to many young, aspiring Negro intellectuals in the South. But perhaps the best-known alumnus of South Carolina State College was David (Deacon) Jones, a member of the "Fearless Foursome" of the Los Angeles Rams and one of several former State College football players who made it with the pros.

Like many another state-supported, traditionally Negro college in the South, South Carolina State found it easier to get adequate funds for athletic and band activities than for academic programs—and the former diverted attention from the deficiencies of the latter.

South Carolina had done less than any other southern state to provide higher educational opportunity for Negroes, even on a separate basis. According to a 1967 report by the Southern Regional Education Board entitled *Negro Higher Education in the South*, 60 percent of the white college students—compared with only 28 percent of the Negro college students—attended state-supported institutions. For Negro students it was the lowest percentage of any state in the seventeen-state region.

A study made by the Southern Education Reporting Service in May 1969 showed that a higher percentage of Negro college students from South Carolina attended school out of state than did students from any other state in the region. In South Carolina, 28.7 percent of the Negroes who went to college attended out of state, compared with only 13 percent from the region as a whole. South Carolina State College turned down 540 qualified applicants for the fall 1967 semester, while all qualified students were admitted to the state's predominantly white colleges and universities.

The students at State College came predominantly from poor families. Most of the middle-class students there were sons and daughters of State College alumni, many of them teachers and ministers. Sons and daughters of most of the state's small Negro upper-middle class went out of state to college—usually to the more prestigious Negro colleges in Atlanta or to Howard University in Washington. A few went to predominantly white universities in the North, and most of them remained in the North.

The son of President Benner C. Turner of South Carolina State College went to Harvard as his father had done. Turner, also a graduate of the Harvard Law School, was dean of the law school at South Carolina State before being named president in 1950. The state had established the law school after a Negro applied for admittance to the University of South Carolina Law School. And it was disestablished in 1966 after the U.S.C. Law School had begun to admit Negroes.

An aloof, somewhat shy autocrat, Turner, sixty-one, was the target of a student protest in February 1967 against the high-handed suspension of three students who had led a demonstration in front of the president's home on campus.

The original protest by students came after they learned that contracts would not be renewed for three popular young white professors, Woodrow Wilson teaching fellows, who had begun to raise doubts in the minds of students about the quality of the education they were getting. The appointment of the teaching fellows had brought hopes to some student leaders that the campus would eventually attract enough white students to the college to persuade state political leaders to think more about the quality of education at the school.

After demonstrations by Negro college students in Orangeburg in the early sixties, Turner's administration had erected a fence topped by three strands of barbed wire to separate the State and Claflin campuses. To students, it was known as the "Berlin Wall." Life at South Carolina State was highly regimented. Freshmen and sophomores were required to attend Friday chapel services and Sunday vespers. Students were assigned seat numbers so professors could check easily for absences. There was a limit of three unexcused absences a semester and students faced disciplinary action if they missed more than three times. Men were required to wear coats and ties at the Sunday dinner meal. The faculty had little voice in the affairs of the college.

One of the three young teaching fellows, Dr. Thomas Wirth, was appalled as he came to realize he was teaching students limited by an inferior, segregated public-school system. Wirth, who had a doctorate from California Institute of Technology, felt the system was self-perpetuating because many of the students would return as public-school teachers after an inferior college education.

Of twenty-seven full professors listed on the South Carolina State academic faculty for 1967–1968, twenty-three had doctorates, thirteen of them in education. Only two of twenty-six associate professors had doctorates. None of the forty-one assistant professors or twenty-five instructors had doctorates. Faculty salaries for equivalent positions were less than at the traditionally white state-supported colleges.

Wirth also was appalled at the lack of awareness among the students of what was going on in civil rights. Turner's administration had actively discouraged formation even of a campus NAACP chapter. Wirth and a group of activist-minded students drove to Atlanta one weekend to visit the national office of the Student Nonviolent Coordinating Committee (SNCC), a civil-rights organization which spearheaded the sit-in demonstrations of the early 1960s, but which had abandoned its goals of integration in 1966 in favor of a policy of militant black self-determination symbolized by its new slogan, "Black Power."

The protest against the nonrenewal of contracts for Wirth and the two other white teaching fellows—one a female who was reprimanded by President Turner after he learned she had a male visitor at her quarters one evening—spread rapidly after the suspension of the three students for protesting in front of the president's home. The four class presidents organized more than 80 percent of the student body in a two-week boycott for "the cause"—a vaguely defined protest demanding that the state provide quality education at State College. The campus leader for "the cause" was Isaac Williams, senior class president and one of eleven children of a Baptist minister from Charleston. (Williams later served in Vietnam as an Army lieutenant and in 1969 was named NAACP field secretary in South Carolina.)

Governor NcNair delicately negotiated a settlement in which students gained concessions and neither the state nor the students compromised principles. Although additional state police had been sent to Orangeburg by McNair as a precautionary measure, they generally were kept out of sight of the campus where their appearance on one occasion had been provocative to students.

Among those involved in the painstaking negotiations were the president of the state conference of the American Association of University Professors, Professor Robert Moore of Columbia College, the chairman of the Higher Education Commission, John K. Cauthen, and the chief legal counsel for the state NAACP chapter, Matthew J. Perry. The negotiations resulted in the return of students to classes with promises that long-standing neglect of Negro education would receive attention.

A major break in settling the boycott dispute came at a secret meeting in the governor's office between McNair and the four class presidents. The meeting was set up by Isaac McGraw, a state Department of Education employee and vice chairman of the South Carolina State College Alumni Association, who had volunteered his services to McNair. He set up the meeting after interviewing more than 100 students to learn their grievances and meet their leaders. Isaac Williams said later that McNair listened to the class presidents with an attitude of understanding and demonstrated a desire to work out a solution. A settlement was reached the next day; it included amnesty for those who missed classes.

The three suspended students were readmitted after Matthew Perry won a court order from Judge Robert Hemphill of the United States District Court in South Carolina, who ruled that the college handbook regulation under which the suspensions were made put a "prior restraint on the right to freedom of speech and the right to assemble" in violation of the First Amendment. Williams won approval to organize a campus NAACP chapter. He got help from Henry Smith, then a freshman, who worked closely with Williams in "the cause" and who recruited NAACP members among freshmen and sophomores.

Meanwhile, Negro political leaders urged that Turner be dismissed, and he announced his early retirement in May. M. Maceo Nance, vice president for finance, was named acting president. A special committee, with Furman University President Gordon Blackwell as chairman, was appointed by Cauthen, the Higher Education Commission chairman, to study State College's student and faculty rules and regulations. When classes resumed in the fall, Nance implemented the committee's major recommendations. Students were named to all standing committees of the college, compulsory chapel attendance was abandoned, and students were allowed to dress as they pleased for meals.

In addition, a small group of students organized the Black Awareness Coordinating Committee (BACC). Its presence created considerable apprehension among both faculty and staff members and among the Negro middle-class community in Orangeburg. A major force behind the organization of BACC was Cleveland Sellers, Jr., a native of Denmark, a town twenty miles from Orangeburg, and organizer for the Student Nonviolent Coordinating Committee. Sellers and other SNCC members had been on the State College campus during the spring uprising against Turner, but left at the urging of Williams and other student leaders after the boycott began.

In April, after Sellers had been involved in the State College protest, the all-white Bamberg County draft board notified him to report for induction. He reported May 1 to an induction center in Atlanta, but refused to step forward and take the oath. He contended that Negroes were excluded from draft boards in South Carolina and Georgia and that he had been called for induction out of turn because he was a militant civil-rights worker. Three weeks later he was charged with violating the Selective Service Act, but released on bond.

Sellers, then almost twenty-three, returned to Orangeburg in October to promote BACC. His reputation as a black militant and organizer of resistance to the draft had brought him under FBI surveillance earlier and now the FBI office in Columbia was alerted to monitor his activities in Orangeburg. He was accompanied by his wife Sandy, a slim, attractive SNCC worker with an Afro hair style. They moved into a small frame house that faced Claflin College across some railroad tracks and a highway. The house had spare furnishings, with sleeping mats on the floor and a wall poster of Huey Newton, a former SNCC associate of Sellers who had become national defense minister of the Black Panther party, then a new group of armed, young black revolutionists who believed in retaliatory violence.

Sellers, tall and slim, with a goatee, mustache, and bushy Afro hair, was a frightening figure to Orangeburg whites. And middle-class Negroes were almost as uneasy. Some of them quietly asked the city police chief, Roger Poston, if he could run Sellers out of town. Poston told them the law did not cover a person's appearance or beliefs and that Sellers had a right to be in Orangeburg as long as he did not violate the law.

Orangeburg was a fountainhead of white ultraconservatism. It was the state headquarters of both the John Birch Society front organization, TACT (Truth About Civil Turmoil), and the South Carolina Association of Independent Schools, an organization of segregationist, private schools that sprang up as a result of public school desegregation. It also was the home of Southern Methodist College, a small school operated by the Southern Methodist Church, a denomination which espoused Biblical sanction of segregation.

George Wallace's 1968 presidential campaign manager for South Carolina was owner and manager of local radio station WDIX, which editorialized in support of Wallace's American Party: "The people of the United States need a party which will stop tolerating and supporting the Communist subversion of America through agitation of racial turmoil in our streets and schools."

Orangeburg had an unusually large Negro middle class because of its two predominantly Negro colleges. Many blacks in the urban area lived outside the city limits, which cut through the middle of the State College campus. The city population was 60 percent white, but the 1960 census showed a county population of 68,559 that was 60 percent Negro. Since 1960, the traditional agricultural economy of the county has shifted sharply to a broadened industrial base, with several new high-wage plants creating job opportunities for the white population and, to a lesser extent, the Negro population.

Sellers came to Orangeburg as an organizer, but he had previously served SNCC as national program director, working closely with Stokely Carmichael and H. Rap Brown, whose very names conjured up images of black anger and violence not only in the minds of the whites of Orangeburg, but in the minds of most white and many black Americans. Three years earlier, SNCC had mobilized more than 2,000 white and black college students for sit-in demonstrations that crumbled segregation barriers in many parts of the South. But in 1966, with the election of Carmichael to succeed John Lewis as chairman, SNCC became more militant and kicked out its white members. Lewis, who resigned from SNCC in disillusionment, said Carmichael's cry of "Black Power" was a slogan intended to "scare the white man." SNCC's violent rhetoric, which in many places included threats to "burn the town down," succeeded in frightening white America.

In the fall of 1967, black students throughout the country were just beginning to demand courses in black history and culture and other black studies. Sellers worked to organize groups to promote such studies and black awareness on all six Negro college campuses in South Carolina, as well as at the state university in Columbia. He helped organize at least three black college units as well as an Afro-American group at the University of South Carolina—a group similar to those being organized by black students at predominantly white colleges in other parts of the country. His second project in South Carolina was to organize resistance to the draft, but he got virtually nowhere with that.

At State College, Acting President Nance granted a

charter to students seeking campus recognition for the Black Awareness Coordinating Committee. The name was similar to that of the State College Student Coordinating Committee, an ad hoc group that had organized "the cause" the previous spring. A few of the more militant BACC members were surprised when Nance approved their charter. They had believed a denial would have given them an issue. Dr. Rubin F. Weston, chairman of the Department of Social Studies and president of the new faculty senate, supported the charter and became faculty advisor to BACC.

An article in *The Charlotte Observer* in December quoted Weston as saying: "It was my position that we had to hear these young people out. If we denied them or tried to suppress them, it would cause an explosion . . . It was not logical to deny black students on a black campus the right to organize simply because they are concerned about blackness." Weston explained that the goals of the group were primarily "to seek a greater commitment among educated Negroes toward the plight of the Negro masses and to develop a pride in racial heritage through study of Negro history and literature and trying to change the concept that black is evil."

He continued: "While they seemingly talk about black separatism, they are really interested in getting into the mainstream . . . They want to commit themselves to other Negroes, not to desert other Negroes after getting an education." Weston acknowledged that the relatively large Negro middle class in Orangeburg considered the new group a threat to their security, but he said the BACC students were interested "in identification with and not desertion of the masses by people who can help."

Steve Moore, editor of *BACC Speaks*, a mimeographed publication of the group, wrote that the primary aim of BACC was "the development of a sense of black consciousness among students in South Carolina" and that the group intended to "move into the mainstream of the revolutionary struggle that black students are beginning to wage throughout America." Another BACC member, Sarah Bankhead, said, "I feel that unless black people have race pride and black unity we will not emerge successfully in this white power structure."

Sellers, a soft-spoken, polite youth who did not share the flamboyant rhetoric of such SNCC leaders as Carmichael or Brown, relished a quote by Professor Paul Puryear of Fisk University in discussing the impact of black awareness: "It could result in a reexamination of integration so that integration will become a force of cultural exchange rather than a force for cultural absorption."

BACC attracted only eighteen members, many of whom also belonged to the student NAACP chapter, which that fall had more than 300 members. The first BACC chairman was an ROTC cadet colonel.

Historically, an aristocratic racism had dominated the white South Carolina social and political structure—a racism in which Negroes were looked upon as children rather than as a lower class of being and in which lower-class whites were also looked down upon. It contrasted with the democratic racism that prevailed in the Deep South in which all whites shared a sense of equality because they were white.

Degrees of the two varieties of southern racism were found in all southern states, but the system of aristocratic racism, which gave more value to an orderly society, prevailed in South Carolina, an Old South state. The state, whose percentage of Negroes in the population was second only to Mississippi's, generally had responded to the assault on segregation with legal resistance through the courts and legislature, or sometimes with economic reprisals, in contrast to the violence that frequently rocked the Deep South.

South Carolina had been one of the original thirteen colonies, and its lowcountry planters and wealthy men of commerce in Charleston had attempted to develop an aristocratic society. A certain amount of the aristocrat's sense of noblesse oblige remains to this day. In race relations, it developed as paternalism.

Before Eli Whitney's invention of the cotton gin in 1793, there had been manumission societies in South Carolina that promoted freeing of slaves. The cotton gin accelerated the settlement of the Deep South states of Alabama and Mississippi, and the new opportunities and lust for money through slave labor brought an end to notions in South Carolina that slavery was wrong. In his 1964 book, *Who Speaks for the South*, native South Carolinian James McBride Dabbs quoted a friend who had long observed the South as saying, "Mississippi was conceived in sin, but South Carolina fell into it."

Many of the early nineteenth-century settlers of the raw frontiers in the newer Deep South were aggressive farmers from the South Carolina upcountry, men who put into practice John C. Calhoun's theories on race—that the existence of black slaves provided the basis for a white democracy, and that their skin color provided a badge of equality of all whites. The corollary was that the blacks were a little less than human. Although Calhoun married a Charlestonian, the cavalier neoaristocrats of Charleston in the lowcountry never took such theories seriously. They regarded "white trash" as being as lowly as the slaves, who were viewed more as children who never grew up.

In South Carolina, the planting of cotton—and the use of slaves—had stretched to the state's westernmost counties in the Appalachian foothills. Thus, on the subject of race there was unity, and the more populous white upcountry deferred to the lowcountry planters and neoaristocrats and their paternalistic tradition. As in the rest of the Deep South, race was the dominant force behind social and political decisions, but there evolved from this aristocratic racism a white social structure which seemed to value stability almost as highly as segregation.

After the Supreme Court desegregation decision in 1954, South Carolina's leaders correctly read the meaning of the extremism of Arkansas, Mississippi, and especially Alabama. "They saw both its futility as regards integration and its danger as regards the economic future of the state," wrote Dabbs, and he added, "It is true, there has been, and there is, mean legal and economic infighting in South Carolina; but violence itself, even the suggestion of violence, is quickly condemned." The state's political leaders reflected the mood of the people.

Thus, South Carolina fought integration every step of the way. But a few days before Harvey Gantt entered Clemson as the first Negro to break the state's segregation barrier in education, outgoing Governor Ernest F. (Fritz) Hollings told the legislature:

> As we meet, South Carolina is running out of courts. If and when every legal remedy has been exhausted, this General Assembly must make clear South Carolina's choice, a government of laws rather than a government of men. As determined as we are, we of today must realize the lesson of one hundred years ago, and move on for the good of South Carolina and our United States. This should be done with dignity. It must be done with law and order.

Gantt was admitted to Clemson a few days later in quiet dignity, a few months after the eruption of violence when James Meredith was admitted to the University of Mississippi. Gantt, who after graduation would remain in the South as an architect in Charlotte, North Carolina, commented, "If you can't appeal to the morals of a South Carolinian, you can appeal to his manners."

The handling of Gantt's admission to Clemson was more than a reaction to the violence at Ole Miss, however. In the summer of 1962, before Meredith was admitted, South Carolinians were electing a moderate governor at the same time that George Wallace was riding to victory in Alabama with his promise "to stand in the schoolhouse door." One of the gubernatorial candidates in South Carolina was fiery state Representative A. W. Red Bethea, an articulate segregationist who promised, "If they try to do to the University of South Carolina what they did to the University of Georgia [admit Negro students], I'll close it so tight you can't get a crowbar in." Meanwhile, former U.S.C. President Donald Russell, a brilliant lawyer and later a federal judge, gave lip service to segregation and said the state needed "the best legal mind" to deal with its problems. A third candidate was Lieutenant Governor Burnet Maybank, Jr., son of a former governor and United States senator. He was supported by much of the state's political establishment.

Bethea was a well-known figure who twice had run strong in elections for state secretary of agriculture. He figured to get enough votes to force a runoff between Russell and Maybank in which he would be able to bargain with them for his support. However, he received only 7 percent of the vote, and Russell won a smashing victory.

At his inaugural a few days before Gantt was admitted to Clemson, Russell set the tone for his administration with a surprise announcement that the social function for the inaugural would be a barbecue luncheon on the grounds of the governor's mansion—which sits on the border of a poor

Negro neighborhood in Columbia—and that "all of the people in South Carolina" were invited. Thousands turned out, ranging from Negro maids clad in house dresses to society matrons in furs.

By the late 1960s, Negroes in South Carolina were finding new job opportunities in textiles and other industries. The state's conservative Negro leadership patiently accepted legal victories and began developing a sense of political sophistication as blacks moved actively into political participation, sometimes holding the balance of power in statewide political races.

To Cleveland Sellers, however, oppression in South Carolina was "greater than anywhere else" because Negroes had not pushed hard enough for change. "Their minds are chained," he said in the fall of 1967, and when a newsman asked if there would be violence, he answered with a soft smile.

2 : MONDAY—A DAY OF CHALLENGE

JOHN STROMAN was a determined young black man who loved to bowl, and Harry Floyd was a determined southern white man who believed it would cost him business if he allowed blacks to patronize his bowling alley. Those were the seeds of discord that bloomed into a major confrontation in Orangeburg in February 1968.

For several years, Negroes in Orangeburg had pleaded, cajoled, and even begged Floyd to be allowed to bowl at his bowling alley, the only one in the city. The white establishment as well as Negroes had urged Floyd to desegregate. In the late 1960s they saw his policy as dynamite for a small southern city in which two Negro colleges were located.

Students at Claflin and South Carolina State colleges had staged mass protests against segregated lunch counters in 1963, and police had made mass arrests and used fire hoses on the protestors. The events had upset the tranquility of white Orangeburg, and in the late 1960s the mood of black America was more militant and less patient. The bowling alley had become the most visible and volatile symbol of segregation in Orangeburg, where other segregationist traditions were gradually crumbling as they were in the rest of the South.

A strong-willed senior from Savannah, Stroman considered his rights the same as those of any other American. As a black student, he was contemptuous of the Orangeburg Negro middle class. "Instead of trying to educate the less fortunate Negroes, most of our leading educators and businessmen segregate themselves from them," he once wrote. "This is their way of satisfying themselves; so long as they are doing better than the average Negro and the white man gives them a little more respect, they don't care about what happens to their race." In Savannah, he had been a league bowler, but as a student at State College he would have to drive forty miles to Columbia if he wanted to take a date bowling and then be confronted with an early curfew for coeds.

In Orangeburg, Stroman found students had two outlets for night life, the movies and the night clubs—and Negroes weren't admitted to the drive-in movies. "If you go to the movies one night during the middle of the week," he observed, "then you have a choice of seeing this movie again or going to one of five night clubs, at three of which you are lucky if you are not cut or shot."

On the night of February 5, Stroman led a group of students to Floyd's All Star Bowling Lanes, where only a few months before the "For White Only" sign had been replaced by one reading, "Privately Owned." To Negroes, the meaning was the same. The students entered through the rear and about forty got in before Floyd locked the door. Floyd moved in front of Stroman and tried to hold him back. Stroman shoved Floyd's hands away and strode to the snack bar. As on a previous occasion, he was refused service. Floyd called for police and wanted the students arrested for trespassing. Told he would have to swear out a warrant, he departed for the home of the local magistrate.

Floyd's white patrons were clearly disturbed, but Stroman and his group were determined. Police Chief Roger Poston, who in the past had told Stroman he would be protected if he wanted to picket or otherwise protest through any peaceful and lawful means, arrived and quickly concluded the situation was explosive.

City Administrator Robert T. Stevenson arrived at the A&P Shopping Center on Russell Street, the main street of Orangeburg, about the same time as Poston. Floyd's bowling alley was located in the corner of the L-shaped shopping center, several store fronts away from the A&P supermarket, the dominant store. A large parking lot was framed on two sides by stores and on two sides by city streets.

Stevenson concurred with Poston's evaluation of the situation, and agreed that Poston should order the bowling alley to close for the night. The students returned to the campus, but vowed to continue their desegregation efforts.

Although the 1964 Civil Rights Act contained a section on public accommodations, it only covered establishments engaged in interstate commerce and the intent of Congress was not clear insofar as bowling alleys were concerned. Some liberal Republicans, opposed to extending the limits of the interstate commerce clause, argued unsuccessfully to put public accommodations under the Fourteenth Amendment equal protection clause, contending it gave Congress the authority to require anyone offering to serve the public to serve all—or at least not to exclude anyone on the basis of race, color, or national origin. Nineteenth-century Supreme Court Justice John Marshall Harlan had made the same argument in a dissenting opinion in a case involving a Reconstruction era civil-rights bill. With a tough fight ahead in Congress, the prevailing opinion in the Kennedy administration was that the interstate commerce argument could be more successfully defended on constitutional grounds.

The lofty arguments in Washington did not take into consideration early curfews for coeds and the problems of young blacks who just might like to bowl; nor did they take into consideration the symbolic meaning of an establishment that refused to admit people because of their skin color when other establishments serving the public admitted all people because that was the law.

Orangeburg was moving away from segregation, white leaders in the community would tell you, but Harry Floyd believed the attitude of white bowlers was such that he would suffer financially if he voluntarily allowed Negroes to bowl. The Negroes in Orangeburg who bowled were traditional southern conservatives. They did not want to cause trouble. They even asked Floyd to let them bowl one night a week for their league.

Problems arose soon after the 1964 Civil Rights Act became law. Floyd always was emphatic that the law did not require him to let Negroes bowl and that anyone who disagreed could take him to court. On April 20, 1965, after Floyd had made his position clear, Dean of Men Oscar Butler at State College wrote to Director Leroy Collins of the Community Relations Service in Washington. A former athlete at the college, Butler wrote as a member of an all-Negro bowling team. He explained that his team had bowled in a league in Columbia after getting special permission from the American Bowling Congress. However, the bowling alley they used there had closed and Columbia league officials suggested the Orangeburg team comply with an ABC regulation recommending the normal jurisdiction of a chartered association be an area within a twenty-mile radius. Floyd's bowling alley was the only one within a twenty-mile radius of Orangeburg.

Butler related how his team brought the regulation to the attention of Harry Floyd, representative of the management of All Star Bowling Lanes, in September 1964. Floyd promised to present their request to bowl as individuals or as a team to his superiors and contact them two weeks later. He did not contact them, and the bowlers telephoned him in November and again in January. At that time, Floyd said the owners did not feel the Negro bowlers should be allowed to use the bowling alley because it did not cater to "tourists" and did not use goods or machinery covered by interstate commerce regulations. He told them the ownership was unwilling to consider their request.

In his letter, Butler asked to be informed whether or not the bowling alley was covered by the 1964 Civil Rights Act and said that any assistance or suggestions to aid in the solution of the problem would be greatly appreciated. "We are still hopeful that something can be worked out without creating any further confusion in our community," he said. On April 20, Chief Counsel Samuel W. Allen of the Community Relations Service advised Butler that

> a bowling alley, as such, is not covered by the Civil Rights Act of 1964. However, if there is operated in connection with the bowling alley an establishment which serves food for consumption on the premises to patrons of the bowling alley, and that establishment serves food to interstate travelers or a substantial portion of the food which it serves has moved in interstate commerce, then the bowling alley would be subject to the provisions of the Civil Rights Act of 1964.

Allen advised that, if this were the case, a person denied access because of his race could file a civil action in federal court, but that legal counsel should be consulted because the Community Relations Service did not provide legal services in such matters.

After the Civil Rights Act, Negroes in Orangeburg grew accustomed to formerly "white only" restaurants and other establishments being open to all. The bowling alley—located only five blocks from the State College campus—became the leading symbol of white racism in Orangeburg.

In August 1966, students from State College went to the bowling alley and were turned away. Black bowlers continued to drive to Columbia to bowl, and middle-class Negro leaders sought help from city officials and business leaders to persuade the bowling alley to change its policy.

In June 1967, Floyd became owner of the bowling alley he had managed, and Butler and businessman Earl Middleton talked with him again about opening it to Negroes. Floyd, a thin, nervously energetic, middle-aged man whose large, shell-framed glasses dominated his bony face, said later he attended a two-and-a-half hour meeting on campus. His position was that he had a right to operate his business as he saw fit as long as it was not in violation of the law, that he would not integrate his bowling alley voluntarily, and that Negroes could go to court if they felt he was violating the law.

Floyd's policy proved an embarrassment that summer for the city when Orangeburg was host to the Little World Series of the American Legion-sponsored junior baseball program. Some members of a California team went to the bowling alley, and Floyd refused to admit Negro members of the team, marring an event that emphasized good sportsmanship.

In September, Butler and Middleton went to Mayor E. O. Pendarvis and to chamber of commerce leaders. Pendarvis promised to try to use his influence to persuade Floyd. In addition, a chamber of commerce leader and a representative of an industrial group contacted Floyd on the matter. Private store managers in the shopping center were also asked to see Floyd.

At State College, Butler, more than any other official, was in close contact with the students and was familiar with the new concept of pride in blackness. To most of the college officials and especially to the city's middle-class Negroes, the presence that fall of Cleveland Sellers and the Black Awareness Coordinating Committee had become ominous. The Negro middle class was almost as afraid as the whites of the new "Black Power" slogan and were just about as uninformed about it. Butler knew the attitudes of students were changing and that there was growing impatience at delay in getting rights and freedoms they felt belonged to them.

On September 27, Butler again wrote to the Community Relations Service, referring to the earlier exchange of correspondence and asking if court rulings had since altered the status. Butler said the bowling alley served food for consumption on the premises and that the bowling equipment was transported into Orangeburg through interstate commerce. He made it clear he and others were denied use of the facilities because they were Negroes. On November 3, he received a one-paragraph reply that his complaint had been referred to the civil rights division of the Department of Justice.

In the meantime, a student NAACP chapter was organized at State College which wanted to take action on the bowling alley. Dr. Charles H. Thomas, an education professor at the college and local NAACP president, said that voter registration was the most important NAACP activity, but that the NAACP might take up the bowling alley after a registration drive. Dr. Thomas also felt the matter should be handled by adult Negro bowlers in the city, rather than by students. He believed that in the past it had always been the students who took action on rights for Negroes in the city and that it was time for the adults to help themselves.

In October, the NAACP set up a meeting to discuss the bowling alley and brought in Matthew Perry, the state NAACP legal counsel from Columbia, to explain the legal aspects of the situation. The NAACP in effect offered to provide legal counsel. Perry stopped short of actually asking someone to make the complaint, but he felt he made it clear that he would file a civil suit if a complainant stepped forward. To those less familiar with the subtleties of the law, however, perhaps it was not so clear. Butler, who already had written his second complaint to the Community Relations Service, recalled later that he would have been willing to make a complaint in his name if someone had been asked to step forward, but the question was not asked.

As it was, Butler appealed to the chief of police, the mayor, and the city administrator. He talked to a board member of the bowling association that sponsored league bowling in Orangeburg. The board member already had talked to Floyd and had been called a "nigger lover." However, he suggested that Butler write the American Bowling Congress. The ABC's reply was that they had no jurisdiction over the operations of local managers.

City Administrator Stevenson went to several industrial plants and talked at least one into withdrawing from league participation because of Floyd's policy. A boycott and picket of the entire shopping center was threatened, but Dr. Thomas pleaded against it because a Negro worked as a checker in the A&P, previously a job for which only whites would have been hired.

By December, almost any time a conversation on the State College campus dealt with the subject of racism, the bowling alley was brought up. For example, when a coed in a sociology class took the position that things were getting better for Negroes, another student interrupted to ask, "Why can't we bowl then? Because we're black, that's why!" And other students shouted approval.

Sometime in December or January, two FBI agents dropped in to see Floyd, and one of them asked if he would close his snack bar rather than integrate. "I said I would, and one agent looked at the other and I knew what they meant," Floyd later recalled.

John Stroman had kept himself informed of efforts to integrate the bowling alley. He planned to seek advice when he returned home to Savannah for Christmas holidays.

Meanwhile, another student, James P. Davis—an Air Force veteran and a Charleston minister's son—had been angered by the racism he found in Orangeburg and began circulating a petition among students to picket the bowling alley. Davis, a twenty-six-year-old father of two, had put aside his Air Force sergeant's uniform in the spring of 1967, after six years in France and Italy, and looked forward to seeing how the 1964 Civil Rights Act had changed the South. He was quickly disillusioned. "It was like stepping out of heaven into hell," Davis said in describing what happened to him when he returned home.

With plans to enter South Carolina State (where he later won academic honors as a foreign language major), Davis noticed on his first day in Orangeburg in April a small frame house with an "Apartment for Rent" sign. He knocked on the door, and the white woman who answered snapped, "It's not for rent to niggers." A few days later, he was shocked to find a "For Whites Only" sign on the door of the bowling alley. Davis, who is slightly built and wears glasses, entered to talk to the owner about it, but was told to get out.

A few days before Christmas holidays, he developed a sinus infection. He went to a local specialist and was confronted with a sign "Colored Waiting Room in the Rear." Davis entered the front door into a comfortable room with upholstered sofas and a rack of magazines and newspapers. A nurse told him he was in the wrong room, then showed him to a small room with a few straight-backed wooden chairs.

Furious, he left, returned home, and composed a long open letter to the students, faculty, and administration of both State College and Claflin. His message was clear: Negroes at the two institutions should be ashamed to continue to accept without protest the racism in the community. Davis soon collected more than 300 names on his petition. However, Stroman did not sign the petition because he did not want to take action without more detailed strategy. He told Davis he was not going to do anything until returning to college after the holidays. Davis's plan to picket the bowling alley shortly before the holidays was called off because of a conflict with exams.

When Stroman went home, all he could think of was the bowling alley. He talked to several bowling alley managers in Savannah and found them surprised that such a place existed. On his bus trip back to college, an idea occurred to him. Floyd had removed his "For Whites Only" sign, replacing it with another one, "Privately Owned." Whenever Negroes attempted to enter to bowl, Floyd had adopted a policy of refusing admittance on the grounds that the bowling alley was a private club and they were not members. Stroman's idea was to get the college's lone white male undergraduate to go bowl, then have a group of students confront the owner with what he meant by "privately owned."

The white student agreed to the plan and on Monday, January 29, he left the campus about 4:30 P.M. and went to the bowling alley. About fifteen minutes later, Stroman, Davis, and about ten other students arrived. Dean Butler heard of the plan and met them at the shopping center to observe. About six of the students were able to enter the bowling alley before the door was locked. They went directly to the lunch counter and ordered food. They were ignored.

Two of the students went to the desk and asked for lanes. They were told the bowling alley was private. Pointing to the white student, they asked how could the bowling alley be private when a classmate was bowling and he was not a member. The white student was ordered to stop bowling and the students were told to leave. They refused.

About this time, Floyd came over to Butler and said, "Oscar, get these students out of here." Butler replied, "Harry, I did not bring them here." One of the students had put a coin in a juke box and selected a record. Others began to purchase soft drinks from a vending machine. Floyd and his brother unplugged the machines and returned the money, which some of the students refused. The students waited for Floyd to call the police. He did not call, and the students left under Butler's eye.

Later in the week, Stroman sought the support of the Black Awareness Coordinating Committee, of which he was a member, but they felt the bowling alley problem was not of importance. Davis and other students returned to the bowling alley to confront the manager, but Floyd's position remained unchanged. Butler went to Negro leaders and city officials and pleaded for effective action.

On the next Monday—February 5—Stroman received an answer to a letter he wrote to the American Bowling Congress; they said they had no control over Floyd's policy. Stroman knew Monday was a league bowling night. He went around campus that afternoon getting names of students willing to sit in at the bowling alley. Stroman had been one of the three students suspended by President Turner the previous spring and he knew that some students, such as Henry Smith, could be counted on for support. A rangy sophomore, Smitty had been unflagging in his loyalty to "the cause" the previous year. If he believed in something, he committed himself.

Stroman got about forty-five names, but only Smitty and about a dozen others showed up when they were to meet at the student center. Heading out of the campus, Stroman's group went by Lowman Hall, the last building on their route, and got about two dozen freshmen to join them on their way to the bowling alley.

That night, after Floyd returned with his arrest warrants, he found the bowling alley had been closed under Chief Poston's order. Floyd angrily called city officials to protest that his right to run his business as he pleased wasn't being protected. He felt he got a run-around from city officials that night, but he was promised a hearing the next day when a regular meeting of the city council was scheduled.

About 9:30 P.M., he called Governor Robert E. McNair in Columbia to tell his version of what happened; he later recalled he told the governor that the situation was serious, that it was tense, and that "I know it will happen again." Floyd remembered the governor telling him, "You will be provided protection of the law."

3 : TUESDAY—A DAY OF CONFRONTATION

TUESDAY NIGHT John Stroman returned to the bowling alley with another group of students. This time the doors were locked, and the students were confronted by about twenty law enforcement officers, including some members of the state highway patrol who carried riot batons—narrow, hardwood sticks almost three feet long, designed for self-protection and use by police in formation to break up crowds. To the students, they looked like ax handles or clubs. Before the night ended, they were used as clubs.

While South Carolina had consistently resisted desegregation through legal strategems, law enforcement practices had changed with the law. Now the law seemed unclear. Did Harry Floyd have the right to deny Negroes admittance to his bowling alley or did Negroes now have the right to use his facilities as a place of public accommodations covered by the 1964 Civil Rights Act?

Floyd had gone to the Orangeburg City Council earlier Tuesday and demanded protection of his right as a property owner to serve whomever he wanted. He had presented a bill asking several hundred dollars for business he had lost the night before because the city had closed his bowling alley. And he had severely criticized Robert Stevenson, the city administrator, for ordering the bowling alley closed. But Stevenson heatedly told Floyd that if there was another confrontation that night, he would again order it closed.

At the council meeting, Floyd accused Chief Poston of having told him Monday night, "I am not going to risk my life and my boys' lives to protect your property." Poston denied the statement and told the council that what he actually said to Floyd was, "I am not going to ask my men to violate the law in interfering with those who are not breaking the law by being in your place."

However, City Attorney C. Walker Limehouse had concluded that bowling alleys probably weren't covered by the Civil Rights Act. Although Limehouse defended Chief Poston for his action the night before, he warned the council that the law was in a "very shadowy field." And he advised that the police would have to make a trespass arrest if Floyd asked an individual to leave and he refused to do so.

Limehouse had read the transcripts of several federal court cases during the day and had called the state attorney general's office before reaching his conclusion. State Attorney General Daniel R. McLeod said later that because of conflicting court decisions, "you simply couldn't tell" whether the bowling alley was covered. McLeod knew the bowling alley was covered if there was a restaurant, but was uncertain whether Floyd's snack bar met the criteria of the public accommodations section of the Civil Rights Act.

Accepting Limehouse's recommendation, the city took the position that Floyd's claim that he had the right to choose his customers was more valid than the students' claim that they had the right to be served.

Floyd told the council that he had been in touch with the governor and with Chief J. P. (Pete) Strom of the State Law Enforcement Division (SLED)—an agency under the governor's direct control. According to Floyd, Strom had promised to pay a visit that afternoon to help obtain protection.

As the state's top law enforcement officer, Strom had the reputation of being the J. Edgar Hoover of South Carolina. For years he had been Mr. Law Enforcement in the Palmetto state. When McNair was sworn in as governor, he immediately signed an order reappointing Pete Strom as chief of SLED. McNair was the fourth governor to appoint him as chief. Strom, who knew Hoover personally, even bore a physical resemblance to the FBI director. A heavy-set man with a muscular paunch and a bulldog face dominated by baggy, slightly protruding eyes, Strom spoke in rustic idiom, and his appearance in conservative, loose-fitting suits and a crossed-pistols tie clasp was such that folks back home in tiny McCormick County—where his father had been sheriff —would never accuse him of putting on airs.

Strom had been a central figure in South Carolina's record of racial peace. He had played a key role in breaking the influence of the Ku Klux Klan in the 1950s and in sending a grand dragon to prison. In the 1960s Strom won respect for his handling of civil-rights demonstrations. In 1964 he coolly handled an explosive situation that occurred when an integrated group of college students showed up to picket George Wallace at Columbia Municipal Airport. It was before the Goldwater nomination, and the Alabama governor, then considering a presidential campaign, was greeted by several hundred enthusiastic supporters. They turned with anger after spotting the students. A burly man in khaki work clothes moved forward with clenched fist cocked. Strom moved in, flashed his badge, and ordered the man to move back, then turned to the students and told them that they had a constitutional right to picket, but they could not violate any laws. He directed them not to block the street or sidewalks and to march not more than two abreast. He asked them to select an area in which to picket and assured them of protection. The students moved into a grassy area at the front of the Wallace crowd and began marching in a ring with anti-Wallace signs while singing freedom songs. Wallace supporters waved Confederate flags and loudly sang "Dixie." That was the scene that greeted Wallace as he stepped from his plane a few minutes later.

Under NcNair, however, Strom had shown less tolerance when antiwar demonstrators protested at the University of South Carolina over the granting of an honorary degree to General William C. Westmoreland, a South Carolina native then in command of United States troops in Vietnam. Strom ordered pickets hustled away from the campus chapel, where the ceremony was being held, after they had been threatened by a large crowd of pro-Westmoreland students. Asked later why police moved against the pickets, who had been peaceful, Strom indicated the governor wanted no antiwar demonstrations to mar the ceremony.

On Tuesday, February 6, 1968, Strom went to Orangeburg at McNair's direction to confront students challenging Harry Floyd's segregation policy. When Stroman and the other students arrived at the bowling alley, Strom and Chief Poston were waiting for them. Attorney General McLeod had advised Strom earlier in the day that the state should not make any charges under the trespass law. McLeod said that if the bowling alley owner personally wanted to prefer charges under the state law, he could do so and run the risk of being in violation of the Civil Rights Act. McLeod reasoned:

> The difficulty was that if this establishment was under the Civil Rights Act, you could not refuse admission to a person on account of race; he had a right to come in there. Consequently, you couldn't turn him down and prosecute him under the state trespass law if he refused to leave. So you were in a quandary as to whether police officers could sign a warrant. I advised they should not do it. There was nothing to prohibit the owner of the establishment from prosecuting people for refusing to leave after notice to do so by him. The owner, rather than the officer, would then run the risk of violating the Civil Rights Act.

In front of the bowling alley's locked doors, on which the words "Privately Owned" were neatly lettered, Poston and Strom explained to Stroman that Floyd had the right to file trespass charges against the students if they refused his request to leave. When Stroman passed along the explanation to the other students, one said, "If we can defend this country that has places like this, then we should be able to enjoy them."

The doors were opened, and Stroman led a group of more than thirty inside. Some were coeds. They lounged around for about fifteen minutes before Floyd asked that they leave. Strom advised Stroman that it was not necessary for a lot of people to be arrested, that they could take the matter to court if only one or just a few were arrested. Stroman told the coeds to leave and advised other students to leave if they did not want to be arrested. Police began escorting the remaining students to patrol cars. Fifteen had submitted to arrest when a student on the outside cursed a policeman and was arrested for it. Other students protested angrily. One of them hurried back to the State College campus, five blocks away, and told hundreds of students attending a movie in the auditorium that police had arrested a group of students at the bowling alley. Students poured out of the auditorium and headed downtown. Along the way, a few picked up bricks from a site where a building was being demolished.

When Dean of Students Henry Vincent got word of what was happening, he rushed to the front of the campus and persuaded about seventy-five students not to go downtown. Several faculty members hurried to the bowling alley to observe. When Dean of Men Oscar Butler arrived, he found several hundred students milling in the parking lot, clamoring for the release of those arrested.

Butler approached Poston and Strom, who agreed to release the students in Butler's custody with an understanding that those under arrest would then return to the parking lot and get the other students to go back to the campus. Butler, student body president Robert Scott, Faculty Senate Chairman Rubin Weston, and two other college staff members went to the jail. They explained the proposition to Stroman and the others, who discussed it and agreed to return and get the other students to leave the shopping center parking lot.

There in front of the bowling alley, roughly 300 to 400 students, including some from Claflin, confronted the police demanding the release of the arrested students. Some jeered, "Hey, honky," and a few yelled, "Burn, baby, burn," a cry that had achieved notoriety in the Watts riots of 1966. Inside, Orangeburg whites continued bowling as if nothing was happening—and they were to continue to bowl uninterrupted all evening despite the trouble outside. When Stroman and the others who had been arrested returned to the parking lot, they began to fan out into the crowd. Stroman enlisted the aid of several football players in persuading the crowd to disperse, and the students began to go back toward the colleges, satisfied that those arrested had been released.

Meanwhile, Chief Poston as a precautionary move had ordered a fire truck to come to the shopping center and had instructed the firemen to come as quietly and inconspicuously as possible down a side street. Poston had been in Orangeburg only three years and had earned a reputation for professionalism, but he was unaware that Claflin and State College students had been sprayed with fire hoses in a sit-in demonstration in 1960. When the fire truck arrived, the students felt they had been tricked. Their mood changed from conciliation to anger and hostility. The night was cold, and the students thought the fire hoses were going to be turned on them. A large group surged toward the fire truck. The hoses remained on their reels, but students began jeering at the firemen. "Hey, man, where's the fire?" some shouted. Others, lighting matches or cigarette lighters, yelled back, "Hey, here it is—over here." A student waved a lighted cigarette lighter under a detective's nose.

Stroman climbed on top of a car, waving his arms and urging students to return to the campus. Strom already had called for reinforcements, and perhaps fifty law enforcement officers now were on the scene. Highway patrolmen wore riot helmets and carried their long riot sticks, some with leather-thonged loops that slipped over the patrolmen's wrists.

Chief Poston, sitting in a highway patrol car with Patrol Captain Carl Fairey, had unsuccessfully urged over a loudspeaker that the students return to campus. Several students rocked the car from side to side, someone slashed the tires, and a message was scratched on the trunk: "Go to hell." Stroman climbed on top of another car, waving his arms and urging students to return to the campus.

Strom, who had been present at the 1960 demonstrations, knew immediately the fire truck was a mistake. Dean

Butler also knew it was a mistake. When he learned it was Poston who called for the fire engine, Butler went to him and urged that it be sent back. Poston ordered the fire truck to leave, but by now, in the words of Professor Weston, "the situation had been rendered nonnegotiable."

When police moved away from the bowling alley to cover the fire truck, a group of students broke for the front door, chanting, "Hey, hey, let us in." To Harry Floyd, standing inside near Strom, it appeared as though they were trying to unhinge the door. Some grabbed at the hinges with their hands. One darted forward and kicked a narrow glass window beside the door, then moved back into the crowd. Many in the surging crowd did not see him, but heard glass shatter. Strom pointed out Arthur Dodson, Jr., a State College freshman, as the individual who kicked out the glass, and Lieutenant Jack Kemmerlin, resident SLED agent in Orangeburg, moved in and arrested him. Some students maintained Dodson had not kicked the window, and many thought the glass was broken by someone pushed forward by surging students.

Police had moved back to cover the bowling alley, and students pressed forward, protesting the arrest of Dodson. Several spat in the faces of officers. Strom later was to testify that when Dodson was arrested, "that is when the officers moved in and fists and clubs began to fly."

Patrol Sergeant John S. Timmerman, thirty-eight, a sixteen-year state patrol veteran who normally was desk sergeant at patrol headquarters in Columbia, was pushing three students back, using his riot baton in front of him. Suddenly, one of them ejected a caustic liquid in his eyes—apparently liquefied tear gas. Timmerman, momentarily blinded, instinctively swung hard with his riot baton, hitting someone. (Timmerman, later promoted to lieutenant, suffered permanent impairment of his vision in the incident.) Chief

Poston thought the police responded after being pushed back against store fronts. Whatever triggered it—the protest of Dodson's arrest, the spraying of Timmerman, or the crowd pressing against police—clubs started swinging and students ran for the street.

A State College student who was confined at the college infirmary after treatment for head injuries later said, "I was standing by the bowling alley and a policeman hit me and knocked me down, and I got up, and I got hit and knocked down again." Through all of this the bowlers inside continued bowling.

Henry Lake, former legal aide to the governor, had come over from his home ten miles away in St. Matthews to observe. In the confusion that followed, Lake—a portly lawyer and one-time highway patrolman—accidentally sprayed tear gas, which he carried for protection, in the face of an Orangeburg city detective, but without serious injury. NcNair several months earlier had promoted Lake to director of the legislative council and later was to name him as the governor's personal representative at the Orangeburg crisis, but Lake was in Orangeburg Tuesday night on his own.

Professor Weston, who was standing near the edge of the action, saw highway patrolmen "move into the students, swinging their clubs." He saw a tall, husky patrolman with his riot stick raised over his head move toward Mrs. Ida Dash, head nurse at the State College infirmary, as she stumbled away from the turmoil. Weston and Lieutenant Colonel Walter Mebane, ROTC commander at South Carolina State, stepped forward and one of them said sharply, "That's not necessary," and the patrolman moved away. Butler and many others saw one patrolman hold a coed while another patrolman beat her. Several other coeds were clubbed.

The students retreated toward the street. Stroman was

among the last to leave. He saw two patrolmen beating a fellow student and tried to help, but was sprayed in the face with a chemical and knocked to the ground by a blow to the stomach.

"When I fell to the ground, one of these cops, a big fat one I'll never forget, started to hit me, but the chief [Poston] saved me," Stroman recalled later. "All he said to me was 'I told you some shit like this would happen, but you wouldn't listen.'" Stroman said, "I saw a policeman beat Emma McCain while two others held her. It made Smitty sick. I saw a policeman run out in the street and pull a gun, but Chief Poston stopped him." Poston testified later that the officer pulled his gun instinctively after being struck by a piece of lead pipe and knocked to the ground. The officer, William Long, was taken to the Orangeburg Regional Hospital for treatment.

On their way back to the campus, the students vented their anger on white-owned businesses, throwing bricks, rocks, and sticks of firewood. They knocked out plate glass windows at a furniture store, a florist shop, a tax office, and two filling stations. They scraped bricks along the paint of half a dozen or so parked cars, cracked windshields, snapped off radio antennas, and broke out windows at an auto display room. They bombarded the East End Motor Company, a Lincoln-Mercury dealer at the corner of College Avenue and Russell Street, four blocks north of the bowling alley and a block from the State College campus. They broke all the windows in a large display room of the motor company and damaged cars parked behind a fence. Total damage at East End Motor Company was $1,800, at least four times that of any other establishment.

Battered and bloodied students, some of them half-carried by other students, stumbled into the State College infirmary. Mrs. Bernice Daniels, the nurse on duty, had never seen anything like it. One student, William Stackhouse, bled profusely from a deep gash across the back of his head. "We got clubbed at the shopping center," a student sobbed to Mrs. Daniels. Emma McCain bled from a lacerated ear and other cuts and was bruised on the face and body. Others had bloodied and bruised faces.

Mrs. Daniels immediately called the campus physician, a white doctor in Orangeburg, and asked him to meet her at Orangeburg Regional Hospital, which still maintained separate emergency rooms for whites and blacks. Eight State College students were given emergency treatment, and Stackhouse was admitted to the hospital. Miss McCain, another coed, and half a dozen male students remained overnight in the college infirmary. Other students were treated at the infirmary and returned to their dorms. Several Claflin students also were treated for injuries, and one coed there was released with her heavily bandaged arm in a sling.

Strom, who had called Governor McNair earlier when the crowd at the shopping center grew large and boisterous, reported to him again after the outbreak of violence. Strom later testified that the police could not use tear gas to clear the parking lot because the wind was blowing "directly into the bowling alley" and that women and children were inside. Poston said that the use of tear gas was discussed, but that many officers didn't have gas masks—this even though trouble was anticipated.

Lieutenant Governor John C. West, attending a dinner across the street from McNair's office in the state capital, got word there was an emergency and walked over to the governor's office about 9:30. West said later:

> I've never seen him more upset than he was. He
> reported he had talked to the law enforcement people and
> that a real tense racial situation had developed and

*erupted to the point of violence, that a police car had been
attacked and officers spat upon, that bricks had been thrown
and store windows knocked out . . . I remember very vividly
he told me Chief Strom said he had never been in a
situation in which he feared more for the lives of his men.
What stands out in my memory was that the police officers
were really concerned about their personal safety . . .*

    *The governor's concern at that time, I remember, was
the fact that this bowling alley had not admitted Negroes.
As I recall, he commented, "My goodness, if it's a violation
of the Civil Rights Act, I would hope that they would
file suit. It would be a shame if the actions of one person
that could be determined right or wrong in the court marred
our race relations." The governor, all of us, had been very
proud of the fact that we had had no violence. We had gone
through a great many tense situations, and I remember
the governor's commenting that it would be a shame if a
little incident such as a bowling alley—which seemed
insignificant when compared to school integration problems
—triggered a situation. He said then it could be a real nasty,
dangerous situation although I don't think either of us had
any idea it would develop into what it did.*

    *I remember him being quite concerned that we might
be put in an almost untenable situation, that we were being
asked to protect a business that might be found guilty of
violating the civil rights law, and he said this in expressing
his desire that there be some determination whether
Negroes had a right to go into this bowling alley or not.*

Before West left, McNair had issued a call for about
250 Orangeburg area National Guardsmen to report for
standby duty at an armory less than two miles from the State
College campus. Strom had heard there were threats to burn
down the shopping center, and he expressed fears that public
utilities might be attacked. Angry white businessmen had
called Poston, demanding protection. For months, McNair and

Strom had attended conferences on dealing with civil disorder in the wake of the major riots that caused millions of dollars in damage at Watts, Newark, Detroit, and elsewhere. The South Carolina National Guard, which was more than 99 percent white, had undergone special riot-control training. McNair told West it was a question of maintaining order in the streets of Orangeburg. It was the first time in memory the National Guard had been called to duty in South Carolina for a racial problem. West did not recall any mention by the governor of students being injured or coeds beaten.

Officials quickly blamed the violence on "outside agitators." Strom later testified that SNCC organizer Cleveland Sellers "took over . . . I wouldn't have believed one man could do it," and that Sellers was on the hood of an automobile talking to the students before the outbreak of violence. However, FBI agent William J. Danielson, who was assigned to cover Orangeburg and who knew Sellers and had followed his activities since the previous October, watched Sellers closely that evening, but never saw him on a car. Danielson later testified:

> [*I saw Sellers*] *walking around, I never heard him say one word because there was a lot of noise and he did not yell out at anyone, but he was talking to groups; and from my observations he talked to a small group of eight or ten and he would walk away, and as soon as he left they would start yelling and jeering and raising cain. When they sort of tired out, he would go to another group and it was very interesting and so I did really observe him. I kept my eye on him pretty good. He did this on several occasions with different groups in the parking lot. When he would leave, they would start up, and then he would go around to another. But I never heard him say one word. I don't know what he told these people or anything else.*

A SLED agent commented later that Sellers harangued the students not to leave after the fire truck arrived and told them that dignity was involved, that "your mammas and daddies have slaved in the fields . . ."

Sellers, who came down to the bowling alley after the arrests, had been in Columbia the night before. Earlier, when he had been approached for assistance by Stroman, Sellers told him the bowling alley was not important. Sellers said later he was leaving the parking lot with the students when the fire truck arrived.

After returning from the bowling alley, many of the students gathered at White Hall, the auditorium where the movie was being shown. They talked about what to do, and Sellers—who had been involved in demonstrations in Mississippi and Alabama—discussed techniques of resistance. He suggested that students form a human blockade across College Avenue (U.S. 601) by linking their arms together and sitting in the street. Assistant Dean of Men William Hammond, who attended the meeting, recalled Sellers could muster no followers. "He didn't move students here," Hammond said. The students discussed Sellers's suggestion of a human blockade and rejected it as foolish and dangerous. Recalled Joe Lambright, a student from Charleston and a Marine Corps reservist, "He didn't go over too good, then or afterwards."

In front of the campus, some students hurled rocks and other objects at passing cars driven by whites. A city policeman whose car was hit stopped in front of the campus and fired a shotgun into the air as a warning, then radioed his action to Poston. In the campus interior, students hearing the gunfire dived for cover, and word quickly spread that a policeman had shot into the campus.

M. Maceo Nance, acting president of South Carolina

State, got a call at his home off-campus from Dean Butler after the violence at the shopping center erupted. Nance immediately drove to the campus and stopped by the infirmary, then went to the hospital where two students were still in the emergency room. He was shocked to see Stackhouse with the deep gash across the back of his head as though his skull had been opened.

Nance then went to the jail to help get bond for Dodson, whose release Nance thought would help cool the situation on campus. When told that Lieutenant Kemmerlin of SLED had made the arrest, Nance went to the bowling alley to see him. When Nance arrived at the parking lot, he was detained at the sidewalk and forced to wait while a patrolman sought out Kemmerlin. To Nance, it seemed a long wait before Kemmerlin came over and told him a judge would have to set bail before Dodson could be released.

Nance returned to the campus, where several hundred students still milled around White Hall. Some wanted to return downtown, but Nance counseled against it and they remained on campus, most of them drifting back to their dormitories.

Henry Smith, who had been hit on the head but not seriously injured, returned to his off-campus apartment. He told his roommate, Bobby Burton, what had happened and described in detail how two girls he knew had been beaten. The beatings seemed to prey on Smitty's mind.

Several student leaders and others, including Dean Butler, gathered at the home of Professor Roland Haynes, head of the psychology department and faculty advisor to the student NAACP chapter. Sellers attended, but said little. Stroman also attended, as did the student body presidents of Claflin and State College. Two television newsmen from Columbia sat in for part of the meeting. Fear was expressed that unless students had an outlet for their frustrations, they would attempt to return downtown the next night and further violence might erupt.

They discussed other grievances based on segregationist resistance in Orangeburg, ranging from job discrimination to segregated waiting rooms at doctors' offices. Finally, it was decided that the student bodies from both colleges would stage a mass march to city hall Wednesday and present a list of grievances to city officials.

Calls were made to inquire about a parade permit. Mayor Pendarvis made no commitment, but agreed to meet in his office at 8:30 in the morning with a committee of six from the two colleges, including the two student body presidents. The meeting at the Haynes residence broke up about 2:30 A.M., and it was agreed the march would be held, with or without a permit, and that the students from both colleges would gather at 9 o'clock at White Hall.

4 : WEDNESDAY—A DAY OF FRUSTRATION

AT 9 A.M., White Hall, the old auditorium on the State College campus, was packed. Students and faculty from the two colleges filled all 600 seats and lined the walls. Newsmen joined students sitting on the floor. Classes were cancelled. Plans were to march downtown to protest the beating of the students the night before and to present a list of grievances to city officials. There was a special sense of outrage over the beating of the coeds, but also an air of excitement over the anticipated protest march.

Acting President Nance told of his shock in going to the hospital and seeing a student with "his head split open," and of first-hand accounts from staff and faculty members of a coed being beaten by one policeman while being held by another. He emphasized that damage to property the night before came "only after our students were set upon by police."

The forty-four-year-old educator showed strength and a

willingness to take decisive action throughout the Orangeburg crisis. As a graduate of South Carolina State he had
worked his way to the top from his first job as a clerk in the
college bookstore. He returned to the college after earning a
master's degree in business administration at New York University. Despite his lack of academic credentials, Nance read
widely, kept abreast of the rapidly changing mood in the
black community, and surprised many of his critics by independent decision-making and efforts to bring more freedom
to the campus and to provide students and faculty with mean-
ingful roles in the life of the college.

Wednesday morning's Orangeburg *Times and Democrat* headlined an article at the top of page one, "Policeman
Injured in Racial Scuffle." A subhead read, "Others Hurt,
Not Seriously, During Protest," and a smaller headline added,
"Windows Broken, Some Arrested." The story reported that
"for a brief time rocks flew and glass broke" and named four
establishments in addition to the bowling alley where windows were broken. It named the city policeman who had been
injured and reported that "he and nine others were treated
and released."

While Nance and the students met at White Hall, the
six-member grievance committee representing the two colleges ran into an unexpected problem in their meeting at city
hall. Edgy city officials refused to grant the parade permit
and suggested as an alternative that they go to the campus
instead and meet with students. City officials were not in a
habit of making official appearances on the State College
campus, and the offer came as a surprise to the committee.

City Manager Robert T. Stevenson, whose voice was
usually dominant in setting city policy, maintained that officials were afraid that because of the ruckus the previous
night, which they labeled a "riot," aroused whites might
create a disturbance. Stevenson later testified that the per-

mit was not granted for fear the students would get out of hand, and that college officials had been unable to control them the night before.

Several hundred National Guardsmen already had been placed on alert, and Dean of Men Oscar Butler suggested there were enough troops to keep order. He later recalled warning Stevenson, "You're not going to be talking to a group of farm kids. These kids are sharp and many of them are angry."

The grievance committee had agreed to support the march only if a permit were granted, Butler said, "because we didn't want to get anybody hurt." After the parade permit was denied, Nance proposed a boycott of downtown Orangeburg until the grievances were met, partly to put some pressure on the city to act on grievances, but also to encourage students to remain on or near the campus. Students cheered and applauded when Nance recommended the boycott and told them, "This is where Mr. Green speaks."

Stevenson, Mayor Pendarvis, and several white business leaders arrived at White Hall at 10:30, and the meeting soon turned into a debacle. The students listened restively when Pendarvis said, "We do not condone police brutality and there are courts to prevent it if it occurs." The first time Pendarvis, a soft-voiced, white-haired merchant, said "Nigra," they began booing and hissing. Like many white southerners, Pendarvis used the traditional pronunciation he had learned for the word "Negro," but sensitive blacks, hearing the word "Nigra," believed whites using it really meant "nigger."

Students continued to hoot at the officials when they were unable to give specific answers on the grievances. BACC Chairman Wayne Curtis asked questions from the floor while holding a microphone, and other students laughed and jeered when the embarrassed white officials tried unsuccessfully to answer. Some of the questions concerned matters outside the jurisdiction of the city officials, such as segregated waiting rooms in physicians' offices.

Cleveland Sellers stood along one wall of the auditorium, enjoying the predicament of the whites, but he asked no questions. However, the white officials apparently assumed he was playing a major role and thought he was the person with the microphone. Stevenson later testified it was Sellers who held the microphone.

Nance told Pendarvis the bowling alley was "just one of several things we are quite concerned about in the community." With the city officials listening, Nance told the assembly, "I do not condone destruction of property, but for the record, it happened after the young ladies were hit."

The officials, somewhat shaken at the end of the meeting, agreed before leaving to consider the grievances and to meet later in the day at city hall with the negotiating committee. A cartoon that later ran in the State College newspaper showed how the meeting looked to students. The cartoon pictured the mayor on the stage saying, "To my knowledge . . . that is . . . er—ah . . . oh yes . . . uh I . . . uh can't help you . . . uh with that . . . problem. It's . . . uh beyond the jurisdiction of my . . . uh office." Nance, commenting on the trip to the campus by the white officials, later observed, "Their visit served no good purpose at all. They had no concrete proposals."

Stevenson, who did not think the group that came to the mayor's office really expected to get a permit, agreed the meeting was a mistake. He said later the city officials had expected to meet with class representatives, not the student body. He believed that Nance had not realized that the city officials had not seen the list of grievances before the meeting.

After the meeting, Nance called McNair in Columbia to seek assistance in getting bond set for Arthur Dodson, the student charged with breaking the glass at the bowling alley.

Nance told the governor that the situation on campus was very tense and that the confinement of Dodson aroused great concern. McNair replied that Attorney General Daniel R. McLeod was flying to Orangeburg and suggested that Nance meet with him to arrange for Dodson's release. At the airport, Nance saw SLED Chief Strom and Police Chief Poston, who were also awaiting McLeod's arrival, and they helped arrange the release of Dodson.

There were more meetings. At 1 P.M., most of the group that had met at Haynes's house met again. At 2 P.M., the State College student body met and discussed marching, permit or no permit. One student rose and shouted that marching had gone out of style, that "violence is what they do today." At that point, student body president Robert Scott observed white reporters standing in a doorway and ordered the door closed.

Also at 2 P.M., the faculty met and discussed the growing seriousness of the situation. At 4:30, the official committee from the colleges met again at city hall to formally present the following list of grievances, expressed in language not even remotely resembling black power rhetoric:

1. Close down the All Star Bowling Lanes immediately and request the management to change his policy of racial discrimination before reopening.
2. Police brutality—The action taken by the SLED officers was uncalled for, especially the beating of young ladies.
3. Immediate suspension, pending investigation, of the officer who fired a shot unnecessarily into the State College campus.
4. The establishment by the mayor of an Orangeburg Human Relations Committee of a biracial nature, with the recommendation that each community select their own representation.
5. A request should be made for a public statement of in-

tent from the Orangeburg Medical Association as to its determination to serve all persons on an equal basis regardless of race, religion, or creed.

6. Formulate or integrate a fair employment commission in the city of Orangeburg.
7. Change the dogmatic attitude of the office personnel at the Health Department and the segregated practices used there.
8. Extend the city limits of Orangeburg so as to benefit more than one segment of the community.
9. Give constructive leadership toward encouraging the Orangeburg Regional Hospital to accept the Medicare Program.
10. Eliminate discrimination in public services, especially in doctors' offices.
11. The integration of drive-in theaters.
12. Fulfill all stipulations of the 1964 Civil Rights Act by leading the community so that it will serve all people.

Immediate action was asked on the grievances, but no priority indicated.

In the meantime, Attorney General McLeod had met with city officials, Chief Strom, and National Guard Commander Colonel Robert McCready. They all agreed the bowling alley should close for the night, but were not sure whether Floyd would cooperate. Mayor Pendarvis stepped out to phone Floyd and returned with word that Floyd would close the bowling alley. "Everybody breathed a sigh of relief," McLeod later recalled.

Mayor Pendarvis, in describing his reception on campus as "rough," told McLeod that Sellers had used a microphone in the auditorium.

From the mayor's office, McLeod called Stephen Pollak, an assistant attorney general in charge of the civil-rights division in the Department of Justice. McLeod, who had dealt with Pollak on official matters in the past, knew a complaint about the bowling alley had been made to the Department of Justice. Pollak told him he had the matter on his desk. McLeod replied, "For Lord's sake, put it on top of the pile and get the thing rolling."

Various court decisions had been divided on whether or not bowling alleys were covered by the Civil Rights Act of 1964. McLeod and Pollak both were uncertain, but Pollak said he believed the courts ultimately would conclude bowling alleys were covered under the public accommodations section of the act. This section was based on the interstate commerce clause of the Constitution rather than the broader "equal protection" clause of the Fourteenth Amendment, which would have required an end to racial discrimination by an establishment serving the general public. If a bowling alley contained a restaurant that served food shipped in interstate commerce, the bowling alley automatically was covered, but McLeod and Pollak were uncertain whether Floyd's snack bar fell into that classification.

"We wanted the federal government to institute the action, and bring it quickly as possible," McLeod later recalled, "so as to bring this matter to a head. We believed that if the federal court said the place was under the Civil Rights Act, it would compel the bowling alley operator to let everybody in . . . if the federal court said he could exclude whoever he wants to, it would at least clarify the legal situation."

While at city hall, McLeod several times heard fire trucks roar out of the adjoining fire station. He finally asked what was going on. "That's been going on all day yesterday and all day today," someone said, "practically all of them false alarms."

Although McLeod had been sent to Orangeburg by the governor, the city officials asked him not to attend the meeting with the college group. They indicated to McLeod they did not want to give the impression to the Negro delegation of being overly concerned. During the meeting in the council chambers, McLeod remained hidden in the mayor's office. There, he called McNair. The governor especially wanted to know whether the bowling alley was covered by the Civil Rights Act and McLeod told of his conversation with Pollak. McNair later made calls to the White House to try to speed up action on the case by the Justice Department. Pollak already was preparing a letter to Floyd asking for voluntary compliance, a routine step before filing a formal complaint, and the letter was mailed late Wednesday.

Inside the council chamber, Pendarvis told the delegation from the colleges that he would not call a special meeting of city council and that he would not use the mayor's office to appoint an official human relations committee for the city. Instead, he suggested they appear at the next meeting scheduled for city council—almost two weeks away. Pendarvis did inform the group that the bowling alley would be closed that night. The other grievances either were deferred until a human relations council would be named or else were declared not in the jurisdiction of city officials.

On one matter of concern, Chief Poston explained that the officer accused of firing unnecessarily into the campus had shot into the air as a warning to rock-throwing students. He offered to have the officer take a lie detector test if student witnesses would also. City officials said reports of police brutality should be made to the FBI. The college group returned to the campus in frustration, able to report only that the bowling alley would not open that night.

The lack of communications between the city and the colleges distressed McLeod. The next day in Columbia, he told the governor, "You have two camps sitting down there, one out at the college, one uptown, both of them belonging to the same country, the same state, same county, same city, and it's a hell of a note when you have two groups of people parleying back and forth like a couple of warring nations."

The Wednesday afternoon *Columbia Record* ran an Associated Press wirephoto of an angry-faced State College student pointing, the night before, toward law enforcement officers, and the caption said the students dispersed only after breaking windows and overturning cars, and after a policeman was hospitalized for injuries. In fact, no cars were overturned; all property damage except the broken glass at the bowling alley occurred after the students were beaten and were returning to campus, and total property damage amounted to less than $5,000.

The angry students involved were black, and the response of the state was to a "little Detroit" rather than to a severe case of college students letting off steam. Hundreds of additional National Guardsmen and highway patrolmen poured into Orangeburg Wednesday.

A statement issued in Washington that day by Representative Albert W. Watson, an archconservative Republican whose congressional district embraced Orangeburg, reflected the temper of the times. Based only on fragmentary information, Watson's statement was bound to appeal to his conservative white supporters, many of whom saw all protests by Negroes as communist-inspired.

> For the past few years we have heard a great deal about legitimate dissent. The civil disturbance which occurred in Orangeburg, S.C., Tuesday night, and which still threatens to erupt again, can, under no circumstances, be termed legitimate, and it was certainly not peaceful dissent.
>
> What is occurring in Orangeburg at this moment is just another step in an overall plan to disrupt this entire nation.
>
> Hearings before the House Committee on Un-American Activities, on which I serve as a member, have proved without

a shadow of a doubt that these riots are planned long in advance by so-called civil-rights leaders and groups which are bent upon destroying the Democratic process.

Law enforcement officials on the scene in Orangeburg are to be highly commended for their magnificent efforts in putting down this threat of anarchy. The chief of police and his department, the Orangeburg County sheriff and his deputies, Chief Strom and the South Carolina Law Enforcement Division, and the South Carolina Highway Patrol acted swiftly, positively and courageously in putting down this riot.

Certainly the entire nation can look to the example set by these gentlemen in Orangeburg, S.C., and gain an insight into the proper way to curb a serious civil disturbance . . .

Watson went on to mention "such despicable characters as Martin Luther King, Floyd McKissick, and Stokely Carmichael."

Back on the campus, dusk was settling. In White Hall, student body president Robert Scott arrived late from the city hall meeting and found that student NAACP president George Campbell had already informed the students the bowling alley was closed. But Campbell was unable to answer other questions, and disgruntled students had begun walking out when Scott arrived.

At the student center, a lone male student watching a seven o'clock newscast from Columbia heard Governor McNair express concern over the situation in Orangeburg and blame the trouble mainly on "outside agitators." The student stalked out, cursing, "Man, you don't know what the shit you're talking about."

Scott walked briskly out of White Hall, scowling and obviously agitated, and told a reporter he was too busy to talk. Other students ambled out of White Hall, frustrated and with no plan of action. A few minutes later, a barrage of rocks and pieces of brick struck a white news photographer's car as he was driving off the campus. Students moved to the front of the campus and began throwing rocks at passing vehicles, but Dean of Students Henry Vincent and several student leaders persuaded them to return to the campus interior. Vincent, believing the situation had quieted down, drove to his home a mile and a half from the campus.

However, restless students later returned to the front of the campus, which faced U.S. 601. There, they pelted several cars with rocks and bottles, and a roadblock was ordered by law enforcement officials to divert traffic around the area.

At the corner of 601 and Russell Street, the south end of the roadblock, Patrol Corporal Norwood F. Bellamy was approached by a white station wagon whose left rear window had been shattered by a soft drink bottle that lay on the back seat. Gasoline was splattered over the cargo area. A white man at the wheel, obviously upset, huddled a deaf-mute boy under his arm. Bellamy directed him to Police Chief Poston to make a report on the incident. National Guardsmen with fixed bayonets helped patrolmen man the roadblock at the 601-Russell Street intersection and also blocked off the shopping center parking lot in front of the bowling alley.

At the other end of the roadblock, three blocks to the north, two cars containing women and children were struck by missiles before Lieutenant Jesse A. Spell's squad could close the road. Later, more than 100 students massed on the Claflin campus near Spell's squad, yelling obscenities, shouting, "Honky, hey, honky," and throwing things at the patrolmen.

A soft drink bottle landed near Lieutenant Spell, and he ordered his men to back up. Now, they were too far away for the students to hit them, but the students kept throwing. Many students still were talking angrily about the girls' being beaten the previous night.

About two blocks from the State College campus, a

group of Claflin students ventured near a white man's house and were greeted with a blast of birdshot. Three were treated for wounds at Orangeburg Regional Hospital and released. The man telephoned city police and reported he had shot at a group of Negroes after he heard a commotion in his yard and objects hit his house. Police found debris in the yard and minor damage to a vehicle.

A little after 10 P.M., campus security chief B. E. Evans received a call that a car had left something behind Miller Hall, a women's dormitory on the western edge of the State College campus. Investigating, one of his men found two soft drink crates less than half-filled with crude Molotov cocktails, made from soft drink bottles filled with gasoline and stuffed with rags. The firebombs were turned over to the FBI.

Meanwhile, a fire slightly damaged a vacant house adjoining the front of the campus. Firemen also found smoke, but no flames, in answering a call to a warehouse across the street from the Claflin campus. They put out a small fire at a liquor store and found evidence of a possible firebomb. They answered five false alarms after 9 P.M.

Just after 11:15, a car carrying two white teenage brothers slipped into the main campus entrance from 601. It sped through the campus, and one of the occupants fired a pistol several times. Suddenly, the youths found they had turned onto a dead-end street. As the driver turned around, students bombarded the car with rocks, bricks, and boards, cracking several windows.

Captain Evans and two of his men jumped into a patrol car and chased the vehicle as it sped back off campus and headed north on 601. Evans fired two or three times, shooting out a tire with the last shot. A highway patrol car that had joined the chase arrested the youths and took them to the sheriff's office, where they were charged with reckless driving.

The next day, Evans added a charge of shooting firearms on a public street.

At 11:28 P.M., the Orangeburg Fire Department received the report of the fire at the unoccupied house adjacent to the State College campus. Another fire was set three hours later, both causing minor damage before being doused by firemen. The sprawling fourteen-room house was owned by Mrs. Jenny Brunson, an eighty-two-year-old white woman who fourteen months earlier had moved into a nursing home.

Across the railroad tracks from the Clafin campus, four highway patrol cars—with two patrolmen in each car— parked in front of the wooden frame residence of Cleveland Sellers. McLeod headed for Columbia at midnight, after driving in Orangeburg all evening with a SLED officer. By 1:00 A.M. the college area was quiet, and Lieutenant Spell directed his men to clean up their end of 601. They removed rocks, bricks, bottles, glass, sticks, and several pieces of metal pipe.

The students who had been throwing at patrolmen from the Claflin campus had dispersed. Most of them returned to dormitories, where a great majority of the students had remained throughout the evening. Many still clustered in the dorms, discussing the night's events, especially the shooting by the white boys on the State College campus and the shooting of the three Claflin students.

After leaving the Claflin campus with a group, Henry Smith joined other students in a dormitory lounge, sharing their continued sense of frustration. A little after 2 A.M., Smitty called his mother at home in Marion, South Carolina, a small county-seat town 110 miles northeast of Orangeburg. To his mother, the rangy sophomore—six-feet-four-inches tall and weighing 180 pounds—was "Peanut," a nickname he picked up because of his brittle bones. On Tuesday, he had written her a letter headed, as usual, "From the desk of

H. E. Smith"; it began, "My dear Mother," and told of taking the ROTC test and of plans to go into advanced ROTC if he passed. He wrote of finding a new peace of mind that semester, "something everybody wants—once you find it you are ready to live not only for yourself but for the people you care for." The letter ended: "Write soon and pray for me."

His mother—a hard-working, proud, independent woman of deep religious conviction and faith—had raised Henry and three other children in a four-room shotgun house (one in which you can fire a shotgun through the front door and out the back, shooting through every room without hitting anything). It had an outdoor privy. Her husband had left the family when Henry was a small child. Every Sunday, Mrs. Smith, her mother, and the four children all walked three miles to church.

When Henry was deeply troubled, he always turned to his mother for guidance, and he was deeply troubled when he called home more than two hours past midnight. He told her, "The way those policemen beat those girls, I could just see 'em beating you, Mother . . . I wish you had been here; it was shameful . . ."

Mrs. Smith, who prays on her knees and "ain't ashamed of it," advised her son not to go back in the streets any more, but to take the grievances "to the highest authorities." He replied, "Mother, we've already gone and we just get talk, talk, talk."

"Sit tight on the campus," she told him, "but if you have to go, pray."

5 : THURSDAY—A DAY OF FOREBODING

AN ALMOST eerie calm settled over the campuses of Claflin and South Carolina State colleges on the morning of February 8. Class attendance was near perfect at State College, and in each classroom the following memorandum from Acting President Maceo Nance was read:

> I called to your attention yesterday that the situation in Orangeburg was very tense and dangerous and we appealed to the student body to remain on campus because of the dangers involved. We again impress upon you that your personal safety is in jeopardy, and we are requesting that all students remain on campus and refrain from going to the periphery of the college's campus, throwing brickbats and bottles as was the case last night. The shooting last evening bears out the danger involved in this kind of violence and destruction.
>
> The faculty and staff of South Carolina State College met yesterday and indicated to the president of the student

body that they would support your grievances as listed, but it must be understood that by no means would they or could they support violence and destruction.

Until some semblance of order is restored, students are requested to remain in the interior of the campus. I sincerely hope that we can have your cooperation in this matter.

In Columbia, Governor McNair was trying to get the White House to pressure the Justice Department to act on the bowling alley. McNair also was being urged to intervene personally, but he refused to do so. An aide said McNair expressed "continued concern."

Albert Dawson, a sophomore from Charleston, later recalled about Thursday: "By that time we had a lot of other grievances. After Wednesday night, frustration shifted to the police action; the bowling alley dropped out of it. I don't think a suit would have had much effect at that time." It was a day of growing tension. Dawson also said—and other students agreed—"If Governor McNair had come and met with student and faculty groups, there wouldn't have been a problem. If he had just put in an appearance, it would have changed everything."

But there was no action on the grievances except for a call from City Manager Stevenson to college officials that the Justice Department had been contacted. Nance was given no directions, either by McNair—who never called him during the day—or by the college board of trustees.

The student government leadership was virtually discredited because of the failure to get any action on the grievances. Resentment and frustration continued to build on campus. White newsmen who ventured onto the State College grounds were harassed and cursed by increasingly hostile students. Most of the newsmen were looking for Cleveland Sellers, whom McNair was pointing to as the cause of trouble.

Sellers had spent Wednesday night in a dormitory room,

and Nance instructed the dean of students to prohibit "un-authorized persons" from entering dormitories or the student center. Before noon, Sellers returned to his home across College Avenue and the railroad tracks. He was accompanied by several BACC members. The patrol cars were gone. Commenting on the attention being focused on him, he told newsmen who found him at his home, "Everybody is looking for a scapegoat." He spent Wednesday night on the campus because he was afraid to go home with the patrol cars stationed in front of his house, he said.

As for SNCC's role, Sellers said his organization was interested in the situation, but not directing it. He said he had been in touch on the average of every other day with Stokely Carmichael and that Carmichael "probably will come to Orangeburg if they incarcerate me." Sellers gave the impression he hoped that quote would get into print and that the police then would cut down their harassment of him.

To Sellers it was a "drastic error" for students to have called off a march on downtown Orangeburg Wednesday after city officials refused to grant permission. He attributed rock-throwing by students Wednesday night to their having no plan of action. "The students have just cause to be very angry," he said. "Everybody forgets they got beat up two nights ago." He thought a march should be held, but only in the daytime. "It would be suicide at night," he said, and called the situation "extremely dangerous." That afternoon, Sellers tried to enlist support for a downtown march, but again he had no followers.

Sellers later recalled February 8 as "a strange day on the campus. If you believed in signs and witchcraft, you could feel it. People were walking, not saying much, going to class, and nothing was happening. But you knew something was going to happen."

Off the campus, Orangeburg was bristling with armed

men. McNair activated 110 additional National Guardsmen. To add to the tension, bowling alley operator Harry Floyd said he would reopen and that he planned to stay open until the normal midnight closing time. "My policy has not changed," he said in regard to allowing Negroes to bowl. A letter to Floyd from the Justice Department was in the mail, but would not arrive until Friday morning.

About 5 P.M., after pressure from city officials, Floyd agreed to close the bowling alley. Earlier that day, Floyd had told the Associated Press that Negro students want to "strike a match to my place so they can light fires all over town." Rumors swept the white community, whipping up mass fear that militants would try to burn down the city. Floyd later said, "The shopping center was planned to be burned down Wednesday night. My boy's life was threatened . . . it's been quoted that Sellers said the bowling alley owner was going to die tonight." Actually, Sellers would not venture off the campus at night because of his fear of the police. He told newsmen, "My people say the police have orders to 'shoot the long-haired niggers first.'" Other rumors also spread among the students.

McNair's reaction was to continue to escalate force. In previous months the governor had been to conferences to discuss the McNamara plan to utilize the National Guard in event of large-scale civil disorder—and that was the view McNair apparently was taking of Orangeburg. National Guardsmen were sent to guard public utilities. SLED Chief Strom later testified it was done "because we know that's the plan of the Black Power people—to do away with your waterworks, lights, telephone service, so forth, gas and such things as that."

A headline Thursday morning in the Columbia *State*, South Carolina's largest daily, said, "We Have No Intention of Letting Things Get Out of Hand—McNair." The story reported that the governor told a hastily called Wednesday afternoon press conference, "We want to avoid property damage and injury to anybody."

Relatives of Mrs. Brunson, the eighty-two-year-old woman who owned the unoccupied house that had been set afire, called Orangeburg police and requested assistance in moving out all furniture of value. Before noon, the furniture was moved out.

Thursday afternoon, Colonel P. Frank Thompson, veteran commander of the South Carolina highway patrol, drove to Orangeburg, met with senior patrolmen, and instructed his men to use firearms only as a last resort if their lives were in danger. That decision, it was implied, would be left to each individual patrolman. Colonel Thompson then returned to Columbia.

Orangeburg City Manager Stevenson reported threats had been made to burn down the Livingston warehouse across the railroad tracks from the Claflin campus and also a warehouse owned by Mayor Pendarvis.

Citizens stopped Police Chief Poston wherever he went to tell of new rumors, often accepted by them at face value —black militants from other states were moving in; Rap Brown and Stokely Carmichael were on their way; there were plans to burn Orangeburg. These and other tales spread throughout the city. False fire alarms sent sirens screaming through the streets. Businessmen in the campus area armed themselves. A gas station operator allowed newsmen to use his restroom, waving them inside with a pistol. Store owners had loaded shotguns behind their counters.

Reporter David Bledsoe of the Columbia *State* entered a small funiture store across the street from the bowling alley late Thursday and talked to an angry proprietor and several people with him. They showed Bledsoe two or three high-caliber rifles, two shotguns, a pistol, and a box of double-

ought buckshot shells for the shotguns. When another newsman called the city police department to find out if charges
had been pressed in the shooting of the three Claflin students,
a police lieutenant said, "That man had every right to shoot
those people."

While state officials were pressing the Justice Department, Earl Middleton of Orangeburg turned to another federal agency, the Commission on Civil Rights. Middleton, a
Negro businessman in Orangeburg and a member of the
commission's South Carolina State Advisory Committee,
called Washington in the afternoon and told a staff representative the situation was exceedingly volatile and expressed
fear someone would be killed if immediate relief were not
obtained. After the call, the commission contacted the Justice
Department immediately to ask about the legal status of the
bowling alley, but was told by an attorney in the Community
Relations Service the question still seemed "up for grabs."

In Orangeburg, seventeen people showed up at 5 P.M.
at a baseball park a mile from the campus for a special
prayer service called by the Reverend Eddie Hightower. A
boyish-faced man in his late twenties from Denmark (the
home town of Cleveland Sellers), Hightower was a student
at the Orangeburg college of the Southern Methodist Church
—a denomination that preached Biblical sanction of racial
segregation as doctrine. Hightower prayed for good Christian white people to support Mr. Floyd and his bowling alley
and for the Almighty to deliver Orangeburg from its
troubles.

A group of student leaders drove to Columbia early in
the afternoon to meet with civil-rights leaders there in an attempt to get help on the grievances. Mrs. Modjeska Simkins,
long-time matriarch of the civil-rights movement in South
Carolina, later recalled that George Campbell, student
NAACP president, said he feared there would be bloodshed

if something wasn't done. "He had a foreboding something would happen," she said.

Later in the afternoon, Mrs. Simkins and NAACP leader Billie Fleming, of Manning, met with John Cauthen, chairman of the state Higher Education Commission. The meeting had been scheduled for weeks, and the objective of the Negro leaders was to boost Dr. Charles H. Thomas as a candidate for president of South Carolina State College. (Dr. Thomas was president of the politically influential statewide Voter Education Project and a professor of education at South Carolina State College.) However, the conversation with Cauthen dwelt on the deteriorating situation in Orangeburg. Cauthen found Mrs. Simkins and Fleming deeply disturbed.

During the meeting, which lasted almost three hours before breaking up after 5:30, there was emphasis on the tension that had been growing on the campus for the preceding six weeks, caused by the failure of the trustees to name a permanent president and to act formally on the Blackwell report. Cauthen immediately called McNair, who agreed to call a meeting of the board of trustees the next week, and Cauthen relayed this to the Negro leaders. However, upon returning to Mrs. Simkins's office, they reported to Cauthen that the students had gone back to Orangeburg after hearing that conditions on the campus had worsened. Cauthen left a telephone number where he could be reached if needed.

Also in Columbia, Attorney General McLeod suggested to the govenor that he bring in Orangeburg city officials to meet with Greenville Mayor David Traxler, who had set up an effective biracial council in his city to deal with grievances. McLeod called Traxler away from a banquet table that night to set up a meeting the next morning in the governor's office. Orangeburg city officials had agreed to attend.

In Orangeburg, word had spread among the students

that the Reverend I. DeQuincey Newman, state NAACP field secretary, would speak at a 6 P.M. meeting on the Claflin campus. Actually, Newman knew nothing about it. Two BACC members, who later said they thought it might reduce tension to get the students talking, planted the rumor that Newman would talk in order to draw a crowd.

Several hundred students went to the Claflin gym for the scheduled meeting, but were told Newman would not appear. Several BACC members walked in with posters, such as "Let the Bricks Swing." Someone said that white people with guns were parked near the campus. No one was in charge of the students and no leader emerged from the speakers. Finally, Blinzy L. Gore, a Claflin dean, told the students they had to leave. Many left, grumbling that they had heard nothing but "a lot of talk."

Meanwhile, Newman had come to Orangeburg for a strategy conference near the campus with NAACP officials, including student leaders. Unsuccessful attempts were made to call McNair, whom they wanted to intervene personally. Newman had been a key contact for the governor with the Negro community, but he was never consulted during this week of crisis.

After the meeting at Claflin, Albert Dawson returned to his dorm for more clothing. It was a near freezing night. Henry Smith led a group of students who tried to build a bonfire about 7:30 on Watson Street, just in front of an embankment at the edge of the State College campus.

Watson Street, a block-long side street, forks off U.S. 601 (College Avenue) at the southwest corner of the campus. The streets join at the end of State Street, the main entrance to the campus. The bonfire site was a few yards from the apex of a triangle of land bounded by Watson Street, College Avenue, and Russell Street. East End Motor Company, the scene of Tuesday night's major damage, was located at the base of the triangle, a block south of the campus entrance. The bowling alley was located four blocks west on Russell Street.

The intersection of Russell Street and U.S. 601 had become "Checkpoint Charlie," main command post for the law enforcement officials. National Guardsmen and highway patrolmen stood beside barricades that blocked traffic from passing in front of campus rock throwers.

Dawson was in his dormitory room when he heard the bonfire would be built. He joined other students going to the front of the campus. Students took wood from a construction site and picked up other scraps of wood and piled it all in the middle of the street. Police had stayed away from the campus, but a city police car drove up. A policeman jumped out with a shotgun. A fellow officer took the wood out of the street and placed it on the sidewalk at the foot of the embankment. The students, about fifty of them, scampered up the embankment and jeered. Dawson remembers them shouting, "What you want, honky? What you want, man? Can't we build a bonfire?" Some of the students remained outside in the cold night air griping about their latest plan being thwarted. Other students went back to their dormitories.

Dean Butler toured both campuses and found "everything was unusually quiet." Here and there small groups of students milled around, and some complained because police had blocked off U.S. 601 in front of the campus to prevent them from hurling objects at white motorists.

A few minutes past eight, Patrol Lieutenant Jesse Alfred Spell, who was to play a leading role in the night's events, was called at his motel room to report with his seventeen-man squad to U.S. 601 and Russell Street, the "Checkpoint Charlie" intersection. There had been a report that a group of students were getting ready to march off campus, a reference apparently to the group of fifty or so that had gathered for the bonfire attempt.

The forty-five-year-old lieutenant, ruggedly handsome, his wavy gray hair flecked with brown, easily carried 190 pounds on a large-boned, six-foot-two-inch frame. He had been a patrolman for twenty-one years. He later told of fearing the students "would do considerable damage to property and possibly citizens"; he moved his squad to block Watson Street at the corner of Russell, the rear of East End Motor Company, to head off any attempted march.

About 8:30, Isaac McGraw arrived in Orangeburg and went directly to see Chief Strom. McGraw, who had arranged the meeting between McNair and the class presidents the previous spring, was called late Thursday afternoon by SLED. Until then, McNair had ignored those who had helped settle the earlier crisis. Strom wanted McGraw to try talking to the students, but McGraw concluded the students were in no mood to talk to anyone and that the situation was too tense to venture on campus.

Shortly before nine o'clock, a student group had moved to the edge of the Claflin campus and had begun to hurl rocks and other objects at patrolmen stationed at Livingston's warehouse and at a freight depot located across College Avenue and the railroad tracks that ran parallel to the highway. Just after nine, someone began sporadic firing of a .22-caliber weapon from the Claflin campus, shooting over the heads of patrolmen across the railroad tracks.

Patrolman L. G. Dobson, stationed in front of the warehouse, heard periodic shots "and occasionally you could see a flash resembling gunfire from the campus. And also we could hear the bullets whiz over our head, also heard them slam into the building behind our back . . . they were continuously throwing rocks, and pieces of brick, and Molotov cocktails at us."

FBI agent Nelson L. Phillips heard two or three bullets hit the warehouse above his head. One bullet whined over the depot, apparently aimed at a street light behind it. A rock bounced off Dobson's helmet. The men in front of the warehouse were ordered to move behind it. Someone ran into the street and hurled a crude Molotov cocktail that hit the warehouse. From the campus came the cry, "Burn, baby, burn." Flames flared a few seconds, then flickered out. Two blocks away, Lieutenant Spell left his post and ran a short distance to the "Checkpoint Charlie" command post to report the warehouse fire and possibly call a fire truck, but then saw the flames had gone out.

Behind the depot, UPI reporter Max Ford heard a loud explosion and walked over to a patrol sergeant to ask what the noise was. It was a shotgun blast fired into the air from a riot gun as a warning. Near the depot, a gray bus with metal bars was parked, a "cattle car" from the South Carolina Department of Corrections, on hand for possible mass arrests. On the Claflin campus, the shooting ceased, and students stopped throwing things. Minutes later, Patrolman Dobson and the rest of the District Two squad were instructed to move to the "Checkpoint Charlie" area, two blocks away.

About 9:30, a bugle sounded from a window in Lowman Hall, a dormitory 400 feet across Lowman Field from the embankment. The bugler sounded "Charge" and students milling around the campus interior moved down to Lowman Hall to see what was going on. Someone said, "Let's go build a bonfire," then everyone seemed to say, "Yeah, let's go build a bonfire."

Cleveland Sellers appeared at Lowman Hall, then drifted back to another dormitory when a group started down for a second attempt to build a bonfire. Once again students piled wood in Watson Street, and Henry Smith threw a gasoline-filled bottle. It did not break. Someone threw a second bottle that broke and a match was tossed on the gasoline. More wood was added and the blaze grew, attracting other students. Smith and others warmed their hands around the fire. Someone yelled, "Hey, honky, come roast some marshmallows with us." There were other yells of "Floyd's a bastard. Get him, honkies, go get Floyd . . . hey, honky, here we are."

Albert Dawson remembers there was concern not to let the flames get too high for fear they would burn the wires overhead. "Everyone was enjoying the fire," recalled Dawson. "Everyone was joking, gleeful, cracking jokes." About 200 students eventually gathered on the embankment. They jeered at the police and sang "We Shall Overcome" and "We Shall Not Be Moved," traditional songs of the civil-rights movement—songs disdained by young black militants since they began preaching "Black Power" in 1966. For the students, the bonfire was an act of defiance, an outlet for frustration, at last a means of visible protest of grievances.

Henry Smith threw a rock against a billboard near East End Motor Company, then a bottle at a traffic sign on College Avenue. Later, he and others ripped down several traffic signposts, and tossed them into the fire.

Other students ripped out window shutters and shattered the windows of the vacant house on Watson Street at the edge of the campus, about forty feet from the embankment. Earlier in the day, police had removed all valuable contents from the rambling frame structure. The shutters, a bannister railing, and other wooden objects torn from the house were hurled on the fire. Several heavy, two-foot bannisters from the railing were left in a pile on the campus near the embankment.

From the bonfire, Smith dragged a burning signpost out into U.S. 601 and heaved it into a patch of dry grass between the highway and the railroad tracks. Students around the bonfire shouted gleefully as the grass caught fire. Smitty seemed to be everywhere at once. Later, numerous witnesses would tell how the lanky sophomore dashed around, tossing objects, helping build the fire, shouting at the patrolmen, and encouraging other students to protest.

"We never thought about being arrested for anything," recalled Dawson. "We were just frustrated and couldn't do nothing . . . We just had to do something to let it out. The bonfire was it." Someone lit a rag wrapped around a stick and threw it at the house. There was a brief glow under the house, then it flickered out. Another of the crude torches flamed out as it bounced off the side of the house.

At Orangeburg police headquarters, Henry Lake—the governor's former legal aide—"could feel tension building up from reports coming in from all units." A little after 10 P.M., he went down to "Checkpoint Charlie."

Several coeds joined in at the bonfire. One of them, Louise Kelly Cawley—a married senior—went down to the front of the campus "to voice my opinion" because of what happened at the bowling alley. "I wanted to be there personally myself to participate in the bonfire," she later testified, "and if we were going back down to the bowling alley, I was going to go down there, too."

Earlier, Henry Smith had talked of marching to the bowling alley. "Hey, man, you better cool it," BACC leader Steve Moore told Smith at the time. "You gonna get killed. These crackers gonna kill you." Dawson recalled, "Smitty said, 'Let's go down to the bowling alley,' but he was just saying it; we weren't going to go."

Not only had the bowling alley closed, but all of downtown Orangeburg had been blocked off to traffic after the shooting from the Claflin campus. National Guardsmen manned barricades at all intersections. The confrontation at the campus attracted scores of cars filled with whites. Whole families and teenagers with dates parked near the college grounds to watch the unfolding drama. In one car, two couples munched popcorn as they watched from across the railroad tracks. An occasional pickup truck with a gun mounted on a rack behind the driver patrolled, then parked near the campus.

A campus patrol car intermittently drove down State Street near the bonfire, but reported to campus security chief B. E. Evans no imminent danger. Oscar Butler had moved to the campus police information office with Captain Evans more than two blocks from the bonfire.

To Nathaniel Abraham, a Negro magazine editor from Columbia, the situation looked ominous. Abraham had gone to Orangeburg at the request of Mrs. Simkins, the Columbia civil-rights leader. He arrived there after 8 P.M. and found "everything in turmoil." Apprehensive over the large number of police and National Guardsmen near the colleges, Abraham went on campus and talked to student leaders, telling them civil-rights groups in Columbia had the ear of the governor. He told the students that another twenty-four hours were needed to talk over the problem with the governor. Most of those milling around the campus returned to the dormitories, but some drifted down to the bonfire.

The students at the bonfire told Abraham they would stay as long as the National Guard remained in the street. He talked to SLED Chief Strom, Patrol Captain Carl Fairey, and Police Chief Poston, and they told him to tell the students to move back from the front of the campus. "I don't know what the alternative was," Abraham recalled. He went back, but the students refused to leave. Abraham found them in a jovial mood.

Across the street, several State College coeds who lived in a private residence stood outside and watched the bonfire. Carrie Tyson, the only white coed at the school, suggested leaving after a half-hour, but one of the other girls said,

"Let's stay, something's going to happen tonight; something's going to happen tonight, child."

A few minutes before 10:30, Strom and other officers at "Checkpoint Charlie"—after observing the grass fires and the tossing of flaming objects at the vacant house—conferred and decided to call a fire truck to douse the bonfire for fear it might spread further. With siren wailing, the truck arrived at Russell Street and 601 at 10:30. Patrolmen were ordered to move up with it to protect the firemen. National Guardsmen were ordered to deploy between 601 and the railroad tracks opposite the bonfire. The truck proceeded slowly.

Lieutenant Spell and his squad were directed to move up Watson Street; they scrambled up an embankment as they came to the vacant house. Strom and Captain Fairey, the senior patrol officer on duty, sent in four squads altogether— sixty-six highway patrolmen in all. Fairey then began to trot toward the bonfire. The sixty-one-year-old patrolman, bespectacled and somewhat slightly built, suffered from chronic bronchitis and began to wheeze and cough. He stopped, gasping for breath.

Strom, the officer in overall charge, moved briskly toward the bonfire. SLED Lieutenant Leon Gasque, Strom's number one assistant, accompanied by SLED Lieutenant Carl B. Stokes and FBI agent-in-charge Charles H. DeFord, drove up near the bonfire in the SLED command car. It was equipped with a powerful loudspeaker system and mobile telephone for direct contact to the governor, and it contained a supply of tear gas grenades in the trunk.

On the campus, Cleveland Sellers had heard the siren and he walked out of a dormitory in the campus interior, toward Lowman Hall and the bonfire, to see what was going on. As the troops moved up with the fire truck, students retreated from the bonfire and ran up the embankment, then began heading back toward Lowman Hall, cursing as they went. Several rocks and bottles fell around Lieutenant Spell's squad.

At 10:33, Patrolmen David Shealy and Donald Wayne Crosby, two men in Lieutenant Spell's squad, moved up together from the embankment to the vacant house. Shealy moved in front of Crosby and started around a bush, Crosby right behind him. Crosby saw two white bannister posts coming through the air, "coming down like they were falling out of the sky almost, and I ducked and I saw one coming for Patrolman Shealy. It was too late to do anything about it."

6 : "THE MASSACRE"

TENSION and confusion swept through the ranks of the patrolmen after Shealy fell, and if anyone was in overall command, it was not apparent. Several patrolmen shouted that Shealy had been shot. Others ran from their posts on the embankment to where he lay by the vacant house.

Sergeant Sidney C. Taylor, hearing someone yell, "Shealy's been shot," ran a few feet to his side and rolled him over on his back to find he was "bleeding profusely around the mouth and nose."

Corporal Norwood F. Bellamy ran from District Five's position on the embankment and "observed his face covered with blood and his gasping, giving the appearance of a man who was dying." Another District Five member, Patrolman J. W. Brown, got only a glimpse of Shealy but "it was my impression that he had been shot" and Brown dropped behind the embankment.

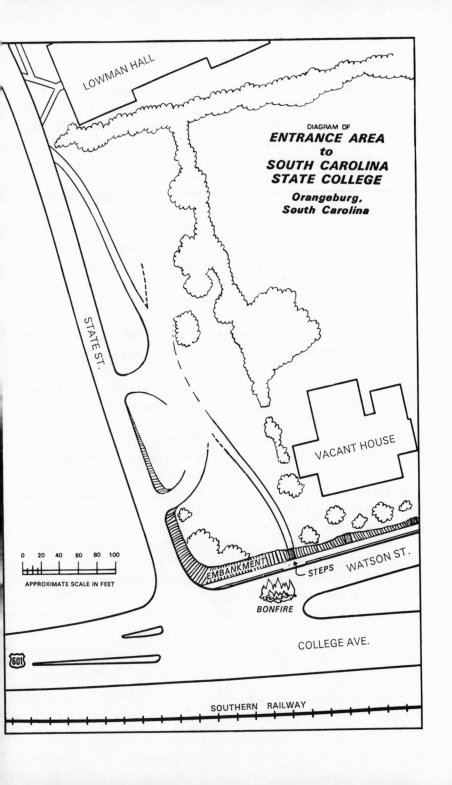

DIAGRAM OF
ENTRANCE AREA
to
**SOUTH CAROLINA
STATE COLLEGE**

*Orangeburg,
South Carolina*

LOWMAN HALL

STATE ST.

VACANT HOUSE

EMBANKMENT

STEPS

WATSON ST.

BONFIRE

0 20 40 60 80 100
APPROXIMATE SCALE IN FEET

601

COLLEGE AVE.

SOUTHERN RAILWAY

Sergeant Henry Morrell Addy, who was directly behind
Shealy, saw a bannister fall at the patrolman's feet as he
keeled over, but "assumed he had been shot" and "saw that
he was bleeding profusely about the face and observed him
to be unconscious, and his entire body was jerking rapidly."
If Addy had looked at the heavy, three-foot-long bannister,
he would have seen teeth marks and a smear of blood.
Shealy was struck on the mouth and bridge of the nose.

Lieutenant Spell ran to Shealy's side, then ordered
Sergeant Taylor and another patrolman to take him to a
patrol car. Patrolman first class Louis B. Judy, Jr., of Lieutenant Spell's District Six squad "rushed to the fire truck to
ask them to radio for a rescue truck." The call was logged at
10:34 at the fire station.

Three patrolmen peered over the embankment, shoul-
dering their weapons and aiming them at the shadowy figures
now fleeing back toward Lowman Hall. Other officers
dropped behind the six-foot embankment or crouched behind bushes, and still others remained standing, fidgeting with
their weapons.

The official ostensibly in charge, SLED Chief Strom,
along with FBI agent Charles DeFord and SLED Lieutenants
J. Leon Gasque and Carl B. Stokes, had been parked in a car
a block away. Strom stepped from the vehicle and walked
briskly toward the fire engine and "the first thing I heard was
a patrolman had been hit. I looked on the ground and there
on the ground lay a patrolman. His face was bloody, and I
didn't know what caused his injury, but he was injured and in
a little bit an automobile drove up and they picked him up
and carried him to the hospital."

Still gasping for breath because of a coughing spell,
Captain Carl Fairey, the senior patrol officer, had been unable to reach the scene from "Checkpoint Charlie" a block
away.

Nathaniel Abraham, the Negro editor, had noticed the patrol moving toward the campus and had run to a pay telephone across the railroad tracks from the campus to call Mrs. Simkins, the civil-rights leader. She and Fleming, the NAACP leader, called Cauthen, the Chairman of the Commission on Higher Education, and asked him to try to get through to the governor.

Cauthen telephoned the governor's mansion; when a butler answered and said the governor was not in, Cauthen asked to speak to Mrs. McNair. The butler said she was out of town too, then asked if he knew Mrs. McNair. Cauthen replied that he knew her well and that he had some emergency information about Orangeburg; the butler said to hold the phone a minute. Then the governor got on the line. Cauthen told of his call from Mrs. Simkins and Fleming and said they had Abraham holding on a telephone in Orangeburg.

"They say you've got a terrible situation down there," Cauthen told McNair. "The militia's drawn up to the campus and the students are confronting them, and the students have Molotov cocktails, and all hell can break loose any minute, and they would like something out of you that might calm the situation down. Is there any message I can give them back?"

Cauthen later recalled that McNair replied that the troops had orders to contain the students on the campus because they were going to burn down Orangeburg if they got off the campus. He said McNair told him, "You can tell them for me that if the students will draw back, preferably go back into their dormitories, then I'll order the militia, the patrol and all, to back off from the campus."

Cauthen called Fleming and Mrs. Simkins and gave them the governor's message, and they said they would call Abraham back. Mr. Simkins recalled Cauthen telling her the governor said the students "were going to burn down a white lady's house and it's got to be protected."

Meanwhile, Abraham had made an unsuccessful attempt of his own to call the governor, then rushed back across the tracks to appeal again to Strom. Noticing patrolmen on the bank raising and lowering their weapons, Abraham "grabbed Chief Strom by the arm." He pleaded to be allowed to use a bullhorn to talk to the students in an attempt to "keep my people from being hurt." "I tried to get him to stop it," Abraham said later. "I told him there was no need. I was excited, but as near as I remember, he said, 'You're too late.'"

By now most of the students had run back to the vicinity of Lowman Hall, about 400 feet from the embankment. Some were embarrassed at having retreated. There were grumbles that it was their campus and that the police had no business there, and some students began drifting back toward the embankment.

Basically, it was a question of honor—of asserting their manhood in the presence of the all-white police power that had clubbed black girls. But if there was a spirit of bravado, there was also a feeling among most of the students of being secure as long as they were on the campus. "Hey, man, they can't do nothing to us on our own campus," one student cried out.

Some students started back down simply because that was where the crowd was going and because they wanted to see the firemen putting out the bonfire. The students apparently were unaware that a patrolman had been injured. A few who saw Shealy being helped down the embankment thought it was a student being arrested.

If those who headed back down—and a few remained to linger outside Lowman Hall—could not stand up physically against the overwhelming power they faced, they at least could dare to hurl the vilest of epithets. As some ambled along casually and others almost trotted, there were shouts of "honkies" and "motherfuckers." A few carried rocks, bottles, and bricks, but other students yelled for them not to throw.

Among the crowd were students who had never been involved in a civil-rights demonstration, not even in the bowling alley protests. Most of them were from South Carolina State, many were from Claflin, and a few were from Orangeburg's Wilkinson High School. Several State College football players were there, although their coaches had urged them to refrain from protest activities.

A rescue truck pulled up near the fire engine, its siren wailing. The driver parked the vehicle after being told the injured patrolman had already been taken to the hospital in a patrol car.

It was now 10:38 P.M.—at least five minutes since Shealy had been injured—and the bonfire had been doused, although smoke continued to billow from the charred wood. The students, numbering about 150, were strung out on Lowman Field for about 100 yards—from 100 feet away from the embankment back to Lowman Hall. They were proceeding roughly along a narrow footpath usually used by students to cut across campus, although some were scattered out for several yards on either side.

To the patrolmen they were only silhouettes on the darkened campus, outlined by the headlights of several patrol vehicles and a street light on Watson Street, and by two utility pole lights on campus—one on State Street about halfway between Lowman Hall and the embankment and the other a powerful light in front of Manning Hall just beyond Lowman.

On the students' left, although most of them were unaware of it, was Lieutenant Spell's squad, deployed mostly around the bushes of the vacant house—sixteen men, now that Shealy was gone. Three of them—Spell, Addy, and Taylor—were armed with shotguns; the others had revolvers and riot sticks, and some had carbines.

Near the embankment and to the right of the students were several members of Lieutenant R. M. Sullivan's seventeen-man District Five squad, most of whom were stationed along the embankment. At the extreme left flank of the squad was Corporal Joseph Howard Lanier, one of four squad members armed with shotguns. Lieutenant Sullivan and Sergeant C. C. McDonald of Sullivan's squad were armed with carbines.

Also stationed along a 100-foot stretch of the embankment, from a point near the bonfire to a clump of bushes at the entrance of State Street near where Lanier crouched, were twelve District Seven squad members and twelve District One squad patrolmen. Some of them had dropped low, using the embankment as a shield, and not even their silhouettes were visible to the students.

Altogether, there were sixty-six state patrolmen, backed up by forty-five National Guardsmen armed with M-1 rifles and fixed bayonets. In addition, some of the twenty-five SLED agents in the area, several members of Orangeburg's twenty-eight-man police force, and several sheriff's deputies were nearby. At the moment of ultimate confrontation there were about as many lawmen and Guardsmen as there were students. In addition, sixty-one other state patrolmen and 395 other National Guardsmen were on duty in Orangeburg that night. Maceo Nance, the state college president, later observed, "With the police power on hand, they could have arrested the entire college community if they had wanted to."

Some students chanted, "Your mama's a whore, your mama's a whore." Several patrolmen repeatedly raised and lowered their weapons, as though taking aim. And the three patrolmen on the embankment who had taken aim after Shealy was hit shouldered their weapons.

The patrolmen's shotguns were loaded with deadly buckshot used to kill deer and other heavy game. The buckshot ranged in size from Number 1 to the largest manufactured—double-ought, which is about the size of a .32-caliber slug.

Although some patrolmen later claimed the students were charging at them like a thundering herd, throwing bottles and bricks and other objects, the evidence was overwhelming that few objects were being thrown, that there was no shooting, and that the students were not running.

Ellis MacDougall, director of the Department of Corrections, whom Strom had called to the scene in the event of mass arrests, was struck in the leg by a rock and at first thought he had been shot. No one else was struck by a missile, and witnesses were to testify later to seeing only three other objects thrown—two bannisters and a dirt clod.

The front ranks of the students now were within about 100 feet of the embankment and about the same distance from Spell's squad on their left and from Corporal Lanier and several other patrolmen on their right.

Suddenly a carbine fired. Patrolman first class Judy, who had returned to his post by the vacant house after calling for the rescue truck, heard the gunfire to his left. Other witnesses later told of hearing the same gunfire—several shots fired into the air in rapid succession by a patrolman, apparently as an intended warning.

Most of the students, still scattered all the way back to Lowman Hall, turned to run. Some held up their hands and others dropped to the ground. Almost simultaneously a volley of shotgun blasts and the crack-crack-crack of a .38-caliber pistol caught them in a cross fire.

Spell, Addy, and Taylor blasted away with shotguns from the students' left side. Corporal Lanier opened up with a shotgun from the bushes on their right-front side. Corporal Bellamy and two other District Five squad members—Patrolmen John William Brown and Colie Merle Metts—fired shotguns over the embankment. So did Patrolman Allen Jerome Russell of District Seven, at twenty-four one of the youngest riot squad men on the scene and apparently the only member of his squad to fire. Patrolman Edward H. Moore of the District Five squad, who believed the patrol gunfire was "a spontaneous reaction to the situation," also fired over the embankment—six times with a .38 Colt police special. All of the patrolmen were to later say they had not fired at any particular target, but had just shot into the crowd of students.

Johnny Bookhart, nineteen, a soft-spoken sophomore "too busy to be involved in civil-right demonstrations," had been writing a theme in his room at Lowman Hall, but had stepped out on the dormitory porch just before the gunfire erupted to see what was happening. "It was like a wave of soldiers falling down, like a scene out of a war movie," said Bookhart, who was felled by a pellet in the knee as he stood on the porch.

Henry Smith was in the first wave. He had never retreated very far toward Lowman Hall and that was one of the reasons some of the students had started back toward the front of the campus. Smith caught the brunt of several shots from both sides, was spun around by the force, then shot again in the back, a slug entering behind his right shoulder and exiting through the left side of his neck. A physican later counted five separate wounds.

About twenty feet to the left and front of Smith, Savannah Williams, nineteen, a State College sophomore, caught a load of buckshot in the left shoulder. Another State

College sophomore, Charles W. Hildebrand, nineteen, who had started back toward the embankment "after someone said Smitty was down there," first thought the patrol was shooting blanks "to frighten us." He later testified:

> So I turned when I heard the gunfire and then somebody next to me hollered, "Oh, Lord, I'm hit." So immediately, I fell to the ground. Upon falling, I felt a blow in the back of my leg which felt like a piece of brick or something had been thrown against it. So I stayed on the ground maybe a half-second and got up and ran a step or two farther and was hit in the hip. I got up and ran again . . . and was shot a third time in the arm pit . . . I hid behind a trash can.

Other students ran or crawled in panic as buckshot continued to riddle the area. Some hid behind trees and utility poles and others behind trash cans. Some lay still on the cold ground.

Samuel Hammond, eighteen, a stocky football player, was shot in the back. Delano Herman Middleton, seventeen, a high school student whose mother worked as a maid at the college, suffered seven wounds—three in the forearm, one in the hip, one in the thigh, one in the side of the chest, and one in the heart.

A freshman, Robert Lee Davis, Jr., nineteen, a towering linebacker for State College who had been scouted by pro football teams, hit the ground about 100 feet from the embankment and the vacant house as the gunfire erupted. He crawled toward Lowman Hall for several seconds, "then I got up under a street light, took two steps and I got hit in the back and felt like I was floating. Everything came up in my stomach." A buckshot slug physicians at first mistook for a rifle bullet lodged next to his spine.

Tall, bushy-haired Cleveland Sellers had just stepped into the light of the utility pole on State Street, about 250 feet from the embankment, a little closer to the vacant house. "I turned around and so many people were hollering for help that I grabbed one and then let him go and grabbed another one who seemed to be in worse shape," Sellers said later. "They kept shooting and I was getting ready to hit the ground when I felt something hot hit the back of my arm. It burned and my arm started getting numb. I saw men coming and I ran behind a tree and then a garbage can."

The student Sellers tried to help probably was Thompson Braddy, twenty, a Claflin freshman who was felled by buckshot that tore into his right elbow and left leg as he turned to run about twenty feet in front of Sellers.

Henry Smith's roommate, Bobby K. Burton, twenty-one, a sophomore, whose parents were schoolteachers, was in the middle of the group of students when he was hit in the right hand. He fell and was struck twice more—in the left arm and right leg. His arm was paralyzed.

Richard McPherson, nineteen, a State College freshman, was near the front ranks and had just looked back over his shoulder after hearing students cautioning others not to throw anything. "I was hit in the back of the head," he later testified, "and I was unconscious for maybe thirty seconds, maybe longer, maybe shorter, but when I awoke this person was crawling over me and when I came to, the shooting was still going on, and as I was getting up, heading back toward campus, I heard this person over there saying help me because he couldn't walk. So I reached out to help him. I started back towards campus, I got shot again in the back . . ."

A few feet in front of McPherson, Joseph Hampton, twenty-one, an Army veteran and former State College student, turned to run and was struck in both legs, and a few feet behind McPherson two other students—Samuel Grate, nineteen, a Claflin sophomore, and Harold Riley, twenty, a State College sophomore—were cut down as they tried to flee. Grate was struck in the buttocks and pelvis and Riley in the pelvis and right knee.

About 150 feet from the embankment, several feet to the right of Grate, Bobby Eaddy, seventeen, a State College freshman, dropped to the ground as the shooting erupted. Seconds later he was hit in the back of the right shoulder. A few feet away buckshot ripped into the right arm and right thigh of Ronald Smith, nineteen, a Claflin junior who had tried to run.

Two State College students—Joseph Lambright, twenty-one, a junior, and Thomas Kennerly, twenty-one, a senior—were walking near the front ranks, a little more than 100 feet from the embankment and about the same distance from the vacant house. "I saw some officers coming around a tree by the vacant house," Lambright recalled later. "I was concentrating on them and I didn't even see those on the embankment. Someone had suggested we sit down and watch and I was in a crouching position fixing to sit down when they shot. I hit the ground and started crawling. I crawled for about twenty yards and felt a sharp pain in my right shoulder."

Kennerly hit the ground immediately and lay still. He later explained: "I naturally thought they were shooting over our heads when it started, but the way I knew they weren't was a guy about ten yards away from me said, 'Oh, Lord, I'm hit.' Students were yelling and hollering and crying in pain—Oh, Lord." As he lay on the ground Kennerly was hit in the upper right arm, left hip, and left big toe. Just behind Kennerly, Robert Watson, nineteen, a Claflin freshman, was shot in the foot, thigh, and buttocks.

A few feet behind Watson buckshot tore into Frankie

Thomas's left cheek, knocking out fifteen teeth and splitting his tongue. The eighteen-year-old Claflin freshman also was struck in the leg and the back of the arm. Behind him Herman Boller, Jr., nineteen, a Claflin sophomore, turned to run, "got about four of five steps . . . was shot in the thigh twice . . . fell on the ground and stayed about ten, fifteen seconds, then was shot in my left foot."

Robert Williams, nineteen, a State College freshman, and Jordan Simmons, III, twenty-one, a State College senior, were in the rear ranks, about 300 feet from the embankment and almost that far from the side of the house.

"All I saw was fire from their muzzles and students falling on the ground," Williams later testified. "I started scuffling on my stomach like everyone else. I thought they were shooting over our heads, but while I was scuffling something hit a bottle next to me and it burst. So I got on my hands and knees to make better time. I don't know how far I went . . . but I felt something hit me in the arm. As I moved on, my arm got cold. I reached back and felt nothing but blood on my sleeve."

Simmons earlier had promised his fiancée he would stay away from the front of the campus so he had ventured no farther than 100 feet from Lowman Hall and was standing there when the patrol opened fire. He hit the ground and began crawling toward the dormitory when buckshot struck near his neck, lodging next to the spine.

Albert Dawson, eighteen, a State College freshman, who had been a leader in the week's protest activities, had run back toward Lowman Hall after seeing Lieutenant Spell's squad maneuvering around the house. "I heard someone yell out that they got Smitty," he later recalled, "but I don't know whether they did or not because this was just before the shooting. I was facing the embankment and had an open view toward the bonfire." Dawson started back toward the embankment and was about 200 feet away when he was hit in the chest and knocked down immediately. "I started crawling and other students were crawling and running and one next to me said, 'I'm hurt, oh, God, help me.' "

A few feet to Dawson's right side, buckshot ripped into the left shoulder of Samuel Grant, nineteen, a State College sophomore. Herbert Gadson, nineteen, a lumbering State College freshman, hit the ground near the rear ranks, then got up to run, but dropped again as the shooting continued. Buckshot tore into his left hip as he lay there.

Ernest Raymond Carson, seventeen, a State College freshman, was near the front ranks and "ran and hopped to get away and the first time I got hit I turned sideways. But I kept going and got hit again and fell. Then I got hit in the sole of my foot." Eight buckshot slugs hit him—in the heel, sole, thigh, and back of the right leg.

Two high school students—Harvey Miller, fifteen, and Ernest Shuler, sixteen—and two fellow students had stopped off on the campus to watch the bonfire while cutting across Lowman Field on their way home from a movie. Buckshot ripped into Miller's right leg, chest, and abdomen, and into the back of Shuler's right arm and the bottom of his right foot.

A majority of the patrolmen had not heard an order to fire, although Lieutenant Spell later said he shouted "now" to his squad before firing. As the shooting continued, several patrolmen, including some who did not fire, shouted to stop.

Patrolman James R. Powers of District Seven frantically pulled a whistle from his pocket and blew it in an effort to stop the shooting. Powers was armed with a rifle and a revolver but never took the safety off either one even though he later testified he saw two bannisters "land right in front of me." Patrolman Brown of District Five later recalled that after firing his shotgun twice he heard several patrolmen yell, "Stop firing." Lieutenant Spell recalled "immediately" ordering the District Six squad to cease firing after discharging his own shotgun twice, and Sergeant Taylor said after firing once he yelled several times, "Hold your fire!"

Witnesses likened the scene to a battlefield. CBS-TV cameraman Reginald Smith, whose film of the firing indicated it lasted eight to ten seconds, compared the sound to "a small war." After the shooting stopped, those not too badly injured began making their way to the college infirmary, about a block on the other side of Lowman Hall. Some hobbled without aid, others with the help of students who had escaped injury.

Governor McNair got his first report from Strom immediately after the shooting. The governor later told close associates that he was on the telephone with Strom at the time of the shooting, that Strom left the phone momentarily and then reported, "Governor, I'm afraid something terrible has happened."

Few coeds had ventured on the campus that night and one who did, Louise Kelly Cawley, twenty-seven, a senior, narrowly escaped injury. Mrs. Cawley, a gritty civil-rights activist who had helped start the bonfire, was back near Lowman Hall when the shooting occurred. She later testified:

> All of a sudden I heard one big boom and everybody said, "Hit the dirt," and I hit the dirt and then after that . . . it sounded like machineguns, you know, and a lot of students said they were hit, and I said, "Man, you got to be kidding." I said, "No one would shoot a group of unarmed students," and one guy said, "Yes, I'm hit, please help me."
> So my girlfriend and I went back towards the embankment and helped one student towards White Hall, and when we got to White Hall someone took over that student and carried him to the infirmary and we saw another one laying out on the ground and we went back over there and he said he was all right and he was just too scared to get up. So he got up and went to the infirmary.

Samuel Hammond, the football player who had been shot in the back, was helped to the front of Lowman Hall where he collapsed. Two officers in a campus police car picked him up and drove him to the infirmary.

Henry Smith and Delano Middleton, one of the high school students, lay moaning on the field, one of them calling for his mother. Several patrolmen prodded Smith with their riot sticks, apparently to see if he was alive. Four students later told federal investigators they saw a patrolman strike Smith with the butt of a gun.

Several patrolmen grabbed Smith and Middleton by their hands and feet and dragged them across the field, down the embankment and toward the rescue truck that had been called for Patrolman Shealy. "If you'd been home where you belonged, you wouldn't be in this fix," a patrolman muttered. The rescue truck driver helped put them in the truck, then sped toward Orangeburg Regional Hospital a mile away.

At the college infirmary Mrs. Bernice Daniels was the only nurse on duty in what seemed to her like a long nightmare that kept getting worse. She had been the only nurse on duty Tuesday night when students who were beaten at the bowling alley were brought in and she had been the only one on duty Wednesday night to care for the three Claflin students who had been peppered with birdshot. Now a steady stream of the wounded poured into the infirmary, dripping blood as they came, some moaning, some calling, "Help me, nurse," others looking grim but saying nothing.

Faculty members and students rushed in to help administer first aid, but such mass confusion developed that coaches finally stationed four huge football players outside the infirmary to keep out those who were not injured. Several hysterical coeds fainted and were brought in and given sedatives.

Hammond was moaning "Oh, Lord," calling for his

mother, and talking incoherently. Mrs. Daniels took one look at him, quickly checked and found him "cool and clammy," and ordered him taken on a stretcher to a station wagon to be driven to the Orangeburg Hospital.

With no ambulances available, students began running to their own cars and driving the wounded to the hospital. One of them, Nathaniel Jenkins, twenty-one (a senior who was later commissioned an Army second lieutenant and served in Vietnam), had hit the ground when the shooting erupted and crawled away, apparently uninjured. But after arriving at the hospital with his second load of casualties he felt a sharp pain in his left foot and took off his shoe to find that he had been shot in the left heel.

Physicians at Orangeburg Hospital—only a few were on duty when the first students arrived, but seventeen were there within fifteen minutes—worked rapidly to treat the wounded. The police were there, too. And the hospital was segregated, although it had been under a court order to desegregate since February 18, 1965.

"Who's laughing now?" scoffed an Orangeburg policeman as he walked past injured students in the emergency room. Another, asked by a hospital staffer what had happened, said, "A couple of these niggers got stung with birdshot."

The physicians and most other hospital staffers went quietly and professionally about their work, but several staffers showed little compassion for the injured students. One woman commented, "I don't see what they're hollering about, the niggers got what they asked for."

Most of the students remained quiet, but Thomas Kennerly looked at a policeman who was laughing and said, "You laughing when somebody's dead and you gonna pay for it." Another student told a physician who was removing buckshot from his leg, "You better be ready tonight. We'll be right back, and I'll be back with them. You ain't seen nothing yet."

John Carson, a twenty-five-year-old high school math teacher and a Claflin graduate, rushed to the emergency room after his brother Willie, twenty-three, told him their younger brother, Ernest Raymond, had been shot eight times. John found him in a wheelchair in the hall of the emergency room and asked what happened. "I got shot eight times," his brother told him. "I don't know what happened."

Then he nodded at some highway patrolmen standing beside a Negro deputy sheriff near the exit and said he thought they were among those who fired. John turned to the patrolmen and shouted, "Why did it happen, why did it have to happen?" He was told to be quiet, but kept repeating, "Why did it have to happen?"

A patrolman told John he was under arrest, grabbed him by the seat of the pants and began dragging him from the emergency room toward a patrol car. John dug in his heels and protested. As he continued to resist, a patrolman hit him in the head with a rifle butt and blood spurted out. John's brother Willie, who had followed him outside, took a step forward and several officers stuck guns in his face. The two brothers were hustled into a police car and taken to the county jail by a Negro deputy.

John, dazed and still bleeding, noticed his tee shirt was covered with blood when they arrived at the jail. "I'll die before I go to jail," he told the officers; "I want to go to the hospital." The patrolmen asked the Negro deputy if he thought Carson needed a doctor. The deputy hesitated, then said he thought he should be treated. Before taking John to the hospital, a patrolman directed that Willie be locked up. The two brothers asked why, and the patrolman snapped, "Lock him up, goddamit."

At the hospital, Carson's wound was closed with twenty-two stitches; then he was returned to jail. (He and his brother were released the next afternoon on $500 bond each and charged with assault and battery and resisting arrest. John, whose only prior arrest had been on a traffic violation, later paid a $50 fine. Willie paid a $25 fine.)

A surgeon, Dr. Roy C. Campbell, was treating Patrolman Shealy in the white emergency room when the injured students began arriving in the adjacent emergency room for Negroes. Campbell had found Shealy "semi-comatose . . . not oriented as to what was going on . . . practically drowned in his own blood," and quickly stitched up a gash on his nose. Then he hurried into the Negroes' emergency room to check Henry Smith and Sam Hammond.

Dr. Campbell found five wounds on Smith—two imbedded in the area of the buttocks which were not serious, one in the left neck below the ear, another in the back of the right shoulder, and one which entered the area of the rib cage, made a four-inch tear in his liver, and pierced his vena cava, the main vein leading to both legs.

The physician tried desperately to save Hammond, who had a single wound in the back, two inches to the left of the spine. But the injury was fatal. Hammond died at 11:30 P.M., less than an hour after the shooting.

Meanwhile, Delano Middleton, a 200-pound high school football and basketball star, had called for his mother from a table in the emergency room. Someone telephoned her. She arrived at the hospital with another son, Dureward, a senior at Claflin, while the family physician, Dr. A. B. Wolfe, was preparing to treat Delano.

Mrs. Reather Middleton, a church-going Baptist who raised Delano and Dureward and her two daughters to be the same, grasped Delano's hand as he lay on the table. Blood oozed from a chest wound over the heart.

"Bullets were flying in every direction, Mama," the youth blurted. "Everywhere."

Mrs. Middleton sensed he was dying. So did Delano. "You've been a good Mama, but I'm gonna leave you now," he said. "Tell me the Twenty-third Psalm, Mama."

"The Lord is my Shepherd," Mrs. Middleton intoned, and Delano repeated the entire psalm after her, then said, "Thank you, Mama, I feel so much better now."

Back at the State College campus about 100 students, scared and angry, had stopped off at the police information booth, about a block above Lowman Hall, and tried to get campus security chief B. E. Evans to provide them with guns. He told them he and the other officer there had only their own weapons. The students left and minutes later an electronic burglar alarm sounded in the police booth, indicating the ROTC armory a block away was being burglarized.

By the time campus police arrived, several students had escaped with three rifles and several boxes of ammunition. The students, amid whispered fears that police might rake dormitories with gunfire as police had done at all-black Texas Southern University in Houston in 1967, rushed to a girls dormitory and took up defensive positions. Other students and an ROTC officer appealed for the return of the rifles and ammunition, however, and they were turned in within twenty minutes.

Meanwhile, Mrs. Cawley, the coed who had narrowly escaped injury, ran into trouble while shuttling wounded students in her car to the hospital. On her third trip back to the campus she and another coed were stopped by three officers she later swore were Orangeburg policemen. Mrs. Cawley resisted when the officers tried to force her into the police car "because I was afraid for my life because of what had happened." They beat her and sprayed a chemical in her face, she was to testify. Then, after another coed "told them they could be in trouble for hitting on me and I was expecting," they took her to the hospital. Several of the injured students in the hospital's emergency rooms for Negroes saw her staggering through the door and refusing the assistance of an officer she accused of beating her. "Keep your grubby hands off me," she declared, then collapsed on the floor.

Cleveland Sellers, who was waiting for treatment, later recalled that Mrs. Cawley "came in crying, 'I've been beaten, I've been beaten.' That kind of blew everybody's mind. Then she fell off the table at one point and was yelling and screaming and some of the brothers jumped up to try to help her and one of the deputies—there were five or six armed deputies, all wearing riot helmets—jumped up and said, 'Get back over there—don't let's get started again.' " A week after the incident Mrs. Cawley suffered a miscarriage.

After Sellers was treated for a minor wound in the armpit, a Negro deputy pointed him out to Sheriff Robert Dukes of Orangeburg County. Dukes took him by the arm and said, "Come with me." As they walked through the room Sellers,

---

THE FACING DIAGRAM illustrates the approximate location of all the injured students and all the defendant highway patrolmen at the time the patrolmen opened fire on February 8, 1968. The location of Sam Hammond (number 12) is not shown because there is no evidence where he was located at the time he was shot. Hammond died shortly after arrival at Orangeburg Hospital, but had been helped back from Lowman Field before he collapsed.

The location of the highway patrolmen is based in most cases on their statements to the FBI. The location of Patrolmen Russell and Lanier is based on maps they marked that were attached to their statements. The location of Patrolmen Addy, Bellamy, Spell, and Taylor are based on their statements. Patrolmen Brown, Metts, and Moore were less specific in their statements and their locations on the diagram represent rough estimates based on the location of their squads that night.

The location of the students is based on trial testimony, interviews, and other evidence. All students who testified marked their precise location on a map at the trial.

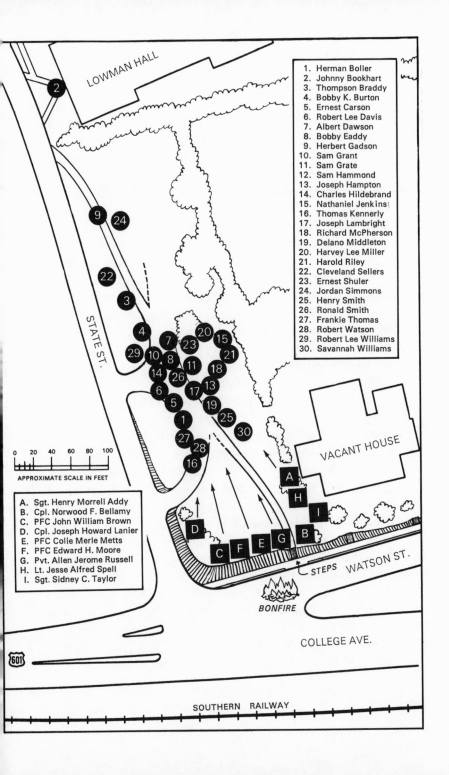

LOWMAN HALL

STATE ST.

1. Herman Boller
2. Johnny Bookhart
3. Thompson Braddy
4. Bobby K. Burton
5. Ernest Carson
6. Robert Lee Davis
7. Albert Dawson
8. Bobby Eaddy
9. Herbert Gadson
10. Sam Grant
11. Sam Grate
12. Sam Hammond
13. Joseph Hampton
14. Charles Hildebrand
15. Nathaniel Jenkins
16. Thomas Kennerly
17. Joseph Lambright
18. Richard McPherson
19. Delano Middleton
20. Harvey Lee Miller
21. Harold Riley
22. Cleveland Sellers
23. Ernest Shuler
24. Jordan Simmons
25. Henry Smith
26. Ronald Smith
27. Frankie Thomas
28. Robert Watson
29. Robert Lee Williams
30. Savannah Williams

0 20 40 60 80 100
APPROXIMATE SCALE IN FEET

A. Sgt. Henry Morrell Addy
B. Cpl. Norwood F. Bellamy
C. PFC John William Brown
D. Cpl. Joseph Howard Lanier
E. PFC Colie Merle Metts
F. PFC Edward H. Moore
G. Pvt. Allen Jerome Russell
H. Lt. Jesse Alfred Spell
I. Sgt. Sidney C. Taylor

VACANT HOUSE

STEPS WATSON ST.

BONFIRE

601

COLLEGE AVE.

SOUTHERN RAILWAY

worried about his own safety, told every student he passed, "Y' all see I'm going with the sheriff. The sheriff's got me."

Sellers was driven to the courthouse where Sheriff Dukes, Chief Strom, and Chief Poston conferred before coming up with multiple charges against him—arson, inciting to riot, assault and battery with intent to kill, destruction of personal property, damaging real property, housebreaking, and grand larceny. City Magistrate Tom Friday set bond at $50,000 and Sellers was hustled into a patrol car and sped to the state penitentiary at Columbia, forty miles northwest.

At 1:10 A.M. Delano Middleton died. News of his death sent a new shock wave through the beleaguered State College campus. Hysteria spread among the coeds, further burdening the infirmary which was still caring for several of the wounded. Nance, the college president, hurried from dormitory to dormitory requesting that radios be turned off so that the coeds would not continue to hear news reports. Some newscasts had put the death toll as high as five.

By now Henry Smith's blood pressure had dropped dangerously low. Dr. Campbell quickly operated and managed to restore the pressure, then stitched him up. For a moment the physician thought Smith would survive.

"He looked up at me with those big brown eyes and for a moment I thought we had him saved," Dr. Campbell later told federal investigators. But sudden hemorrhaging of the neck and shoulder wounds proved fatal. At 1:45 A.M. Smith died, the third fatality of the night. Twenty-seven other students had been wounded, all but two or three shot from the rear or side.

Two television newsmen driving back to Columbia after covering the confrontation listened to their police-band radio as additional patrolmen headed toward Orangeburg; they heard this message to the patrolmen: "You should have been here, ol' buddy; got a couple of 'em tonight."

7 : AFTERMATH

NO ONE had seen any students armed with guns, no firearms or spent cartridges were found on the campus after the shootings, and a bannister—not a bullet—had felled the only injured officer. A great preponderance of witnesses were to testify later that they heard no shooting from the campus for fifteen to thirty minutes prior to the time the patrolmen opened fire. Yet, on-the-scene press coverage, as well as the official version of what had happened, led the nation to believe that a gun battle had taken place.

The Associated Press moved four different leads of its account late Thursday night, and each declared that two students had been killed "during a heavy exchange of gunfire" in which a patrolman had been "struck in the head by a bullet." And that was the account that appeared in most of the nation's newspapers. Although it was based largely on statements by an AP photographer who later said he had

been misquoted, the AP never bothered to run a correction
—except for a clarification of how Patrolman Shealey had
been injured.

The official version of the incident emerged at a 2 A.M.
press conference at the Orangeburg National Guard armory.
Guard officers said the patrolmen had returned fire from the
students, but emphasized that no Guardsmen had fired. In
fact the Guardsmen's weapons were not loaded and most of
the Guardsmen had not even been issued ammunition until
after the shooting.

In contrast to the official version, white-haired Dean of
Men J. F. Lesesne of Claflin told a Friday morning assembly
at the State College that he had watched the confrontation
from near the border of the two colleges and had heard no
shooting by students. He charged that many students were
shot at close range after they fell and that many had back
wounds.

Nance had called the 9 A.M. assembly of students and
faculty members to announce that the colleges were suspend-
ing classes indefinitely. He told the students, "I think under
the circumstances the best place for you to be is at home with
your friends, relatives, and loved ones." Many of the students
appeared dazed as they sat quietly through the assembly.
They accepted without question an offer by state NAACP
officials to provide leadership during the crisis. The NAACP
also made funds available for students who did not have
money for transportation home.

Some students expressed fear of the state highway patrol
and National Guard and were reluctant to leave the campus
to get to bus and train stations. Others were more angry and
hostile than afraid. After the assembly, students cursed and
threatened white newsmen who tried to interview them.

The Friday morning Orangeburg *Times and Democrat*
streamered a two-line headline across the top of page one,

"All Hell Breaks Loose—Three Killed, Many Wounded in College Nightmare." A subhead added, "Officers Blast Rioting Negroes."

Orangeburg resembled an occupied city. One writer termed it the largest concentration of force there since Sherman's march. National Guardsmen in wide-tracked armored personnel carriers that resembled tanks rumbled through the streets and patrolled the campus area.

Meanwhile, state officials in Columbia from Governor McNair down blamed the shootings on riotous conditions caused by "black power advocates." Justice Department officials in Washington from Attorney General Ramsey Clark down believed that even the distorted news accounts indicated at least a case of overreaction by patrolmen. To Clark it appeared it might even be a case of an attempt by law enforcement officers to impose summary punishment, a federal offense.

At a noon press conference McNair announced that because of continuing tension he had declared a state of emergency in Orangeburg and imposed a 5 P.M. curfew. The governor, showing deep concern about the state's image, called it "one of the saddest days in the history of South Carolina." He continued:

> The years of work and understanding have been shattered by this unfortunate incident at Orangeburg. Our reputation for racial harmony has been blemished by the actions of those who would place selfish motives and interests above the welfare and security of the majority. It has become apparent that the incident last night was sparked by black power advocates who represent only a small minority of the total student bodies at South Carolina State College and Claflin College. We commend the large portion of the students who remained on the campus and took no part in the violent and provocative demonstrations.

McNair's statement apparently was based on an account of the incident he had received from SLED Chief Strom, who stood beside him during the press conference. (Both McNair and Strom refused to be interviewed for this book.) The statement indicated the governor had little grasp of what had happened. He stated categorically that the confrontation had taken place *off* the campus and that the seriousness of the situation before the shooting had been compounded by the theft of rifles from the college's ROTC armory—an incident that actually had occurred more than thirty minutes after the shooting. He talked of a firebomb attack on "a private residence" as though someone still lived in the vacant house next to the State College campus, and he said that the patrolmen fired in response to the wounding of Patrolman Shealy, although Shealy was injured at least five minutes before the gunfire. He stated:

> There have been erroneous reports that last night's incident occurred on the campus of South Carolina State College and that the deaths were caused without provocation. The facts are that the confrontation took place off the campus while South Carolina highway patrolmen, SLED agents, and National Guard personnel were protecting a fire truck and fire department personnel dispatched to a private residence off the campus to put out a fire caused by flammable liquid bombs.
>
> The actions leading to three deaths and the numerous injuries came only after an extended period of sniper fire from the campus and not until an officer had been felled during his efforts to protect life and property.
>
> Although the patrolman's injury was caused by some type of thrown missile, there was reason to believe at that instant that he had been shot. The other patrolmen, with instructions to protect themselves and others, responded with gunfire.

The seriousness of this situation was compounded by the theft of several military firearms by students from the ROTC arsenal on the State College campus. The weapons were later returned upon the insistence of the ROTC commander. . . . It is our intention to make all facts in this case public and to put aside rumor, speculation, and propaganda.

Most white South Carolinians accepted McNair's statement at face value. However, some were skeptical. An old college chum of the governor's who watched him deliver the statement on television turned to his wife and said, "I don't know who put that together, but they did a damn good job. Nobody'll ever know exactly what happened, but Bobby'll come out smelling like a rose."

Attorney General Clark telephoned McNair about 5 P.M. Friday and told him he had ordered the FBI to investigate the shooting. That seemed to satisfy the governor and he pledged the state would cooperate. The patrol and SLED had long maintained a close working relationship with the FBI. The patrol riot squads, in fact, had received part of their riot-control training from an FBI agent who was to later testify he heard shooting from the campus just prior to the patrol gunfire.

News accounts of the shooting had fortified, as well as reflected, national disillusionment with the Negro's struggle for equality. Urban disorders and fiery black power rhetoric had already soured much of the public on the civil-rights movement. And civil-rights leaders could not expect a national revulsion like that which followed the police assault on demonstrators at Selma, Alabama, and helped marshal public support for the 1965 Voting Rights Act. However, had the press given a reasonably accurate account of what had happened, there probably would have been some national indignation. As it was, the nation shrugged off Orangeburg.

Editors of *Time* magazine did not find it significant enough even to mention.

In an interview a week after the shootings, Dozier Mobley, the AP photographer who had been quoted in the original AP stories as saying there had been an exchange of gunfire, told the *Los Angeles Times* that he had been misquoted, that he "didn't hear a shot" from the campus immediately prior to the patrol gunfire. "The police panicked," the *Times* quoted Mobley. "I was surprised and disappointed. They lost their composure. They were running around and shouting and hollering. It was bad."

AP not only never retracted its earlier stories, it never acknowledged that Mobley disputed the articles. And a week after the shooting, the wire service was still referring to "an exchange of gunfire" without any qualification. In the spring 1968 issue of *Columbia Journalism Review*, Jim Hoagland of the *Washington Post* cited numerous errors and shallow coverage by AP and by South Carolina newspapers. He concluded that the performance by the press was "a reflection of not only what has happened to the civil-rights movement, and the press' attitude towards the racial struggle in the wake of mega-disturbances of Newark and Detroit, but it is also a reflection of the mood of the newspapers' readers."

Hoagland, who criticized newsmen for failing to report students' accounts of what happened, was clubbed by a Negro on the State College campus two days after the shooting when he went there to interview students. He was not seriously injured, but his head wound required twelve stitches. The assailant was a nonstudent black militant from Ohio who had gone to Orangeburg after learning of the shooting.

The only official source available to newsmen in Orangeburg was Henry Lake, the governor's former legal aide whom McNair named official spokesman and coordinator of law enforcement after the shooting. Lake, a one-time highway patrolman, told newsmen the patrolmen fired "because they had taken it as long as they could, they were going to get hurt, seriously hurt or possibly killed—and they were going to stop them."

Lake, who packed a snub-nosed .38 pistol in his belt, told a reporter he had talked to patrolmen involved and "most of them shot as low as they could and a number of the students fell to the ground and that's the reason some thirty-odd got hurt." He called the patrolmen "trained men" and said, "they could have killed 75 percent of them right then if they had wanted to."

Asked about Dozier Mobley's statement that the officers panicked, Lake declared, "He doesn't understand policemen. They weren't doing any such damn thing. They ran and got under cover, that's the first thing an officer is supposed to do. They had to do that to protect their lives, there was no other way out." Lake said he had "heard" some of the students were shot from the rear and explained: "The shooting was not all at one time. Some of the students were trying to get out of there, they wished to hell they had not been there, and some could have been hit when they turned their backs to run."

Lake accused Cleveland Sellers of throwing the bannister that hit Patrolman Shealy and said of the SNCC organizer: "He's the main man. He's the biggest nigger in the crowd."

A great majority of white South Carolinians felt strongly that the patrol was justified in shooting and that Sellers and other black militants presented a grave danger to Orangeburg. Four days after the incident, McNair's office reported thirty-five messages had been received and "most of them commended the governor for taking quick action to avert trouble and for protecting both the students at Orangeburg and the white people."

A letter to the editor of the Columbia *State* provided a typical reaction from Orangeburg: "Positive action by the governor, the state highway patrol, the National Guard, and the local police prevented another Detroit." Another letter writer from Charleston Heights observed, "Had the National Guard and police not put down the riot, that bunch of people would have really torn up the city of Orangeburg and then looked for new fields to conquer. It will pay to remember Cuba. One day it was free, the next day Castro and his henchmen had taken over." Other letters echoed McNair's comments about black power advocates and Representative Albert Watson's comments about communists.

Some whites viewed the incident in a different light. A Charleston man wrote a letter saying, "As long as we have bigoted individuals we will have our Browns and Carmichaels. We lose sight of the fact that the situation never would have arisen in the first place had Harry Floyd opened his place of business to all people."

In a letter published by the Marion *Star*, William L. McBride, a Negro high school teacher, declared that "Governor McNair should have taken action against the bowling alley," and added, "If the governor had taken positive action to treat the disease rather than the symptoms, he could have spared himself the label of 'murderer of three Negro youths.' "

After the shooting, extremist elements added to the public hysteria over black militants. State Grand Dragon Robert Scoggin of the United Klans of America sought permission to hold a Ku Klux Klan rally near Orangeburg two days later, but SLED Chief Strom told him it would not be permitted and Governor McNair extended the curfew throughout the county.

Three days after the shooting, the *Times and Democrat*,

in an issue that included an article reporting that it had found
no basis for rumors that Rap Brown, Stokely Carmichael,
and Martin Luther King, Jr., were in town, published a full-
page advertisement sponsored by the local TACT Committee
(Truth About Civil Turmoil—a John Birch Society front
group). It was a message by Birch Society founder Robert
Welch "To the Negroes of America," charging that the civil-
rights movement was part of a communist plot to destroy
America. Welch wrote:

> Shameless liars like M. L. King, foreign trouble-makers
> like Stokely Carmichael, perverted characters like Bayard
> Rustin, would-be commissars like Walter Reuther, and dozens
> of other agitators—white as well as black—are working
> ceaselessly to have you arise against your present "bondage"
> (!), and seek "freedom" (!), or "liberation" (!). Right on
> their face these slogans and expressions are all parts of a
> Communist *Big Lie*, of the kind that is used by Communists
> everywhere. They have no real relationship at all to your
> actual situation.

If most of the nation was left with the impression that
there had indeed been a gun battle, Negro leaders thought
otherwise. They clamored for state and federal investigations
of "the Orangeburg Massacre." Roy Wilkins, executive director of the NAACP, sent a telegram to McNair urging a
"prompt and thorough investigation" and declaring, "we are
confident that . . . you would not order troops to fire on unarmed students on their own campus. We don't believe you
would authorize any commander to take such a step."

Rap Brown, chairman of SNCC, wanted revenge, not an
investigation. "The lesson for us is very clear and evident," he
told newsmen in New York. "If we seek redress of our grievances through peaceful and so-called legal means, we will be
shot down and murdered." Brown, who earlier had popu-

larized the comment, "Violence is as American as cherry pie," continued in a diatribe that was extreme even for him:

> *If we must die, let us die with the enemy's blood on our hands . . . let us die like men, fighting back . . . As usual, the Justice Department is acting in a faint-hearted manner after the blood of black youth has flowed in the streets. Three dead and fifty injured is too high a price to pay for a goddam bowling alley. If we are going to be murdered for acting peacefully, we might as well be murdered while trying to kill a few honkies . . .*

At SNCC headquarters in Atlanta, the few staffers still working for it composed a mimeographed statement that indicated how badly the once dynamic organization had deteriorated. Their idea was to "harass honky officials," and they listed the office and home telephone numbers of Governor McNair and other officials, and urged that they be called "collect." The statement also urged: "Organize mass public actions to let honkies know that the black community ain't gonna take their shit!! (Take whatever action is necessary to make this message clear.)"

United States Representative Albert Watson, the Republican segregationist who was attending a dinner in his honor in Columbia the day after the shooting, also called for an investigation—of black power advocates, whom he accused of sparking the violence. He urged that the House Committee on Un-American Activities investigate and declared, "The constant cry of police brutality is the one Communists have used for years. It should be obvious Stokely Carmichael, Rap Brown, and Cleveland Sellers and their cronies would capitalize on such an expression. I'm going to do my part to see that these anarchists are prosecuted to the fullest extent."

The South Carolina Council on Human Relations and the state chapter of the American Association of University

Professors passed resolutions calling on McNair to appoint a biracial, blue-ribbon investigating committee. The AAUP said such a committee "should carry out a complete and impartial investigation into the causes, circumstances, and results of the incident, and promptly and fully disclose its findings and recommendations."

In Atlanta, Police Chief Herbert Jenkins, the only law enforcement official on President Lyndon B. Johnson's Commission on Civil Disorders, viewed the Orangeburg incident as a sign that the nation's police forces were implementing new "get tough" policies toward disorders. Jenkins, whose motto, "Walk softly and carry a sawed-off shotgun," reflected a policy of force and restraint that had contained disorders in Atlanta with relatively little violence, expressed serious concern that buckshot had been used by the South Carolina patrolmen.

After an Atlanta policeman had killed a Negro with a blast of double-ought buckshot during a 1967 disorder, Jenkins ordered that birdshot be used for riot control in the future. His reasoning was that birdshot was lethal enough at close range to stop a rioter and that it could spare lives if used instead of buckshot to disperse rioters at a distance. In an interview after the Orangeburg shooting, Jenkins told a reporter he thought that the police mood nationally was more attuned to buckshot than to birdshot. He said he was not surprised when a Savannah, Georgia, police official told a staff member of the Commission on Civil Disorders that, in case of serious racial trouble, "we'd call out the National Guard and we'd have the biggest nigger killing around here you ever saw."

The Southern Regional Council, an Atlanta-based civil-rights research and voter education organization, conducted its own investigation of the Orangeburg events and on February 25 issued a forty-two-page report saying the shooting reflected new "get tough" policies by the nation's police that "carry into highly volatile situations new elements of danger." The report said the Orangeburg events

> contain in microcosm the history of this decade in civil rights . . . the events also would at least suggest the implications of forces in motion not just in Orangeburg but across America in 1967–68, including black power and white over-reaction to its emotional mood, the tendency to violence by Negroes dismayed by the failure of non-violent and other peaceful protests against social injustice and inequity still enduring, the national tendency nearing public phobia, and a response to Negro unrest with massive police and military force.

The report, based on interviews with numerous witnesses, including students and faculty members of Claflin and South Carolina State colleges, said SRC found no evidence to support McNair's charges that black power advocates were to blame or that students had fired at the state patrolmen. And it severely criticized the South Carolina press and most of the national press for accepting the "official interpretation and justification of the events at Orangeburg" and not investigating further on their own. The report said clarification of the issue and investigations were poor with the exception of those of *The Charlotte Observer*, the *Los Angeles Times* and the National Broadcasting Company.

Also in Atlanta, officials of five Negro colleges and the head of a theological center appealed to President Johnson and other public officials to prevent college and university campuses from being invaded by "the American version of storm troopers." Their appeal, in an open letter to the President, Attorney General Clark, state governors, and local police officials, as published as an advertisement in the Atlanta newspapers, read as follows:

The invasions of college campuses by various police powers in the United States is a trend which can no longer be continued without public protest by responsible educators and other persons interested in preserving the freedom of institutions of higher learning in our country. Incidents of this nature have occurred too frequently in recent years on our college and university campuses, and now at Orangeburg, South Carolina. For more than 600 years in the history of western civilization, the colleges and universities have been the marketplace for the propagation and discussion of ideas without fear of physical violence. Americans added a new dimension to this protection of the discussion and propagation of ideas by fostering the right of people to assemble peacefully and to demonstrate or protest against the ideas which they considered harmful to humanity. A major cause of the American Revolution was the refusal of British authorities to permit demonstrations or to listen to their implications. Demonstrators seeking freedom were killed in the Boston Massacre in 1770: A Negro was the first to die there. In February, 1968, freedom seekers led by Negroes are again fired upon and killed—this time in Orangeburg, South Carolina.

Here in America we seem to have adopted a "get tough" national policy based on the use of armored and armed police and guardsmen in killing American citizens at the slightest provocation. The frustrations of our society which stem from the perplexities of our present involvement in Vietnam coupled with the complexities involved in solving the dual problems of race and ghetto have led many officials to believe that a resort to naked police power and brutality is the proper avenue for handling major social problems. That was the avenue taken by Nazi Germany and other police power states. This has not been the way of modern America.

We, the undersigned, therefore appeal to Americans, both public officials and private citizens, to join us in using every effort to stop this threat to the freedom of colleges and universities—whether they are publicly owned or privately supported. We urge you to stop these invasions of college and university campuses by the American version of storm troopers. We urge you to stop the wanton shooting of young high school and college students. We urge you to bring to justice those who commit such murders. We urge you to remember that police forces can destroy and perhaps even temporarily protect, but they can never build. We urge you to remove from service all armed, untrained law enforcement officers who are prejudiced, brutal, and impulsive. We urge you to remember that a Congress which gives a thunderous ovation to plans for the use of destructive police power and only polite applause to presidential promises for constructive social action creates an atmosphere within which a democratic society cannot long exist. We urge you with all of your power to protect our colleges and universities from armed invasion. We urge Americans to remove the poison of race from our police policy which may result in the murdering of students on and near their campuses. We, the undersigned, make these statements in the full awareness of the responsibility of all citizens to obey the law and follow orderly processes in seeking redress of grievances.

The statement was signed by Thomas D. Jarrett, chairman of Interim Administrative Committee, Atlanta University; Vivian W. Henderson, President, Clark College; Harry V. Richardson, President, Interdenominational Theological Center; Hugh M. Gloster, President, Morehouse College; John A. Middleton, President, Morris Brown College, and Albert E. Manley, President, Spelman College.

A month after the shooting, McNair was still referring to Orangeburg as though it had been a major riot. He told a press conference that in dealing with a riot, "the only way you can control it is to bring in maximum police power and immediately to isolate, control, and contain. Otherwise, you will have Detroits and Newarks."

The governor used the Kerner Commission (National

Commission on Civil Disorders) report to try to justify his action. Although generally critical of the report, which placed major blame for civil disorders on "white racism," McNair said the key part to him was, "Preserving civil peace is the responsibility of government." Concerning any potential riots in South Carolina, he said, "I would much rather be charged with overacting than underacting anytime if I had to make the choice in maintaining peace and order."

In early March, McNair issued a statement saying he had talked with Attorney General Clark "and expressed the hope that a public disclosure of the [FBI] findings of the investigation be made as soon as possible." McNair said that "a full disclosure of the facts is essential because of the concern and confusion over the tragedy and because of the pressing urgency that the facts in this matter be made public."

He said a full report of the activities of SLED, the state highway patrol, and the South Carolina National Guard "will be submitted and a subsequent full factual disclosure of these reports will also be made public as soon thereafter as possible."

However, McNair never made such reports available to the public and in fact refused to allow the authors of this book to examine the SLED report. Colonel Thompson later testified the highway patrol made no investigation or report because it did not want to interfere with the FBI's investigation. The National Guard submitted an official "after-action report," but the Guard was not directly involved in any shooting.

McNair maintained the reason he would not name a special blue-ribbon committee to investigate what happened at Orangeburg was that Negroes would be suspicious of anybody he appointed. But the governor also refused to cooperate with an attempt by the Department of Sociology at the

University of South Carolina to study what happened at Orangeburg, a proposal developed immediately after the shooting.

The proposal had the support of University President Thomas F. Jones, who got prior approval from Chairman Rutledge L. Osborne of the Board of Trustees, a resident of Orangeburg. The seven faculty members of the Department of Sociology in effect offered their professional services to analyze what happened at Orangeburg to develop an understanding that might help prevent violence in the future. They would not release their report to newspapers, but would publish it in an academic journal at some future date agreeable to the governor.

Dr. Charles W. Tucker, who was project coordinator, met with McNair and Jones on February 23, fifteen days after the shooting. McNair was affable, but rejected the offer by the sociologists. He said it would complicate the state's investigation for prosecuting Cleveland Sellers. McNair suggested instead that the group study collective behavior in Columbia, pointing out that there were militant groups at the University of South Carolina engaged in protesting what happened at Orangeburg. Some of the professors agreed the substitute proposal had enough merit to pursue. However, cooperation with that project failed to materialize after a March 13 demonstration at the State House produced a confrontation involving U.S.C. students. The Columbia project was designed to "acquire objective knowledge and understanding of the processes which lead to civil disorder."

McNair left the decision to cooperate to Chief Strom. Strom sent Lieutenant Leon Gasque, his number one assistant, to meet with Tucker and told Gasque to get the educational background on all of the faculty members. Tucker provided the information. In his only meeting with Tucker on March 18, five days after the State House demonstration,

Strom asked, "What do you think about those people calling my police officers motherfuckers?" Tucker said later, "I tried to maintain a social scientist's stance. I couldn't laugh, and I said, 'It would be interesting to know how you train your officers not to respond violently to that kind of talk.'"

Strom was noncommittal about the study. He subsequently failed to contact Tucker again about an appointment to discuss the study, although the sociologist called Strom a dozen times. Finally, on April 30, Tucker wrote Strom a letter. It also drew no response.

Meanwhile, Tucker and Dr. Clark McPhail, a fellow sociologist, had met with McNair again and found he still insisted that a study on Orangeburg by the sociologists might interfere with the state's investigation. McPhail got the impression the governor did not personally object to cooperating on the Columbia study but would approve only if Chief Strom approved—and Strom did not approve. Tucker saw it differently: "The governor was very pleasant about it. It was very diplomatic, kind of a con job."

At the All Star Bowling Lanes the day after the shooting, Harry Floyd, who thought of himself as a "scapegoat," told a reporter he would continue excluding Negroes. "I'm not a segregationist," he said, "but I believe every man has a right to operate his place as he sees fit. I believe every man has a right to tell any man or woman to leave if he doesn't want them in his place. I just want to be left alone. All I want to do is operate my business and to make a living for my wife and children. If that's too much to ask, we've a poor, sad country to live in."

Deputy Assistant Attorney General D. Robert Owen, a ten-year veteran of the civil rights division of the Justice Department, had arrived in Orangeburg about noon the day after the shooting and had gone directly to the bowling alley;

he told Floyd that unless he opened it to Negroes, the department would file a suit against him under the public accommodations section of the 1964 Civil Rights Act. Floyd refused and the next day the Justice Department filed suit in United States District Court in Columbia.

The following Tuesday the Justice Department belatedly acted on another long-time grievance of Negroes—discrimination at the Orangeburg Regional Hospital. The Department moved to intervene in a desegregation suit that had been filed against the hospital on March 24, 1962, by a group of Negroes who charged that discrimination denied them equal protection of the laws. A federal court had finally issued an injunction against the hospital on February 18, 1965, but it had never been enforced. Moreover, on March 25, 1965, hospital officials had given written assurances that they would comply with desegregation requirements of Title VI of the 1964 Civil Rights Act in order to keep receiving federal assistance. The plaintiffs in the case also had gone back to the court on October 30, 1967, seeking enforcement of the injunction after the hospital had continued to ignore the court order.

The department charged that the hospital discriminated racially in the assignment of rooms, floors, wards, and wings, and in medical care, treatment, services, and training programs, all in violation of Title VI. It asked the court to affirm a January 8 order by the Department of Health, Education and Welfare to end federal support for the hospital for noncompliance with desegregation requirements.

Some Orangeburg ministers preached reconciliation at Sunday services, and twenty-two ministers, including some whites, issued a statement urging "restraint and common sense in this time of crisis."

There were some biracial efforts to deal with the crisis in Orangeburg, including the organizing of the fifty-six-member

Human Relations Council, which began to take shape the day after the shooting. And the city's more overt symbols of segregation and racism eventually were dropped. Despite stubborn resistance by a few, physicians who had continued to operate segregated waiting rooms finally abandoned them. Three Negroes were appointed to the official board for the United Fund drive. A Negro for the first time was appointed to the school board. Job opportunities were expanded—but not much.

Many South Carolina whites were shocked by the shooting and the slaying of students. Methodist Bishop Paul Hardin of Columbia scheduled three major meetings and sent notices to ministers to attend and to bring with them prominent lay members of their congregations. Hardin urged Methodists to take the lead in establishing biracial groups in their communities. Groups were formed in many communities, but only a few succeeded in achieving significant results.

The statewide Task Force for Community Uplift sent representatives to cities and towns throughout the state, establishing roughly twenty local groups with varying degrees of effectiveness. In a few cases where there was an honest recognition of mutual need by both the white power structure and the true representatives of the black community, such groups sometimes were effective in establishing communications and reducing suspicion. Occasionally, they were innovative and took the initiative in dealing with grievances and wrestling with the broad problems of social and economic change.

Orangeburg, moreover, had had a profound effect on other Negro colleges. A week after the shooting, students at several Negro colleges in Virginia, South Carolina, and North Carolina burned McNair in effigy and carried wooden coffins symbolizing the three Orangeburg deaths. In Durham, N.C., a protest march erupted into window smashing and rock throwing, but the other demonstrations were peaceful. Negroes also demonstrated in some other parts of the country, including New York, where demonstrators outside Madison Square Garden held aloft a coffin labeled "Orangeburg Massacre."

As tension eased in the days following the shooting, Governor McNair gradually reduced the Guard strength in Orangeburg and eased the curfew. Claflin reopened on February 22 and McNair ordered classes at South Carolina State to resume on Monday, February 26. The governor had steadfastly refused to acknowledge that the state could have been in any way to blame for the shooting, despite a public appeal by the NAACP's Roy Wilkins in a speech at the college a day before classes resumed. Said Wilkins, "I expect that as a man, he is as sick as some of us are about this, but let him say the state was wrong and see where we can go from there."

The day classes resumed John Stroman and James P. Davis became the first Negroes to bowl at All Star Bowling Lanes. Four days earlier United States Judge J. Robert Martin, Jr., had ordered Harry Floyd to stop barring Negroes from the bowling alley.

After bowling a frame, Stroman grinned and told a reporter, "Yeah, we made it." Floyd, asked how things were going, replied, "Everything is going all right. I'm not about to buck a federal judge's order." White patrons continued bowling in the sixteen-lane facility as though having Negroes bowl there had been an everyday occurrence.

The attention of protesting South Carolina State students soon shifted to Columbia where they staged two major demonstrations at the historic state capitol, a granite structure that was completed only after a delay caused by the Civil War.

The first demonstration, sponsored by the Black Aware-

ness Coordinating Committee on March 7, disrupted pro-
ceedings of the state Senate when Steve Moore, a cofounder
of BACC, tried to read a petition from the visitors gallery
and refused to listen when Lieutenant Governor John C.
West tried to restore order. Moore and five others were arrested by SLED agents and charged with disorderly conduct.
(The charges later were dropped.) More than 200 students
came by bus, splitting into three groups—one went to the
Senate; one went to the House and sat quietly; and one went
to the governor's office and huddled on the floor of his reception room. Before ordering the arrests, West rapped his gavel
for order and explained that speeches weren't permitted, but
students could petition in writing and have it read before the
Senate. Students carried signs, some proclaiming "McNair
is a Son of a Birch," "Orangeburg Massacre—a Police Riot,"
and "Needed: Quality Education at South Carolina State."
Several senators talked calmly to students who jammed the
State House after the arrests and advised them of proper
procedures for presenting a petition.

Later the student group attempted to see McNair after
the governor left a meeting of the state's Higher Education
Commission, and he offered to meet with six representatives.
BACC Chairman Wayne Curtis insisted that the governor
first appear before the entire group, but McNair refused after
being advised by Chief Strom that some students wanted to
embarrass him and that there was a possibility of violence.
The students massed quietly outside the governor's office and
Curtis promised there would be no violence. Two Urban
League officials called in by McNair huddled with the stu-
dents and found them reasonable and willing to talk calmly.

McNair's position was that "people don't dictate to the
governor where he will see them" and he refused to appear
before the entire group. The students left in anger and Curtis
declared, "This is war. We want to vote Governor McNair

and men like him out of office." Curtis said he did not think violence would result from the demonstration and he called BACC a "thinking group." But he added, "When we get to the point that violence is extremely necessary and nothing else works, we'll resort to violence."

On a bright, chilly, windy Wednesday six days later, 800 State College students and 200 from other colleges converged on the State House, and several squads of helmeted state troopers with riot sticks lined up in front of the lobby entrance.

The show of force outside the State House created concern among a group of professors and civil-rights leaders, and McNair agreed to meet with five of them. In his office, he told them he had to convince some legislative leaders it was all right to let some of the demonstrators come inside to present their petition of grievances in the proper manner. He insisted there had to be a show of force because "this is the seat of government" and that "people have to learn sooner or later that they cannot disrupt the function of government whenever they feel like it." He said that everyone connected with state government had instructions to lean over backwards to prevent an incident.

When Professor Roland Haynes of State College said he felt the governor had not made himself clear on what the response of the state would be in the future, McNair testily said, "I have made myself crystal clear before and I will make it clear again. We will never initiate any confrontation, but whenever the first brick is thrown, whenever the first rock is thrown, whenever the first firebomb is thrown, whenever the first house is set on fire, then it's *our* move!"

"What would that be?" asked Professor Robert Moore of Columbia College, the former state AAUP president who had helped negotiate a settlement the previous year in the class boycott at State College. The governor replied he didn't know because he didn't know what the circumstances would be. "But you're governor," Moore declared, "you *have* to know what the move would be." The group left the governor's office believing the official response would be all or nothing.

Afterwards, a delegation of fifteen students and BACC faculty advisor Dr. Rubin Weston were permitted to enter the capitol through a side entrance and present a petition of grievances to West. Later they discussed the grievances in an hour-long session with McNair. Weston told the lieutenant governor he knew the presentation of the petition was an unusual procedure and West replied, "There are no precedents for the time we're going through." Nodding toward a window through which almost 1,000 protesting students could be seen marching, Weston—who had been born in Columbia in sight of the state capitol—said, "What you see out there is an expression of outrage by the Negro community."

Outside, the demonstrators split into two groups, those from State College marching and carrying a casket with a sign, "Look, it could happen to any of us." Beside the casket marched a student with another sign, "McNair, you've got blood on your hands." A smaller group of taunting, cursing militants charged up the capitol steps several times to within a few feet of the highway patrolmen. But there was no violence.

McNair later termed the meeting with the students "fruitful" and student body vice president Alexander Nichols told the assembled students, "We educated him to the facts." In an earlier meeting with student government leaders, McNair advised them to have civil suits filed and told them a trial would provide an open forum to investigate what happened the night of February 8. The militants urged the State College students not to leave, but they all boarded buses and returned to Orangeburg—an act that pleased legislative leaders.

The next day the petition was read in the Senate and printed in the *Journal*. And in an unusual move, West sent the petition to all standing committees. He also dictated a 1,200-word letter to Nichols, commending the students for "following established legal methods." The letter discussed in detail the grievances and explained why some of the issues were not within the jurisdiction of the legislature.

"Although the processes of the law sometimes may seem slow," West wrote the student leader, "human experience over centuries has shown it to be the only effective method of human betterment." West followed up by appointing three senators to visit the State College campus and report on the needs of the institution—the first time any group of legislators had ever visited the state college. The lieutenant governor himself also visited the college.

A week after the demonstration, West, in a speech before the Charleston chamber of commerce, publicly commended the students for "following the processes of law and order" and he pointed out they had rejected the militants. He also met privately with McNair and recommended a major bond issue for capital improvements at the college.

On March 23, ten days after the students presented their petition, McNair announced he would recommend a $6.5 million bond issue for the college, including $2 million for dormitories for an additional 350 students.

A bill authorizing the bond issue became an emotional issue in the legislature. House Republican minority leader Jerry M. Hughes of Orangeburg told the House, "You are ramming something down the throats of the people of Orangeburg they don't want," and he said the bond issue was a response to "blackmail" by student demonstrators.

"The white people of Orangeburg do not want this," Hughes said. "People of Orangeburg, especially women, are afraid . . . I'm afraid of black power creating other riots and our little police force not being able to handle it."

However, a fellow Orangeburg County representative, Democrat Lewis Shuler—whose son commanded National Guard troops during the week of turmoil—disagreed. Shuler pointed out that more than 300 qualified applicants had been turned down the previous year at the college because of a lack of facilities, and said, "I don't think 300 more students would mar the city of Orangeburg any more today."

Then, Representative J. Clator Arrants, fifty-one, of Camden, strode to the front of the House chamber and delivered a remarkable speech for a Deep South legislator on the subject of race. Once an ambitious young politician who at the age of thirty-seven ran unsuccessfully for lieutenant governor, Arrants told of having once served as an attorney for the Ku Klux Klan and of having once considered joining the Klan (he never did). Then in a rising voice that filled the hushed chamber, he told the House to forget "fear, hate and prejudice" and to "do what is right" on the bond issue. Appeals to upgrade the college had been made ever since the 1940s, he said, adding, "We're not trying to help outsiders or strangers, but native-born citizens of this state. We'll be condemned and chastised no matter what we do. If I must sacrifice what little political career I have upon the mantle of hate, fear, and distrust or upon what I think is right, the choice is easy."

Minutes later a roll call vote recorded a crushing 95–11 defeat for the first of many amendments aimed at reducing the size of the bond issue. The measure easily passed the House. A threatened filibuster by some Republicans in the Senate fizzled. Senator James P. Harrelson, one of the three senators who had visited the campus, told the Senate it would be "a shame on South Carolina if we don't grant this small token of what they need." (The bill passed in June.)

In the aftermath of the shooting at Orangeburg, a stark analysis came from President Benjamin F. Payton of Columbia's Benedict College. A South Carolina State College graduate who held graduate degrees from Yale, Harvard, and Columbia universities, Payton became the first Negro ever to address a major civic club in Columbia. In his speech to the Kiwanis Club (scheduled before the shooting), the thirty-four-year-old educator declared:

"Was it necessary that three people be killed because 100 of them threw bricks? I have difficulty conceiving in my imagination of the highway patrolmen firing point-blank at students of the University of South Carolina or Clemson doing the same thing."

8 : THE VICTIMS

*In Memoriam—". . . verily I say unto you. Inasmuch as ye
have done it unto the least of these my brethren, ye have
done it unto me."* ST. MATTHEW *25:40*
—FROM THE 1968 BULLDOG, STATE COLLEGE YEARBOOK

SMITTY

"I am living a relatively normal Christian life," Henry
Ezekial Smith wrote to his mother six days before he was
killed. "I am going to church more than I did last year. I am
trying to do unto others as I would have them do unto me. I
think that is about all God can ask of a person."

It was a typical letter "from the Desk of H. E. Smith,"
penciled on a piece of tablet paper, but one passage disturbed
his mother. He mentioned that on his last visit home "it
seemed as if I had been away for a long time and I was a
stranger . . . I hardly recognized anyone."

The fact was that Smitty was getting what his mother had worked and prayed for him to have—"a college education, an opportunity to take a bath like other people and have things that others have"—a chance to escape some of the oppression and narrow life a young Negro faced in Marion, a chance to realize the ambition he mentioned as a life goal in a questionnaire at the college in his freshman year: "Happiness and success."

Mrs. Smith knew the value of an education and "always figured if I couldn't get it, I was gonna have it for my kids. Get them to college and let them get what they needed. I know it helps. My baby brother Cleveland went to Allen University and he's a coach and chemistry teacher in Conway. My older brother Elijah lives in New Britain, Connecticut. He went to Allen University under the GI bill—he was in World War II—and he helped put Cleveland through the university."

But now that new opportunities were opening for Henry, Mrs. Smith worried because "he didn't know how to cope in the man's world. He was tired of women, might as well face it—there's been no men around the house. David [Henry's older brother] even called his underwear 'bloomers' until I told him about it—he didn't know the difference."

In an interview, Henry's younger sister, Ora Sue, who was valedictorian of her high school class and entered the University of South Carolina in the fall of 1968 on an academic scholarship, recalled that Henry "got away from Marion and saw how things were and sort of changed. The family didn't understand him as well. He had a drive we didn't recognize. He wanted to make things better for black people."

Isaac Williams, leader of "the cause" at State College in 1967, recalled, "Smitty was totally activist." When a conservative student group attempted to impeach Williams as senior class president because he had organized a classroom boycott, Henry initiated a drive among other students in his support. Williams said, "Smitty was very concerned at the apathy of many students who did not follow through on 'the cause.' And when his grades began to slump, he started hitting the books to make sure he would be around to work on 'the cause.' "

John Stroman, who had led the drive to desegregate the bowling alley, remembered that "Smitty, if he believed in what he was doing, he'd go all out. He helped me and two other students get back in school after we were expelled in 1967 for leading the student march on the president's house." Bobby Burton, Henry's roommate who was injured in the patrol gunfire, remembered more than anything else that "Smitty was always willing to help a friend."

To Henry N. Vincent, dean of students, Henry was "the kind of fellow who would be known in a short while if he was around. He was outgoing and had a lot of friends." Although Smitty had not been a disciplinary problem at the college, another official recalled that he once "ran into him at a football game when he was drinking and boisterous." And several students said Henry was known to take a drink away from home.

Mrs. Smith and her mother raised Henry, David, Ora Sue, and their younger brother Johnny in one of several shotgun houses on a rural road on the outskirts of Marion. Mrs. Smith's husband left the family and moved to New York in search of employment when the children were young. Once she went to the sheriff's office to ask about swearing out a warrant for nonsupport, but was told, "Just get you a man and call it even."

If her house was tiny and crowded, it still was home and Mrs. Smith kept it neat and as comfortable as circumstances would permit. The outdoor privy did not bother her too much

—it was all she had ever known—but she wanted something better for her children. She worked as a domestic for a wealthy family and at the time of Henry's death was making $6.40 a day (80 cents an hour), plus meals. Because she was strong, dependable, and hard-working, her pay was higher than that of most maids in Marion. Some still were paid as little as $3 or $4 a day.

"I've been lucky," she said in an interview for this book, without a trace of bitterness in her voice over the trials and tribulations she had endured. "But I do work hard. And 'my people' entertained a lot so I got extra for working extra. They were wonderful to me." Since Henry's death, a state legislator had helped her secure a job at a candy factory making $1.60 an hour. She said this would help her pay off the $1,600 bill for Henry's funeral and burial. "It was so high because the body was in such bad shape," she said.

In late 1969 Mrs. Smith finally paid off a small loan company that had lent her $399.66 for Henry's tuition. She repaid the company a total of $600. In 1970 she still owed several hundred dollars on the funeral bill, but said, "I'm paying the undertaker if it takes working all my life to do it."

With a worn Bible opened on the small coffee table in front of her during the interview, and religious pictures and a "God Bless Our Home" plaque on the living room walls around her, Mrs. Smith was typical of many deeply religious southern Negroes who looked to their religion for solace in times of trouble. She taught Sunday school and sang in the choir at the St. John's African-Methodist-Episcopal Church across town on Liberty Street. Every Sunday she and her family would trek the four miles to the church and "hope to get a ride home." When Henry came home on weekends after enrolling at State College, "he loved to wear his ROTC uniform when he went to church."

After Dean Butler telephoned Mrs. Smith on the night of

February 8, 1969, and told her Henry had been shot and was in critical condition, she dropped to her knees and prayed. A few minutes later she told her aged mother, "We better answer the phone."

Mama said, 'It's not ringing,' " Mrs. Smith recalled, "but I said it will because Henry's dead. And it rang and President Nance said Henry had passed and I said I know and I'm on my way."

"My family's always prayed together," Mrs. Smith said. "Henry would call me from school and ask me to pray for him. I guess I might have loved him a little more than the others, although I love them all. But he was fragile, always was, that's why I called him 'Peanut.' He'd break bones, like when he broke an arm chasing chickens in the yard one time."

Henry's letters to his mother reflected not only his religious upbringing, but a concern for his mother and other relatives. "So how is the family doing—Mama, Ora Sue and Johnny?" he would write. Another letter reflected the Spartan life typical of the South's poorer Negro college students: "When I got the meats you sent they were spoiled so I spent part of the $5 you sent me to buy some meats and take some of my clothes to the cleaners. If you can, send me some hamburger meat this weekend." Negro teachers in Marion who were working towards master's degrees at State College on weekends would drop by Mrs. Smith's house and pick up whatever goods she wanted to send to Henry.

His letters, treasured by Mrs. Smith as the most personal things he left behind, also showed that like many college boys he was not adverse to changing his stories when trying to account for a failing grade. In one letter he wrote, "I am doing very well and trying to study harder. The reason I got an F in art appreciation is because I did not go but three times. I just did not like the course and so I tried to get it changed but I was blocked out of the course. My advisor told me not to worry about the course because it did not count." In another letter, written a few days later, he wrote, "As for me lying to you, I did not; I told you I was sick and I was, with a muscular spasm. When I took the x-ray, nothing showed up. But the pain persisted—the doctor did me no good so I stayed in bed until late every morning. That's how I got an F in art appreciation."

In the summer of 1967, after Henry got a job in New York to help pay his second year's tuition at State College, he wrote his mother:

> I miss being home for the first time in my life. I miss you reading the Bible every morning. I miss you telling me not to stay out too late. I miss you and Ora calling every Sunday morning for church. I miss you whistling as you wanted to call us.
>
> Mother, will you find out how much money I need for the first semester? Will you also find out if I got the job at college?
>
> Did the garden grow as well as it did when we were small, trying to get ready for the winter? You do remember, don't you?
>
> I know Mama and Ora and Johnny are fine. I only hope Johnny is not staying out too late.
>
> I will be home August 26.
>
> There is only one thing else—has the price of stamps gone up or is it that the post office burned down?

The letter included this postscript: "Claudia, a friend of mine from school, sends her regards to you and the family. She would like to meet and get to know you."

Among the pictures on the wall of Mrs. Smith's living room was one of Dr. Martin Luther King, Jr. "Henry idolized Martin Luther King," Mrs. Smith said, "and he marveled at the abuse he got and the way he still came back for more."

Mrs. Smith had never heard of Cleveland Sellers until after Henry was killed. The only civil-rights activity she knew her son was involved in, outside of the efforts to desegregate the bowling alley, was "helping people to register to vote when he was a freshman at State." She knew, however, that Henry long had been aware that the law gave him the same rights it gave white people. And she knew he did not mind claiming the rights, even though claiming them did not necessarily mean enjoying them. She remembered that in the fall of 1965, when Henry was a sixteen-year-old high school junior, he got into trouble with a police officer:

> He had gone to wax this white lady's floor and when he got through it was almost dark and he was trying to get to Pope's 5 and 10 before it closed to get some paper for his geometry class. He was running and this policeman stopped him and said what was he doing running in a white neighborhood. Henry said he had constitutional rights and the policeman said, "You damn nigger, you been looking at too much television, don't give me no trouble."
>
> Henry called me on the telephone to come down there and when I got there the policeman told me he didn't know it was my boy or he wouldn't have arrested him. The white people in town all knew me and I got along fine with them. The policeman told me it would be $17.50 to get him out, "That's the best I can do for you," and I paid my rent money to get Henry out. My boys had never been in any trouble with the law and they didn't have a daddy there and I figured I had better pay it. I was the boys' only support and I didn't want to antagonize anybody because they might hurt us. But it was the first time I'd heard of anybody being charged with running in a white neighborhood.

Henry attended Johnakin High School where he was a popular student, made average grades, was president of New Farmers of American and a member of "Future Citizens of Marion," and helped found *The Tiger*, the school's yearbook. His mother was secretary of the school's PTA.

When Marion High School first opened its doors to Negroes under a "freedom of choice" desegregation plan in Henry's sophomore year, he told his mother, "They've got better facilities and they've got better teachers there. And if they got it to give, I want to get it." Mrs. Smith recalled, "I've looked at it carefully since then and it's true and he would have had to walk only a mile to Marion High instead of three miles to Johnakin. But I had to work and everything and we didn't want any trouble, so Mama and I wouldn't let him apply."

Although not one to complain about her troubles, Mrs. Smith long had recognized that "in Marion, it's like this, if you're colored you have to watch it if you want to work. For example, if you're a domestic and working for someone influential, other people won't give you another kind of job because they don't want to offend that person—don't make any difference how hard you work, how much family you got or how much you need it."

Ora Sue recalled that in high school Henry would talk to other students about "why we couldn't eat in the restaurants and why they made us sit upstairs in the theater. They did finally desegregate the theater," she said, "but they would find a reason you couldn't go downstairs and they charged more money downstairs." Henry's sister said, after going away to college, "As long as you walk the white line that the whites draw for you in Marion, you're all right. If you don't, you're a black militant."

However, Henry never really challenged the segregationist practices at Marion. And he and his family were popular with whites, as well as with blacks. After his death the mayor and several other leading citizens called on Mrs. Smith and offered condolences. The weekly Marion *Star* editorialized: "How deeply involved, if at all, this young man was in the Orangeburg tragedy, we do not know. We do know that he came from one of Marion's best Negro families and sympathy goes to that family from all segments of our community." Mrs. Smith proudly called it "the highest tribute that newspaper has ever paid to a black family here."

DELANO

Delano Herman Middleton's "only real interests were sports and church; he never had any interest in civil rights or any of that," according to his mother, Mrs. Reather Middleton, a maid at State College.

"He was a good boy, never bothered nobody," she said in an interview for this book. "He didn't even know the other boys who got killed. Wasn't nothing unusual about him being on the campus that night. I've worked there eighteen years and he grew up around there. He just stopped off there after basketball practice at the high school, like he always did. His being there was just one of those things I guess; I often wonder about it."

Delano was one of four children of a sawmill worker who lost an arm in an accident when the children were young, then moved to Pittsburgh to live with other relatives. Delano grew up in a four-room farmhouse just outside Orangeburg.

His coaches, teachers, and fellow students at all-Negro Wilkinson High School all remembered him as a quiet student who shunned controversy and showed no interest in civil rights, but who was an aggressive athlete and a popular student. His grades were average, but he was considered a leader. He was a member of High Life Society, which promoted citizenship.

Wilkinson's football coach, Shellie E. Wright, Jr., a former State College football player, said, "Delano played three years for me and he was a neighbor of mine. He was a hard-working young man from a rather poor family. He was wrapped up in sports and school work, but he always found time to work around the house and help his grandfather plow. He would have been on the track team except he didn't have enough time because track came during the planting season."

Coach Wright said, "We always prayed before a game and after practice and Delano always was willing to volunteer to lead us in an impromptu prayer. He was just a good, clean-living boy and he no doubt would have been the best football center in the state in his senior year."

The basketball coach, Nelson Brownlee, knew Delano as "one of the best boys I've ever coached—very dependable and never a problem." The day before the shooting at State College, Brownlee "advised the whole team not to get involved, not to go to any protests. Delano never said whether he would go or whether he wouldn't, but if he had said he wouldn't go, then he wouldn't."

Jimmye Williams, a State College student, "played ping pong with Delano at the recreation center on the campus about two hours before the shooting." Williams and other friends felt Delano was merely curious and going down to the embankment because of the excitement when he got shot.

SAM

The faculty and students at Fort Lauderdale's predominantly white Stranahan High School were shocked at news reports that Samuel Hammond, Jr., had been killed in a "riot."

Football Coach Louis Gibson remembered Sam as "a real fine boy, quiet and soft-spoken, never any problem, well liked by his teammates," and Gibson was "surprised that anyone would even think that Sam might be a troublemaker."

In 1967 Sam became the first Negro to letter in two sports at Stranahan. He was an outstanding halfback on the football team and a star sprinter and jumper on the track team.

Sam left the town's all-Negro Dillard High School and enrolled in Stranahan in his senior year—"because it had more to offer in the way of an education," according to his father. Stranahan was in its second year of desegregation under a "freedom of choice" plan, and there were 180 Negroes among its 2,600 students.

Sam, born in Barnwell, South Carolina, grew up in Fort Lauderdale where his father worked as a school custodian and his mother as a nurse's aide at a hospital. His father, a World War II veteran who attended South Carolina State College for two semesters, was anxious for his only son to have a good education, and also planned to send Sam's two younger sisters to college.

Sam planned to be a teacher. On a State College questionnaire, he wrote that the "one big thing" he wanted in life was "education." At the college, Dean Vincent remembered him as being "popular, but so quiet you hardly knew he was around some of the time."

Sam's track coach at Stranahan, Carlos Sasse, found that he "got along well with everybody and had no interest in civil rights as far as anyone knew. Everybody liked him." Sasse recalled an incident when "some colored kids from another school tried to start a little roughness with us during a track meet. They were starting something with John Bogert, our best sprinter, and Sam went over and said, 'There'll be none of that.' And that broke it up." Bogert was attending the University of Florida on a track scholarship when he read of Sam's death. He wrote a letter to the *Fort Lauderdale News*, which published it February 15, 1968:

Last year, as a senior at Stranahan High School, I was captain of our track team. On this team was another senior, a Negro, named Samuel Hammond.

Sam was a tall, strong young man gifted with athletic and intellectual abilities.

Sam and I ran on the same relay teams and against each other in some individual events. We came to respect each other as athletes and friends just as the entire team came to respect him for his maturity and competitive spirit.

Some of the things that Sam did for me shall always remain in my memory as some of the warmest acts of friendship that I have ever experienced. One of these experiences occurred during a meet with another local high school. In a moment of defeat, I returned some of the remarks which were being directed at me by members of the opposing team. They advanced toward me but before they had come two steps Sam was beside me, and, with a few words, my would-be adversaries reversed their steps.

A couple of months later, I pulled a muscle during a race which forced me to fall into the infield. Once again, Sam was the first one there, lifting me to my feet and wrapping me in his own blanket and spending an hour walking me around to keep my injured leg from tightening up.

Sam was a warm and friendly person who did care for the people around him and, as I have illustrated, was ready and willing to help in any way that he could.

·Today (2–10–68) I read that Sam Hammond is dead, killed in a riot at Orangeburg, S.C., by a police bullet. Sam was a student at South Carolina State where, so I am told, he was doing well in his academic work. A Negro riot, the type thing that only occurs somewhere else, had hit home hard. This incident has caused me to take a long hard look at what

I believe to be true. How could I say that what Sam died for
is wrong, how could I condemn the actions of a living, breath-
ing being just as myself, a person that I went to school with, a
person who loved the same things that I did, a person who
was a different color but in every way exactly like me?

I can only sit here and look at the news photo which was
taken while I stood next to him at Lockhart Stadium and feel,
as another student once put it, that someone had killed my
brother.

At a memorial service on February 9, 1969, a new
$1.4 million health and physical education building at State
College was named the "Smith-Hammond-Middleton Memorial Center." A granite marker erected near the center of the
campus and bearing the names of the three students was dedicated to the students who lost their lives "on the South Carolina State College campus, Orangeburg, S.C., February 8,
1968, in pursuit of human dignity."

9 : THE SCAPEGOAT

"EMMETT TILL, that kicked me off like it did a lot of other black boys. That got my psyche. And Mack Parker, too. I remember those cases vividly and I've seen a lot myself. I've worked in counties where it's happened."

Cleveland Louis Sellers, Jr., was discussing why he quit college in 1964 and swapped a relatively comfortable life for the rigors and dangers of the civil-rights movement. He said he brooded over the Mississippi lynchings of Till and Parker and other anti-Negro violence that occurred in the succeeding years in the South and finally decided to join the nonviolent, direct-action movement. At the time he was studying mechanical engineering at Howard University, in Washington, D.C.

At Howard he was a member of the Nonviolent Action Group, an affiliate of the Student Nonviolent Coordinating Committee, and was involved in civil-rights activity in Cambridge, Maryland. There he first experienced a confrontation with police. He was charged with disorderly conduct and trespassing in connection with a demonstration protesting a visit by Governor George Wallace of Alabama.

Over the protests of his father, Sellers dropped out of college and joined the SNCC staff in 1964. And over the protests of his mother, he went to Mississippi that summer. Mrs. Sellers "tried to persuade him not to go; I was afraid for him. But he had made up his mind and thought he had to go."

It was a summer of widespread racial violence in Mississippi—bombings, burnings, and beatings, and finally the Ku Klux Klan lynching of three civil-rights workers in Neshoba County. Sellers, who had known all three of the victims, also worked that summer in Neshoba and other Mississippi counties that bristled with hostility for civil-rights workers. But he escaped personal violence and earned a reputation as one of SNCC's most dedicated and effective organizers.

In 1965 he was elected program secretary of SNCC, the organization's third-ranking post, and in June of the following year he helped popularize the cry "Black Power" during the James Meredith "march against fear" in Mississippi. While Stokely Carmichael and other SNCC leaders were beginning to sound violently antiwhite in their rhetoric, however, Sellers continued to strike a reasonable tone. White newsmen covering the movement found him to be one of the few SNCC figures who remained friendly and cooperative. If toughened and frustrated by his experiences, he was not openly embittered, and he opposed aggressive violence as futile.

During the Meredith march, a group of marchers broke away from the main body, which was headed for Jackson, and traveled to Neshoba County where they demonstrated. Several of them were beaten by police. At a meeting afterwards at Jackson's Pearl Street Methodist Church, angry young militants talked seriously of arming themselves and going to Neshoba to "deal with 'em on their own terms." Sellers turned and looked at a white observer, Kenneth Dean, who served as director of the Mississippi Council on Human Relations (a private group affiliated with the Southern Regional Council), and Dean asked, "Cleve, what do you think?" Sellers replied, "I think that that is foolish. Those people have got bigger guns and bigger bombs and to attempt such a thing is just asking to get more violence heaped upon yourself." After the Orangeburg shooting, Dean recalled, "Cleve Sellers was the one man you could count on to maintain communications after most black militants stopped talking to white people."

In four years of civil-rights activity before Orangeburg, Sellers accumulated a string of arrests, although he spent relatively little time in jail. Charges included: 1966, unlawful entry into the embassy of the Republic of South Africa in Washington, D.C.; trespassing and disturbing the peace in Jackson, Mississippi; and trespassing and failing to move on in Atlanta; and 1967, violation of Selective Service law in Atlanta and carrying a concealed weapon in Baton Rouge, Louisiana.

Sellers' brushes with the law surprised the people of Denmark, who remembered him as a happy, courteous youth who said "sir" and "ma'm" when addressing his elders, black as well as white. He was an active Boy Scout, an acolyte at St. Phillips Episcopal Chapel, and a "B" student at all-black Voorhees High School where he played basketball. He always sat in the balcony of the Dane Theater and never challenged any of the town's other racial barriers.

In the paternalist tradition, his family was considered among "the best colored people in town." His father, a World War II combat veteran, operated a small motel and restaurant and a taxi business, and by Denmark's standards was considered a prosperous Negro. He never bothered the whites, they never bothered him, and he felt that "white people have always been nice to me."

Sellers' mother had a degree in home economics from South Carolina State College and worked as a dietitian at the South Carolina Area Trade School in Denmark. But she spent a lot of time with Cleveland and her only other child, Gwendolyn, who was a year older then Cleveland. She always gave birthday parties for them, and she frequently went fishing with Cleveland in the nearby South Edisto River.

Sellers was raised in a six-room brick house shaded by a cedar tree and two huge pecan trees, with a swimming pool in the back yard. As a child he had a pony and a cart. He fished with a rod and reel, not the cane poles that most Negroes and poor whites used.

As he became older and more serious and read of the lynchings of Till and Parker, he began to brood over anti-Negro violence spawned by the civil-rights movement. He became president of his school's NAACP youth chapter. But he found that he could not discuss the issues with his parents: "They didn't understand me; I guess it was part of the generation gap."

His mother thought of him as "a happy child, never moody and never a problem." And she was unaware that such things as lynchings had influenced him to join the movement: "I never asked him why he got in, what started it all. I wish I had asked him. What he said about it would make sense to almost anyone."

People who closely followed the four days of events in Orangeburg before the February 8 shooting were not surprised when police arrested Sellers. He had been pointed out by Governor McNair and other officials as an "outside agitator" and had come in for increasing attention from the news media. "A cat over WIS TV did me more damage than anybody else," Sellers later recalled. "The day before the shooting he asked if he could have an interview and I said 'no' and he took pictures of me walking with a whole group of students in the background and it looked like I was leading them." Sellers probably would have been surprised if he had not been arrested. As tension increased on February 8 he told newsmen, "Everybody is looking for a scapegoat."

Charges by state officials that Sellers was to blame were disbelieved by people who knew him well. In Atlanta, Charles Morgan, Jr., southern director of the American Civil Liberties Union, told newsmen he knew Sellers as "a gentlemanly person who is easy to deal with," and he said:

> I've seen him at places as varied as my office, a lecture platform at an Ohio college, and the coaches' All-American football game in Atlanta. He is a man of varied interests, and it is inconceivable to me that he would have initiated action which would have been in any way responsible for the tragedy of Thursday night. His sole responsibility, it would seem to me, rests in the fact that he has told Negroes for a number of years that they are entitled to the rights of other American citizens; and since the passage of the 1964 Civil Rights Act, to the pursuit of happiness. This, it seems to me, includes the use of public accommodations such as a bowling alley in a little South Carolina town where the major industry is the education of Negro students.

Dr. Rubin F. Weston, faculty advisor to BACC, the group Sellers helped organize at State College, said of Sellers: "What he's after I believe is equal treatment—no holds barred, the constitution as it is. He's disarming, almost, he's so nice. But he has a streak of stubbornness. If he believes something is right, he'll pay the full price to see something done. He's a good influence on the country."

People who did not know Sellers, but who long had been used to hearing politicians cry "outside agitators" when racial trouble erupted, also recognized his role in the Orangeburg tragedy as that of a scapegoat. A month after the shooting, Harry Ashmore of the Center for Democratic Institutions, who, as an Arkansas editor, won a Pulitzer Prize in 1958 for editorials on the Little Rock school desegregation crisis, spoke of the tragedy in a speech at the University of South Carolina. Ashmore said:

> . . . the saddest dispatch that I have read lately from my native state was not the one that reported the senseless slaughter of Negro students at Orangeburg, but the report that followed a day or so later proclaiming that high officials had concluded that the student unrest was the work of imported black militants. For television purposes, the investigators finally were able to dig up one black man with bushy hair and an African costume to explain why unarmed Negro youths were found dead with police bullets in their backs and in the soles of their feet.

Although Orangeburg further frustrated and disillusioned Sellers with the American system, he still did not lose all faith, as evidenced by a letter he wrote to a staff member of the United States Commission on Civil Rights declaring that the shooting should be investigated. A memorandum dated April 26, 1969, from Gwen Kimbrough, a commission sociologist, to Samuel J. Simmons, field services director, mentioned the letter and declared:

> Cleveland Sellers, and many people like him, have little or no trust in the integrity of government agencies. He does not believe, yet he still dares to hope, that an agency such as ours will take the "risks" of conducting an objective and public evaluation of the Orangeburg situation. I strongly sus-

pect that if the decision is *not* to get involved, the Commission will have confirmed in the minds of many people that we are just another unconcerned, uninvolved, irrelevant federal bureaucracy. If on the other hand, the decision is to get involved, we will have made a step forward (not a very big step admittedly) in beginning communications with the rapidly developing "militant" segments of the Black communities.

Sellers also indicated an interest in working within the system in 1967 by pressing a civil suit in federal court against Governor McNair and Georgia Governor Lester Maddox and other officials of the two states. Sellers charged that Negroes were systematically excluded from draft boards and he petitioned for an order restraining draft board members, who are appointed by governors, from inducting Negroes into service. The United States District Court in Atlanta denied the petition and the Supreme Court, in a 5–3 decision, refused to review the case. Chief Justice Warren and Justices Douglas and Marshall dissented.

The dissenting opinion, written by Douglas, noted Sellers' "uncontested allegations" that only one of South Carolina's 161 draft board members was a Negro and added,

> thus, for a state in which 34.8 percent of the population is Negro, only 0.6 percent participate in the administration of the Selective Service. Moreover, in Georgia, where 28.5 percent of the population is Negro, members of the Negro race constitute only 0.2 percent of the 509 members. Despite these statistics of exclusion, and despite petitioner's assertion that his classification was racially motivated, the District Court refused to enjoin his induction.

Sellers, over the protest of his mother, had refused to step forward for induction and had been charged with violating the Selective Service law. At a trial of the charge on March 29, 1968, seven weeks after the Orangeburg shoot-

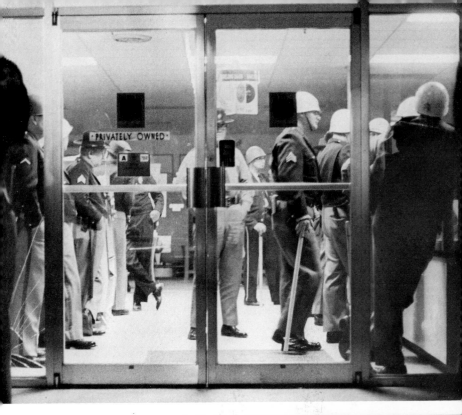

Highway patrolmen stand guard in and around Harry Floyd's all-white bowling alley.

Firemen spray bonfire just before shooting (foreground, two bannisters like those that struck Patrolman Shealy).

Negro editor Abraham talks to Chief Strom (center) and Captain Fairey shortly before patrol opened fire.

Patrolmen deployed on embankment just before shooting.

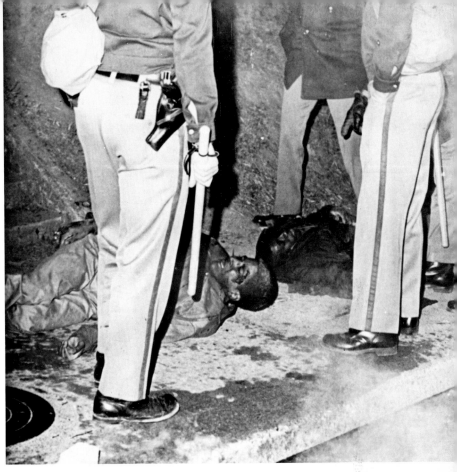

Henry Smith (left) and Delano Middleton lie on sidewalk after being dragged off campus.

Samuel Hammond, Jr.

Delano Middleton

Henry Smith

Photos this page by Cecil J. Williams

From The Desk
OF
H. E. Smith

648 30th Ave
Orangeburg, S.C.

My Dear Mother,

I am living a relatively normal Christian life. I am going to church more than I did last year. I am trying to do unto others as I would have them do unto me. I think that is about all God asks of a person.

So how is the family doing, Mama, Sue and Johnny.

When I was home it seemed as if I had been away for a long time and I was a stranger everyone had grown up so I hardly recognized anyone.

Mother, I will come home Wednesday before Thanksgiving. Oh, yes my meats you gave me spoiled, you see, my bags came in on Monday afternoon, when I got the meats they were spoiled so I spent part of the 5.00 you sent me to buy some meats and take some of my clothes out the cleaners. If you can send me some hamburger meat this weekend.

Your Son
H.E.

Copy of letter from Henry Smith to his mother

Highway patrolmen guarding state capitol during student protest over the Orangeburg killings.

Photo by Bill Barley

Cleveland Sellers (center) leaves the Orangeburg County Courthouse in February 1968, after his arrest on rioting and inciting to riot when two South Carolina State College students and a high school student were fatally shot on the college campus during a confrontation with South Carolina state highway patrolmen. At left is South Carolina Law Enforcement Division (SLED) Chief J. P. (Pete) Strom; at right are Orangeburg County Chief Deputy B. N. Collins and Sheriff R. F. (Bob) Dukes. In the background are two unidentified SLED agents.

Governor Robert E. McNair

ing, Sellers put his character in issue. Two former SNCC officials—ex-Chairman John Lewis and Georgia State Representative Julian Bond—testified in his behalf. So did the Reverend Charles Webster of the American Friends Service Committee, a former chaplain at Clemson University. The government contended that even if Sellers' character were good, it did not excuse "an offense such as this."

A jury composed of nine whites and three Negroes found Sellers guilty. In a presentence statement a month later Sellers told United States District Judge Newell Edenfield of Atlanta that he (Sellers) could only be sentenced by "black people," that the court's decision "has nothing to do with how I move and how I act" and that "it appears that the only solution to my problem is to fight till my death or to fight until I'm liberated."

Judge Edenfield promptly gave Sellers a maximum five-year sentence; until that time the standard sentence in such cases in the Atlanta court had been three years. Sellers appealed the verdict and sentence, but Edenfield, noting the serious nature of the charges against him in Orangeburg, denied him an appeal bond and Sellers remained in federal prisons for more than four months. Finally, Supreme Court Justice Hugo Black directed that he be released on an appeal bond of no more than $5,000, rejecting the lower court's ruling that Sellers was potentially dangerous if left at large, that he was raising a "frivolous argument" about exclusion of Negroes from draft boards, and that he might flee to avoid trial.

Justice Black, pointing out that Sellers had always shown up for scheduled court hearings, noted that the Orangeburg charges were serious, but added: "The state authorities there, however, who are familiar with the facts of that case, have been perfectly satisfied to release him on bail. This record thus fails to establish that serious danger would result to the community . . . if this applicant were released on bail."

Subsequently, after the government acknowledged that the FBI had monitored Sellers's telephone conversations "during the course of two electronic surveillances," the Supreme Court remanded the criminal case to the district court for further consideration. United States Solicitor General Erwin N. Griswold, citing a remanding order in a similar case involving the conviction of heavyweight boxing champion Cassius Clay, had recommended that the Sellers case be remanded.

A grand jury in Orangeburg ultimately indicted Sellers on charges of participating in a riot, incitement to riot, and conspiracy to incite others to riot. But the jury failed to indict him on the original charges of arson, housebreaking and grand larceny, assault and battery with intent to kill, destruction of personal property, and damaging real property.

In January 1970, a state court at Orangeburg granted an indefinite delay in Sellers's trial pending the outcome of a case in the United States Fourth Circuit Court of Appeals challenging the constitutionality of the law under which Sellers had been indicted. The challenge came in a suit filed by the Reverend Ralph David Abernathy, Dr. King's successor as president of the Southern Christian Leadership Conference, who had been arrested in the spring of 1969 on riot charges following demonstrations in Charleston in connection with a hospital workers' strike.

More than two years after his arrest in the Orangeburg case, the state still had not brought Cleveland Sellers to trial. Meanwhile, in 1969 Sellers had completed a four-month period as a lecturer in Afro-American studies at Cornell University. And in 1970 he was accepted as a graduate student at Harvard University for study toward a master's degree in education.

10 : THE GOVERNOR

WHEN A group concerned with civil rights met in the governor's office several weeks after the shooting and suggested to Governor McNair that he should have a Negro on his staff —one who would understand the feelings of black people— he retorted, "I know them. I grew up with them." Recalling his childhood on another occasion, McNair commented about Negro neighbors, "If they were sick, my mother took them to the doctor. If they got in jail, my father bailed them out."

The paternalist tradition of the South Carolina low-country made a strong imprint on Robert Evander McNair, an only child who grew up in the Hell Hole Swamp section of Berkeley County. The area was known throughout South Carolina as a breeding place for moonshiners and politicians.

The McNair farm, 600 acres under cultivation and another 6,000 acres of swampy woodland, was less than a mile from the birthplace of Congressman L. Mendel Rivers, the "swamp fox" of South Carolina politics and chairman of the House Armed Services Committee since 1965, known nationally as a powerful advocate of the military.

The governor's father, Daniel E. McNair, had come as a young man from Scotland County, North Carolina, to manage the land he later purchased. The future governor was born December 14, 1923, out of the county at the home of an aunt, a sister of his mother, Claudia Crawford McNair. As a boy, he sometimes rode his horse down a dirt road to the two-teacher Jamestown Elementary School, and later rode a school bus to Macedonia High School.

In addition to the farm, the elder McNair operated a general store and was a community leader. The governor acquired his father's traditional Scotch-Irish qualities of hard work, responsibility, and stubbornness.

After graduation from high school in 1940, McNair enrolled at Clemson, but transferred after one semester to the University of South Carolina for prelaw study. There, he courted Josephine Robinson, his future wife, of Allendale, played number three guard on the varsity basketball team, and in 1942 entered the Navy V-7 officer candidate program. He ran unsuccessfully for student body president. After getting his commission as a twenty-year-old ensign, he married, then departed for the western Pacific in 1944.

In a few months he was commanding officer of an LST, an amphibian landing craft, with another officer and fifteen enlisted men on board. In the invasion of the Philippines, a Japanese kamikaze pilot slammed his plane through the hold of the mother ship from which McNair's LST was being loaded in Subic Bay. A second plane demolished a companion LST that was loading simultaneously. In the midst of explosions and water aflame from burning fuel, McNair's crew picked up more than 100 survivors, many of them wounded.

After his discharge in January 1946, McNair entered the University of South Carolina Law School. He ran for the legislature from Berkeley County that year—and lost. There were two seats and McNair later recalled proudly, "I ran a strong third in a five-man race." A year after getting his law degree, he moved to his wife's home town of Allendale and became a successful politician and small-town lawyer.

He served as chairman of the board of the First Baptist Church in Allendale and later, as governor, he remained an active layman. Also as governor, he rarely missed a Presbyterian College football game during the four years his son played end. There were three younger children, all daughters.

In 1950, at the age of twenty-six McNair won a tough race for Allendale County's only seat in the state House of Representatives. Five years later, he won the chairmanship of the powerful Judiciary Committee.

South Carolina was entering its period of massive legal resistance against integration—repealing the compulsory school attendance law and voting out the state constitutional mandate for a public school system. As an ambitious young politician from one of the state's smallest and poorest counties—one with a majority Negro population, only a few of whom were then registered to vote—McNair quietly went along.

He showed no special sensitivity on racial matters, but as a legislator was known for doing his homework, working behind the scenes to iron out kinks in legislation, and avoiding open conflict. His horizons were expanding and his innately keen political instincts were developing into those of a consensus seeker and a results-oriented pragmatist. In 1962, he was elected lieutenant governor, and in April 1965, when Donald Russell resigned as governor for appointment to a vacancy in the Senate, McNair moved into the governor's office.

McNair, a man of medium height and somewhat heavy build, still had an enthusiastic, boyish face and youthful appearance, but his wavy, carefully groomed, dark brown hair was beginning to turn gray at the temples.

A survey by political pollster Oliver Quayle for McNair during his 1966 campaign for governor showed South Carolinians more concerned with racial problems than any other issue, with whites basically moderate and Negroes rather conservative. The poll showed only one white voter in five a hard core segregationist who wanted to turn back the clock and withdraw rights from Negroes. By race, 42 percent of the whites and 49 percent of the Negroes considered the pace of integration in South Carolina "about right," but 57 percent of the whites believed integration "too fast" and 48 percent of the blacks "too slow." Quayle observed that white voters "do not want to go any further, but are also realistic enough to know that they cannot turn back."

Tying racial peace with economic progress, McNair successfully campaigned on a theme of peace, progress, and prosperity. He said the greatest problem in South Carolina was "to prepare our people for change." He received roughly half of the white vote and 99 percent of the Negro vote (estimated between 65,000 and 75,000) for a landslide victory over Republican candidate Joseph O. Rogers, former vice chairman of the legislature's official school segregation committee. McNair won 58 percent of the vote, 255,854 to 184,088 for Rogers (who in 1969 was appointed United States Attorney for South Carolina by President Nixon).

Soon after the election, a group of Negro political leaders sought an appointment with McNair, met with him in his office, and came away impressed with his attitude. People meeting NcNair for the first time often found him charming, with a disarming smile and a friendly, ingratiating manner.

Those who knew him better were aware of a sometimes biting wit and a sensitivity to criticism.

In his inaugural address, attended by George and Lurleen Wallace, McNair drew applause when he said, "This is not the time—and South Carolina is not the place—for those who are preoccupied with extremism or petty frustration." He selected "responsibility" as the one word that would be his guide the next four years and pledged his "firm commitment to responsible forward movement."

For his inaugural, McNair restored the traditional formal ball, and tickets were sold for $25 to the public. That night—after the Wallaces had returned to Alabama—a quartet of Negroes sought $5 spectator tickets at the window of Columbia's Township Auditorium. An embarrassed young white woman at the window told them the spectator seats were all gone. After glancing at the skeptical faces, she quickly said that some regular tickets were available for $25 each. One of the men pulled out a roll of money, peeled off five $20 bills, and his group went inside.

Altogether, about twenty Negroes scattered around at the ball hardly created a ripple. It was as though it was the most natural thing in the world for Negroes to be attending the inaugural ball of the governor of South Carolina. The only discordant note of the evening was a white male baritone's rendition of "Short'nin' Bread."

When the legislature convened, McNair proposed reenactment of a compulsory school attendance law. Veteran House Speaker Sol Blatt—a powerful legislative figure—was vehemently opposed to reenactment, but a bill passed. McNair moved to take full advantage of new "Great Society" federal programs and placed his primary emphasis on economic growth and "development of human resources." He began appointing Negroes to state boards and commissions and encouraged county officials to follow his example. And there were little things—like a telegram wishing success to a South Carolina State College coed entered in the Miss Tan USA contest. In the boycott of classes in the 1967 spring crisis, students at State College were promised that the school would be upgraded and given priority attention.

In September at the Southern Governors Conference in Asheville, McNair defended the Southern Regional Education Board report, *Negro Higher Education in the South*, after it was attacked by Governor Lester Maddox of Georgia. In a stinging rebuke of Maddox's position, courtly Governor Mills Godwin of Virginia called the SREB study "a landmark report" and said Negro higher education was "pitiably poor in many institutions throughout the South." Godwin said the situation "cries out very loudly for us to do something about it. We are going to fail miserably if we fail to act."

McNair, the newly elected chairman of SREB, said tersely after Godwin sat down, "I want to echo what Governor Godwin said about the report. . . ." He pointed out that Negro students in South Carolina had protested earlier in the year because of concern with the quality of their education. The report concluded with "the necessity of providing equal higher educational opportunity for Negroes in the South." McNair called the report impressive because of its "depth and honesty" and said it was significant that "we can now talk about the problem and do something about it." He said "priority attention" was needed for higher education programs for Negroes in the South.

Another major item of discussion at the conference was the urban riots of that summer of 1967. The governors met behind closed doors to discuss the calling out of the National Guard in one state for duty in another in the event of an emergency. Earlier in the summer, after the great riot in Detroit that left forty-three dead and caused $50 million property damage, McNair remarked at a press conference that "they waited too late to call in force." He warned that riots would not be allowed to happen in South Carolina. Without fanfare, the state highway patrol had developed a specially trained riot-control force, and the National Guard was put through riot-control training.

In August, McNair had publicly endorsed a proposal by the Reverend I. DeQuincey Newman, NAACP field secretary in the state, for a statewide task force to deal with racial problems. What Newman and others sought was a group with official status to go into an area early if trouble developed, but McNair insisted that it be a volunteer committee that among other things would encourage local communities to establish similar biracial councils. He took no action on another request by Newman and other Negro leaders to seek several hundred new National Guard positions and recruit blacks to fill them. At the time—six months before the Orangeburg shooting—there were only about twenty Negro Guardsmen in South Carolina, and Newman felt it would be provocative if virtually all-white units were to be called out in the event of racial conflicts.

In the fall, McNair presided over a state budget hearing at which Acting President Nance requested what he considered a modest $700,000 increase in operating expenses for South Carolina State College. The state was sitting on a $22 million surplus, and McNair had said only a few months earlier that "priority attention" must be given programs of higher education for Negroes in the South.

There was surface calm on the campus of State College that fall. In December, *The Charlotte Observer* reported the students were adopting a "wait and see" attitude on promises made the previous spring, including adequate funds to improve the quality of education. Student body president

Robert Scott—an articulate, mild-mannered youth from Charleston and a colonel in the campus ROTC unit—said, "If there is not good faith, next spring will be something like last year."

Early in January, an "austerity" state budget was released by McNair that provided no additional funds for South Carolina State College, only a 6 percent increase to correspond with a projected 6 percent enrollment increase. There was new construction going up on the campus, including the 4,000-seat indoor athletic facility, and McNair seemed to think the Negro students would be happy with such visible signs of "progress."

A month before the Orangeburg shooting, *The Charlotte Observer* commented editorially, "It is simply unrealistic at this point to calculate S.C. State's increased appropriations on the increased enrollment factor." Pointing out that Nance was not asking for a giant step the next year, "but for a start toward meeting urgent needs," the *Observer* stated, "It could be tragic if South Carolina ignored his modest plea and the special needs of S.C. State." Student leaders began discussing a petition to the legislature and unrest was beginning to stir on the campus.

Meanwhile, middle-class blacks as well as a few white officials in Orangeburg had expressed concern to the governor's office about the presence of Sellers. During January, McNair mentioned the presence of "outside influences" and emphasized that the state would not tolerate disorder. His tough statements caused concern within the Negro community. Mrs. Simkins, the Columbia civil-rights leader, observed later that "McNair kept saying South Carolina was prepared and he said, 'We are not going to have these situations in South Carolina.' This was interpreted in the black community—I heard it a hundred times—that they were going to kill some Negroes if it took that to put the fear of God in their hearts . . ."

McNair did not personally go to Orangeburg during the week of crisis. An Orangeburg official explained later that Chief Strom had advised McNair it was too dangerous for him to go onto the campus and that city officials believed it would have made matters worse for him to come to the city without going to the campus.

In the weeks after the shooting, McNair's attitude about Orangeburg was that the less said or written, the better, and that what happened should be accepted as an unfortunate incident. In his statement the morning after the shooting, he said, "I hereby call upon all responsible South Carolinians to exercise restraint, responsibility, and reason and to work together to reestablish harmony and good will among all persons." Although he met with adult and student Negro leaders (they complained he did most of the talking and little listening), McNair seemed unaware of or insensitive to the depth of resentment among blacks, who wanted an honest admission of and accountability for mistakes.

Dr. Rubin Weston, the faculty advisor who attended the meeting with McNair and the State College students the day of the mass demonstration at the State House, recalled more than a year afterwards that "the governor said nothing that was racist, but he was ignorant of conditions at the college. He lectured the students on political science, and I asked if he knew that insufficient funds were appropriated to provide a full political science faculty. He said he didn't know —and he didn't seem to care." When Wayne Curtis, chairman of BACC, said at one point in a display of rhetoric, "We could tear this building apart," McNair stiffened and said grimly, "Don't try it." Behind the closed door of the adjoining conference room were two dozen specially selected members of the highway patrol's riot force.

In the weeks after the shooting, the strain showed on McNair. He became increasingly defensive and grew irritable and somewhat despondent. After a *Los Angeles Times* story reporting that at least eighteen of the students were shot from the rear, McNair said testily at a press conference that a lot of the story "was fiction . . . it showed a lack of real investigation."

McNair was in Japan on a presidential trade mission when Dr. Martin Luther King, Jr., was assassinated on April 4. The burden of dealing with new racial tensions—the National Guard was called out and curfews set in half a dozen South Carolina communities—fell on Lieutenant Governor West.

McNair returned from the trip abroad mentally refreshed. He proposed the bond issue that the legislature later approved for South Carolina State College. He also announced he would name a special committee to study State College and report on its academic deficiencies, but the committee was never appointed.

As the months passed, McNair's political instincts were whetted by the upcoming presidential election. He went to the Democratic National Convention in Chicago as chairman of a delegation that included twelve Negroes, one of the few southern delegations whose credentials were unchallenged. At Chicago, McNair made a serious behind-the-scenes bid for the vice presidential nomination, but Orangeburg killed whatever chance he had.

In September 1967, Vice President Hubert Humphrey had come to South Carolina at McNair's invitation, and McNair accompanied him on a flight from Washington. Officially, Humphrey came to dedicate a new mental health facility in Greenville. At the time, the prospects for 1968 presidential politics called for another Johnson-Humphrey ticket for the Democrats. Not a single national newsman covered the visit.

For McNair, however, the visit was significant as a symbol of his efforts to make the national Democratic party "respectable" in South Carolina. After a closed breakfast meeting with McNair and a cross section of education officials and Negro, labor, and industrial leaders, Humphrey called their reports of what was happening in South Carolina "almost inspirational." He said manpower training in South Carolina was "among the most comprehensive anywhere." In his speech at the dedication ceremony, Humphrey praised McNair for "positive and constructive social and economic leadership."

A week before the convention in Chicago a year later—a time for courtship of any politician who controls delegate votes—Humphrey referred on national television to McNair as a representative of the progressive New South and as one of many persons considered suitable for vice president.

McNair was chairman of both the Southern Governors Conference and the National Democratic Governors Conference. At Chicago, his suite in the Palmer House went almost unnoticed as the strategy center for the Democratic governors, who in the end controlled the votes that gave Humphrey the nomination for president. McNair played a key role in holding the convention for Humphrey, but only the *Chicago Daily News* among major media reported the story fully.

On Monday night, a major test vote of the individual strengths of Humphrey and Eugene McCarthy came on the seating of the Texas delegation. A minority report of the Credentials Committee recommended giving 40 of the 105 Texas seats to McCarthy supporters. The minority report was rejected by a vote of 1,368 to 955, a victory margin of 413 votes for the Humphrey forces. Without the challenged Texas and Georgia delegations voting, the remaining fifteen member states of the Southern Governors Conference voted 508 ½ to 88 for the Humphrey position—a 420 ½-vote margin. Only twelve of the remaining thirty-three states had Democratic governors and those states voted 393 ½ to 106 ½ against the McCarthyites.

Thus, the combined border-southern states and those states outside the region with Democratic governors overwhelmingly supported the Humphrey position, 902 to 194 ½. The remaining states supported McCarthy 660 ½ to 466 on the test vote. There was a similar breakdown on two other roll calls that night. It was clear who controlled the power for Humphrey, and it was McNair's coordinating role among the governors that gave credence to his quiet attempt to gain the vice presidential spot.

Immediately after the Wednesday night nomination of Humphrey, former Governor Price Daniel of Texas—official White House liaison man with the governors and one of President Lyndon Johnson's key men at the convention—strolled over to McNair as delegates were streaming out of the convention hall. Daniel placed an arm on McNair's shoulder and whispered in his ear for several minutes. In his hand, Daniel carried a card on which was scribbled the names of Tennessee Governor Buford Ellington, former Governor Farris Bryant of Florida, West Virginia Governor Hulett Smith, and Delaware Governor Charles Terry—each the key man in his state's delegation. Smith and Terry both were close friends of McNair. Earlier in the evening, McNair got a quiet commitment of support from Texas Governor John Connally.

A few hours after midnight, several governors made a trip to Humphrey headquarters. McNair thought they went on his behalf.

Meanwhile, the Reverend A. W. Holman, South Carolina state NAACP president and a delegate, had introduced McNair to other black delegates and to black members of Humphrey's staff. Holman later explained his primary interest at the convention was the nomination of Humphrey and pointed out that McNair was a key figure in getting southern favorite sons to release delegates before the first ballot. Release of the delegates was crucial at the time for Humphrey. "I wanted the black delegates and blacks on Humphrey's staff to know that he [McNair] was very much in Humphrey's corner," Holman said. However, when Holman was asked after Humphrey's nomination if he could actively campaign for McNair, he replied:

No. Were it not for Orangeburg, perhaps he could have been the vice presidential nominee of the Democratic Party. I do believe Humphrey was seriously looking south for a man. Were it not for Orangeburg, I would have supported him. Afterwards, I could not in good conscience ask other Negroes to do so. I'm positive it was a death blow to his chances to get the nomination. Up until Orangeburg, I was very much impressed with Governor NcNair's record.

Some of McNair's advisors in Chicago said privately they believed his handling of the Orangeburg situation, which they considered showed a willingness to use force to put down disorder, would help him in his vice presidential aspirations because of the "law and order" issue.

McNair, who waited in his suite with family and newsmen, stepped into a bedroom at 1 P.M. Thursday to hear on television that Senator Edmund Muskie of Maine had been selected by Humphrey as his running mate. McNair realized only at the last minute that he was out of the running, but accepted it without showing disappointment. A Humphrey aide was supposed to have called McNair to inform him, but in the confusion the call was never made. An embarrassed Humphrey later called McNair and invited him to a private breakfast the next morning to apologize.

Actually, McNair was never in the running for vice president after Humphrey got the nomination. A top Humphrey aide told the authors the decision was made against having a southerner on the ticket before the vote nominating Humphrey for president on Wednesday night.

In a taped interview in *The Charlotte Observer* in April 1969, four years after he became governor, McNair was asked, "Looking back to a little over a year ago when the Orangeburg incident took place, do you now feel or have any regrets as to how it was handled?" He answered:

> *Well, everybody regrets the loss of life, but I know of nothing that was done in Orangeburg that as far as our handling of the situation overall that would . . . I think Orangeburg is something that you can't get into a discussion of the various incidents. Hopefully, we'll never have another recurrence of Orangeburg; we'll never have shooting; we'll never have sniping; we'll never have that kind of confrontation again, because that is most regrettable, and I think we've said over and over that we regret the loss of life; we regret Orangeburg as an incident, and hopefully we won't have any kind of thing like that again in South Carolina.*

He was then asked, "What do you think the impact of Orangeburg has been on South Carolina?" He answered:

> *Well, it would be awful hard to say what the impact has been other than it could happen here—it did happen here, and it made us all aware of that. I think we had been assuming it wasn't going to happen in South Carolina and that it couldn't happen here, and it did. So, of course, people of*

all races, people in all stations of life recognize that it did
happen, and that it can happen. And everybody spends
a lot more time trying to see that there is no cause for a
recurrence of an Orangeburg.

Also in 1969, in the 100-day Charleston hospital strike that ended in June, McNair's initial hard-line, antiunion position—the crucial issue among the strikers, all of whom were black and most of them women—caused him again to be accused of being insensitive to Negro demands for justice and dignity. However, by the end of the strike, McNair twice had met privately with William Saunders, a militant black leader who had helped organize the workers and the one man trusted by black militants in Charleston. Serving on the biracial Charleston Community Relations Council, Saunders won the respect of white establishment leaders and one of them, banker Hugh Lane, set up the meetings between Saunders and McNair.

Saunders had been critical of McNair and had viewed him as the perpetrator of the "Orangeburg Massacre." But by the end of the strike, Saunders said, "I found out he's not the biggest son of a bitch after all; he's about as fair as you can expect from anyone in that kind of business." Saunders added, "I think maybe he took the strong conservative position [on the hospital strike] because he wants to run against Strom Thurmond and he thinks no matter how conservative he is he can get black votes against Strom Thurmond."

Another view of how McNair is perceived was a dialogue between a middle-class black and two whites printed in the *South Carolina Methodist Advocate* in its July 10, 1969, issue. The black was a county NAACP chapter president and the whites were considered liberals in South Carolina:

WHITE ONE: *What was the feeling about Orangeburg?*

BLACK: *If any more trouble had developed, I would have*

done some work with my gun also. I was there—and it was terrible. The governor handled things bad.

WHITE ONE: *In what way?*

BLACK: *He called all that armed force into Orangeburg, and they shot those three boys. He handled that situation badly, just as he has this Charleston thing.*

WHITE ONE: *You sound "down" on the governor. Can you name two or three good things he has done?*

BLACK: *I sure can't, Orangeburg and now Charleston—all is bad news from the governor. What do you think of him?*

WHITE ONE: *I think he's a miracle. When you consider that he came from "Hell Hole Swamp," had a long period of service as a lowcountry legislator, and now has become really a moderate, seeking to be governor of all our citizens, trying to develop programs that will especially benefit the economically handicapped—I think all that is a real social miracle in our times.*

WHITE TWO: *It's very important also to consider what didn't happen in connection with Orangeburg—Governor McNair made no effort to use this to inflame racial feelings or make any political capital out of the unhappy and tragic events. Just consider what a Wallace would have done!*

BLACK: *But, as I see it, he hasn't done one thing to really help us.*

WHITE TWO: *I agree that he has not done many dramatic things that seem to improve things for Negroes. However, in politics things are relative. Just compare the difference in his approach from a Wallace, Faubus or Maddox.*

WHITE ONE: *Yes—and I am certain that his sentiments and feelings are sympathetic to all our citizens. I think I know him well enough to be certain that is true. I have been told, by one of his close associates, how livid with anger be became when some political supporters even mentioned that "they should have shot a lot more of those niggers down at Orangeburg."*

He is trying to develop programs, without saying they are for Negroes, that will especially benefit the economically handicapped. I think he is in error in not realizing that more special attention must be given to those groups, both black and white, but I know he is concerned with developing programs that will motivate and develop all.

BLACK: *These may be good programs, but are they really of any value to us? We just can't see any changes taking place in our community . . .*

WHITE: *I'm a "McNair-man"—but a critical one. I have to agree with you that his good points are not dramatized, that his mistakes became so clear so quickly.*

BLACK: *How do you explain that?*

WHITE ONE: *Several aspects of the governor's "style" and lack of understanding stand out as the basic reasons. I think they are all clearly indicated in the Charleston situation.*

One is his refusal to listen. He says his "door is open to all," and he has met with many persons in connection with these and other matters, but he does all the talking . . . I think a basic mistake is failure to listen more to those who come through the "open" door. A second is that he is a "rigid legalist"—he seems to think that "Law and Order" is strong armed force to coerce legal conformity—not seeming to realize that there are increasingly strong and surging forces of emotionally charged persons for whom elementary justice and the recognition of their human dignity is essential before the mechanics of law and order can be effective and operative . . . Another factor is inadequate advice and guidance. I know that numerous recommendations have been made for him to have a Negro on his staff. Now he has appointed Negroes to many state agencies and boards and he says he looks to them for advice. But he does not have always and continuously available the person who will help him to really understand the feeling and forces, and perhaps even the basic facts, before he takes action . . .

11 : INVESTIGATIONS

THE MORNING after the Orangeburg shooting Attorney General Ramsey Clark arose early at his Alexandria, Virginia, home to make an hour's drive to Airlie House near Warrenton. He was going to speak on riot prevention and control to a group of thirty mayors and chiefs of police. He picked up the morning *Washington Post* and found a disturbing headline: "2 Negro Students Killed in S. C. College Outbreak." The AP story mentioned "an outbreak of gunfire between students and law enforcement officers" and reported Patrolman Shealy had been "struck in the head by a bullet."

Clark found the article "terribly depressing" and he could not help but wish that Terrell Glenn were still the United States District Attorney at Columbia so he could have him on the scene for an investigation. Glenn, known as a "stand-up guy" on civil rights by Justice Department attorneys, had been a favorite of Robert F. Kennedy when he was Attorney General. Clark particularly remembered Glenn as having "performed magnificently" when Harvey Gantt broke the color line at Clemson University in January 1963—less than five months after bloody riots marked the admission of James Meredith at the University of Mississippi.

But Glenn had resigned a week before the shooting to enter private law practice. He had been the attorney for the eastern judicial district, which was being consolidated with the western district to give the state a single district, and he had hoped to be appointed attorney for the new district. But when the Johnson administration delayed making an appointment because of political pressures, he resigned.

The failure to appoint Glenn was to have a significant affect on the government's handling of the Orangeburg case. Clark had strongly preferred Glenn, but United States Senator Ernest F. (Fritz) Hollings (D-S.C.) supported John Williams, attorney for the western division. As a compromise, Senator Hollings finally nominated Glenn's first assistant, Klyde Robinson, a Harvard Law School graduate who had participated in several civil-rights cases. Clark felt Robinson had "performed well" but lacked Glenn's "feel" for civil-rights cases. Robinson later was to refuse to participate in the government's case, a significant handicap to Justice Department attorneys from Washington.

But that was just one problem Clark faced in what was to be an increasingly frustrating investigation for the Justice Department. The civil rights division soon found that some of the FBI agents assigned to investigate the patrol gunfire maintained disconcertingly close relations with state law enforcement officials during the tense period preceding the shooting and even after the FBI had begun its probe.

In fact, state agents participated in an FBI search for evidence around the State College campus the morning after the shooting. The search turned up no shotgun shells, only a few .30-caliber shells. It was not until three months later that civil rights division attorneys—not the FBI—learned that a black free-lance photographer, Cecil Williams, had picked up a dozen shotgun shells at the scene early on the morning after the shooting. The attorneys directed FBI agents to secure the shells, but by that time Williams had only six left and did not know what had become of the others. Of the six he still had, three had been fired from the same weapon, two had been fired by a second weapon, and another possibly had been fired by the second gun. What happened to all the other shells from patrol gunfire—from shotguns, carbines, and at least one revolver—was never learned. Neither was the total number of shots fired ever learned.

FBI agents and SLED agents also jointly searched for evidence across the street from the campus and found several .22-caliber slugs imbedded in the wall of a railroad warehouse. An FBI agent and a SLED agent later were to testify that the bullets had been fired from the direction of where the students were at the time of the confrontation. An FBI crime lab expert from Washington contradicted the testimony.

When Deputy Assistant Attorney General D. Robert Owen, the second highest official in the civil rights division, sought out Charles DeFord, agent-in-charge of the Columbia office, on the morning of February 10, he found him staying in a room at the Holiday Inn in Orangeburg with SLED Chief Strom, the top state official on the scene at the time of the shooting.

In an interview later Owen recalled, "I had a talk with DeFord that night—and in point of fact it wouldn't make any difference with those guys—it wouldn't have made any difference in the investigation. But it was just crazy for them to be staying together and I told DeFord the Bureau was making an investigation of the state patrol and you just have to keep your distance and you can't get in bed with them."

DeFord had been a close friend of Strom's—nothing unusual for FBI and state police officials who often cooperate closely in law enforcement. But both Owen and Clark thought that under the circumstances DeFord should have been more circumspect.

Although DeFord must have been aware that a civil-rights case could develop from a police-student clash, he had closely associated with Strom during the build-up of tension and violence prior to the shooting. So had other FBI agents, at least one of whom had witnessed the clubbing of students by police at the bowling alley.

South Carolina Attorney General Daniel R. McLeod, who had been in Orangeburg the day before the shooting as an observer for Governor McNair, thought that the FBI was so close to the case and was so well equipped as an investigative agency that it should handle any probe of the incident. Besides, McLeod reasoned, a state investigation would be considered suspect by Negroes. McLeod, later recalling that Strom and DeFord were together much of the time on February 7, said in an interview, "Both of them had tin hats on. They were riding in the same car every time I saw them. They were cheek by jowl the whole night long that I was there."

One of the FBI agents closest to the state patrolmen was Nelson Phillips, a native of Elberton, Georgia, who had been stationed in South Carolina for eleven years and who had helped direct training of the patrol riot squads that were on duty at Orangeburg. He later was to testify that he heard gunfire coming from the South Carolina State College campus just prior to the time the patrol opened fire.

It apparently was from Phillips and from some of the other agents who investigated the case that state law enforcement officials got the impression that the FBI investigation would absolve the patrol of any criminal culpability. That undoubtedly was the opinion at the state capitol in Columbia where Governor McNair frequently expressed confidence that the FBI would absolve the patrolmen.

On February 16, William J. Page, southwestern director of the United States Department of Health, Education and Welfare, visited the capitol and found that "the business I wanted to discuss with the governor's office didn't seem to have much perspective because they were obviously pre-occupied over the Orangeburg case." Page later recalled, "There was an atmosphere of real concern because some students were planning to demonstrate at the capitol that day and for the first time there was some open discussion of the possibility that the patrolmen had not actually been fired upon." However, in the governor's office Page "heard some references that FBI agents had been on the scene and that they were supportive of the idea that shots had been fired from the campus before the patrol fired." Page heard a SLED agent say emphatically FBI agents would "support the patrol's account of what happened." Colonel Thompson, commander of the highway patrol, later told the authors of this book that the day after the shooting he talked to Strom and the FBI in Orangeburg and they assured him the patrol had "acted with restraint."

Almost incredibly, the Justice Department itself did not know that at least three FBI agents witnessed the incident. Nor did it find out until almost three months later. Ramsey Clark, in an interview for this book, said, "It was a shame that we probably had quite a bit of trouble with a number of FBI agents as to what they said at different times and we had trouble getting all the interviews we wanted. We also had a terribly difficult time finding out where the FBI people were on the night of February 8—where they were, what they were doing, whether they were eyewitnesses."

Owen said that he specifically asked DeFord and Bill Danielson, an agent assigned to Orangeburg, where they were and "they told me they were in Orangeburg, but they weren't on the scene." Actually, DeFord, Danielson, and Agent Nelson Phillips all had been on the scene.

(DeFord, interviewed by telephone in Seattle, Washington, where he became security director for a bank after retiring from the FBI in June 1968, refused to explain why the FBI misled the Justice Department. "Frankly, I don't care what Bob Owen said," he declared. "I don't want to make any comment as to how soon after it was after it happened that they knew we were there. I don't want to say a damn thing about it. I don't want to get in a pissing match with the civil-rights attorneys." Danielson, interviewed at the FBI office in Columbia, said, "Nobody asked me if I was on the scene." He said the controversy over how long it took civil-rights attorneys to learn of the FBI's presence was "between the Bureau in Washington and the civil rights division." Both he and Phillips, also interviewed at the Columbia office, said they did not know when the civil-rights attorneys investigating the case learned they were witnesses. They said they could not comment further on the matter.)

The motive for misleading the Justice Department—in effect lying to the Attorney General who has statutory authority over the Bureau—was known perhaps only to the FBI. Among Justice Department attorneys there were two principal theories—that the agents were reluctant witnesses because of their extremely close working relationship with the patrol or that they felt they were in no position to acknowledge their presence on the scene because they were there on their own initiative, without specific authorization of FBI headquarters in Washington.

Strained relations between the FBI and the Justice Department's civil rights division had existed for years and it was no secret that as a general rule most agents considered civil-rights enforcement an odious task, especially in cases that involved accusations against local or state police with whom they worked.

"These are hard cases for the FBI because state and local and federal law enforcement are interrelated and each depends upon the other for substantial assistance in performing its duty," Clark commented. "Therefore, when you get a case that involves them in direct conflict, one investigating the other in criminal matters, you can realize how disruptive it can be to general, on-going cooperation and coordination in other matters. You also have to assume that men who have worked together for years, or for months, depend upon each other and rely upon each other in many ways."

Regardless of the motive, the FBI had, at the very least, hampered an important Justice Department investigation. If the department had known FBI agents were eyewitnesses, its attorneys quickly could have established some of the pertinent facts, instead of having to grope for months for an understanding of what had happened. The FBI even submitted a written report of its investigation to the civil rights division two months after the shooting without mentioning that agents had been witnesses.

Moreover, civil-rights attorneys found that the FBI, despite its reputation for thoroughness, did a superficial job in some of its initial interrogations and other investigatory work. The attorneys had to go back to the agents and insist on additional interviews with witnesses, and in late April the civil rights division sent a team of its attorneys to South Carolina to conduct what turned out to be a long, drawn-out investigation.

The FBI's lack of enthusiasm for the case did nothing to deter Ramsey Clark, an extremely sensitive civil libertarian who had shown great empathy for the poor, the black, and the disadvantaged, and who later in the year would become a prime target of Richard Nixon's hard-line, law-and-order campaign for the presidency. Almost from the outset Clark found the police action indefensible and outrageous. Despite distorted press reports of what had happened and an unclear picture even from his own attorneys, he could not bring himself to believe that the patrol gunfire would have occurred if South Carolina State had been a predominantly white college.

Clark drove to his Washington office after the speech at Airlie House and telephoned Governor McNair that afternoon. Clark later recalled:

When I finally got him, I told him I had been hearing and reading about what happened at Orangeburg and I was terribly concerned and wanted to do everything we could to help. I was trying to learn the facts. He told me Chief Strom had been in charge since Tuesday evening. He said all was calm by now and I told him that we would probably file a suit against the bowling alley the next day. That would have been the tenth. I told him that we were going to fully investigate and the FBI was already on the case. He said, "Fine." He said he understood we had to, and I said I thought it was imperative. I tried to find out the names of news people and those who were in the middle of it and he came up with the name of Dozier Mobley [the AP photographer who later said the AP misquoted him in reporting the students had been killed in an exchange of gunfire].

McNair pledged the full cooperation of the state in the investigation and said he would instruct the patrolmen who were on the scene to give statements to the agents. Civil rights division attorneys and investigators for the United States Commission on Civil Rights quickly learned, however, that the pledge to cooperate did not extend beyond the FBI. SLED agents, highway patrolmen, and Orangeburg police officers all refused to be interviewed by anyone other than the FBI. When the civil rights division persisted in its investigation, Colonel Thompson finally instructed his men not to cooperate further—not even with the FBI. By that time, however, FBI agents had already secured signed statements from patrolmen who were on the scene, including nine who said they had fired into the crowd of students and four others who said they had fired carbines, but into the air or over the heads of the students.

Chief Strom did talk briefly with investigators of the Civil Rights Commission on February 12, but he gave them little information. He said, "This thing never would have happened if black power hadn't come in here." An investigator's memorandum also quoted him as saying that no order had been given to fire and that no record had been made of who fired weapons or how often, but that the FBI was investigating and probably would find out.

The South Carolina State Advisory Committee of the Civil Rights Commission quickly turned up evidence to counter McNair's version of what had happened. In a closed-door session with the committee on February 12, Dean Oscar Butler said that not only had there been no shooting from the campus, but that most of the students had been shot from the side or rear.

Everett A. Waldo, a field representative from Washington, headed up the commission's Orangeburg investigation. By February 26, he and the Advisory Committee had completed an initial interoffice report based on interviews with twenty-one persons, including several students who testified they were shot while lying down or running away. The report, which was never publicized for fear of jeopardizing the

Justice Department's investigation, concluded that "without warning of any kind, the armed officers began to fire shotguns at the students . . . most of the injured received their wounds from the back, apparently as they were fleeing."

South Carolina was still left with the "official version," of course, and Governor McNair embellished it in a closed-door meeting with representatives of the Concerned Citizens' Conference, a biracial ad hoc group formed to seek action on the shootings. A Civil Rights Commission document, dated March 11, noted this about the March 7 meeting at the governor's office:

> McNair said that the facts of the FBI investigation would prove to be "very interesting and very surprising" to some people. He went on to say that "you will be surprised at how some of the students were wounded, you will be interested in some meetings that we know about that took place in other parts of the country prior to the disorder and that Orangeburg was mentioned at these meetings."

A member of the group, according to the document, asked McNair if he would take full responsibility for dealing with the patrol if the FBI investigation should show they were at fault in any way, and "he said he would. It was all like arguing with LBJ about Vietnam—he had information we didn't have and he seemed willing to use it to rebut our arguments and objections. He kept talking about how 'these people' just have to learn to obey the law."

McNair, apparently hoping to relieve some of the pressure Negro and civil-rights leaders were exerting for a full airing of the incident, privately and publicly talked about the possibility that he would make public the FBI's report on the case. He publicly said that eventually there would be an inquest into the three deaths, and at the March 7 meeting he said that Attorney General McLeod would soon release a report of a state investigation. None of these things was ever done.

Everett Waldo, in a memo concerning a March 29 meeting he and two other commission representatives had with McNair and McLeod, noted that the governor opposed an open commission hearing on the Orangeburg case and that he "suggested perhaps we could have the information and fact sheet being prepared by the attorney general."

"The governor said one interesting thing," Waldo reported. "He implied that information they had would indicate that it would have been impossible for the state highway patrol to have shot the students." McNair repeatedly implied that his office "would be receiving materials from the FBI," according to Waldo.

Meanwhile, the civil-rights movement continued to exert pressure for official action against the patrolmen who fired and for an investigation to determine the ultimate responsibility for the tragedy. In one of his last communications with federal officials before his assassination on April 4, 1968, in Memphis, Dr. Martin Luther King, Jr. (long a target of FBI wiretapping) had wired Ramsey Clark that the shootings "must not go unpunished."

Dr. King declared the incident "lies on the conscience of J. P. Strom, the officer in charge . . . [on the conscience of] the governor of South Carolina to whom Strom is directly answerable, and on the conscience of all men of good will." He demanded the government "act now to bring to justice the perpetrators of the largest armed assault undertaken under color of law in recent southern history."

In an April 25 memorandum, Samuel J. Simmons, director of the commission's field services division, recommended that the commission hold an open hearing before the end of June. "No adequate clarification of the events . . . in Orangeburg has yet been made," he wrote. "The original 'official version' which included the often-repeated phrase 'exchange of gunfire' and other gross misrepresentations of fact has never been sufficiently challenged or revised. The FBI investigation is not public information and was not designed to be although the governor used the possibility of making it public to his own advantage."

Simmons, who wrote that *the basic issue is one of political accountability in the area of law enforcement*," declared, "Black students and the black community need to know that someone in the establishment is concerned enough to expose injustice and move toward justice." The Justice Department objected that any hearing still would impede their investigation and affect whatever prosecutions might be brought; therefore, the commission decided not to schedule one at that time.

Meanwhile, Charles (Chad) Quaintance, a young, soft-spoken native of Johnson City, Tennessee, had been put in charge of the civil rights division's investigation in Orangeburg. He had begun the role with the distinct disadvantage of not knowing that FBI agents had witnessed the shooting. The FBI had filed a report of its investigation with the Justice Department and apparently believed that closed the case. But Assistant Attorney General Stephen Pollak, director of the civil rights division, ordered Quaintance to go to Orangeburg in late April to launch a full investigation. Soon after he began interviewing witnesses, Quaintance learned of the agents' presence at the scene.

Quaintance found that most of the Orangeburg firemen and National Guardsmen who were on the scene would cooperate, although some "obviously thought we shouldn't be there." He later recalled that one fireman "was very cooperative in trying to locate some records for us, and I was telling him I was trying to avoid having to make him come to court and testify and he said, 'Well, I'm sure glad you're doing it. Goddam, if you put me on the stand, I don't care what you ask me about, all I'll say is that the only thing I'm sad about is that they didn't kill more of them and they should have done it sooner.' "

The fireman then "backed up for a minute," according to Quaintance, "then he said, 'Well, I don't know. Maybe I don't really mean that. I knew that Middleton and he was a nice kid, but those agitators just got them so they were just crazy people or something.' "

Like Clark and other Justice Department officials, Quaintance was upset that FBI agents had misled them in the beginning, but he considered it a "significant accomplishment" that agents had secured statements from all sixty-six of the patrolmen who were on duty at South Carolina State on the night of February 8, including nine who said they fired into the crowd of students.

It was a hit-or-miss proposition as the agents sought to learn who had fired into the crowd, and the way they finally found out was by getting those who did to sign statements. Without the statements from those who fired—the only evidence ever turned up to identify the patrolmen who discharged their weapons—the Justice Department could not have seriously considered trying to prosecute anyone. In addition to the nine patrolmen who admitted firing into the crowd, four patrolmen acknowledged firing carbines, but said they fired over the students' heads.

If what the nine patrolmen who admitted shooting into the crowd said in their statements was the crux of the case the Justice Department was building, it also was at the heart of the state's contention that the shootings were justified. For the patrolmen all said they fired in self-defense. Five said that just before they opened fire they heard gunfire coming from the campus and three others said they "thought" they heard it. Lieutenant Jesse Spell said he gave an order to fire, but only two of the patrolmen who fired said they heard it. All of the patrolmen painted a picture of potential danger on the campus that night.

The FBI secured its first statements from those who shot into the crowd on February 14—six days after the shootings—from the top-ranking officer among them, Lieutenant Spell, and from Sergeant Addy of Spell's squad. The same agents took both statements and the accounts of the two patrolmen were markedly similar. Both contended they heard a great deal more "firing" by students than the other patrolmen stated they heard.

Spell said he "ordered my squad to fire their weapons to stop the mob." He never explained how he verbalized the order and only Addy and Sergeant Sidney C. Taylor said they heard an order—Addy said Spell shouted "now." Taylor said he heard "someone" give the order "now" after several patrolmen had shouted, "Now? Now?"

However, Patrolman first class Louis B. Judy of Spell's squad who was near Spell at the time, but who did not fire, later testified he had heard no order. The other patrolmen who fired into the crowd apparently did so spontaneously upon hearing other patrolmen fire. Patrolman first class Edward H. Moore, who fired a pistol six times, said he thought the gunfire was "a spontaneous reaction to the situation," and Patrolman Allen Jerome Russell, twenty-four, said he fired "after seeing the wood thrown by the students, and hearing some shots fired."

The investigation was painstakingly slow, even though by February 26 agents had secured statements from the nine patrolmen who acknowledged firing into the group of students. There were literally hundreds of witnesses to be interviewed and there was much conflicting testimony.

The assassination of Dr. King further delayed the probe.

So many FBI agents were thrown into the massive manhunt for the killer that there were not enough agents available to adequately investigate the Orangeburg case. Then, too, some of the Justice Department's attorneys were involved in investigating the riots that rocked American cities in the wake of the assassination. And in the summer, some department personnel got bogged down in dealing with the Poor People's Campaign that Dr. King's successor, the Reverend Ralph David Abernathy, took to Washington.

Finally, on July 18, Stephen Pollak, pulled together the voluminous file on the investigative work by his attorneys and the FBI, and then made a tentative decision to proceed toward prosecution. On September 16 he determined that the department should present the case to a federal grand jury. Since there was little coordination between the Civil Rights Commission and the Justice Department, some of the commission's staffers, not knowing Pollak's plans, were getting impatient about the lack of action by the Justice Department.

On September 25, Everett Waldo, who had spent weeks in Orangeburg directing the commission's on-the-scene investigation, sent a memo to field services director Samuel Simmons, asking: "CAN'T WE DO SOMETHING?! Suggestion: Prepare a report for the State Advisory Committee to publish revealing our information and understanding of what happened. To say something, carefully enough to avoid jeopardizing a criminal case (if it ever goes to court!) would be better than any continued silence." However, the commission, upon learning the case was still alive in the civil rights division, chose to remain silent.

When Pollak decided in September to present the Orangeburg case to a grand jury, he was uncertain whether an indictment would be sought. Usually, the government plans at the outset to seek an indictment when it takes a case to a grand jury, but this time there were unanswered questions and conflicting evidence that Pollak felt might be resolved by testimony before the jury. For one thing, law enforcement officers who had refused to be interviewed by the civil rights division attorneys could be subpoenaed to testify.

The burden of presenting the case to the grand jury when it met in October in Columbia fell on Chad Quaintance, who felt deeply about the government's responsibility to prosecute.

United States Attorney Robinson, who apparently felt just as deeply that the government had a responsibility not to prosecute, refused to participate in the case. In an interview later, he explained, "Under the law we are charged with a responsibility that if we don't have enough evidence on which we can sustain a conviction, we are legally bound to decline to prosecute. A review of the evidence in the case convinced me there would be more than a reasonable doubt as to guilt."

Robinson's views varied with the policies and philosophies of Clark, Pollak, and other attorneys in the Justice Department. They believed not only that the evidence was sufficient to sustain a conviction, but that the probabilities of a conviction should not be a criterion in determining whether to prosecute as long as the government believed a crime had been committed and the perpetrators had been identified.

Robinson had been respected by Clark and other Justice Department officials, but they strongly disagreed with his position on the Orangeburg case. After Robinson refused to appear before the grand jury with Quaintance, some of the department's attorneys felt he should resign, and Clark was urged to ask for his resignation. The Attorney General argued with Robinson on several occasions, but never seriously entertained the idea of asking him to resign.

Clark later was to describe his sessions with Robinson as "unpleasant" and another attorney said Clark had "chewed out" the Columbia attorney. But Robinson recalled the sessions as "not unpleasant or unfriendly—he gave me the impression of understanding my position."

The absence of a local federal attorney in the grand jury room had not been lost on the jury, only two of whose twenty-three members were Negroes. The case had quickly shaped up as the United States versus South Carolina, with most of the jurors showing their sympathies almost from the outset.

Students who testified they had been shot while crawling or running away or standing on a dormitory porch found the jurors more interested in what had been done to provoke the attack and in what kind of protest signs the students had carried. "They wanted to know how many signs we had and what the signs said," Albert Dawson told a reporter. "That's the kind of questions they asked. They just beat around the bush, that's all. I don't trust any white man any more."

The grand jury hearing, which lasted for eight days and ended November 7, did develop additional information from patrolmen who had refused to talk to the government attorneys. With Pollak's approval, Quaintance asked for an indictment. But the jury was unimpressed and the government got less than half the twelve votes it needed for an indictment.

The government had sought the indictment under Section 242, Title 18, United States Code, which made it a federal offense for anyone, acting under color of law, to subject anyone to the deprivation of federally protected rights. Clark and the attorneys who had worked on the case were keenly disappointed at the outcome. Governor McNair and highway patrol officials felt that the patrol had been exonerated and that the case was at last closed. McNair expressed hope that the refusal to indict would "put an end to the speculation and uncertainty surrounding the incident."

"We have maintained all along that the matter should be fully investigated and properly aired so as to allow an impartial hearing of all the facts," McNair said. "The federal grand jury provided such a forum. It is my feeling that the grand jury's decision is a conclusive and fair judgment of the incident. I hope that we can now put aside any remaining bitterness and animosity and build upon the foundation of understanding to achieve harmony among all South Carolinians."

The governor's statement "brought grief to my heart," the Reverend F. D. Dawson, of Charleston, wrote in a letter to *The Collegian*, the State College newspaper. The minister, whose son Albert was injured by the patrol gunfire, wrote, "It is my candid opinion had this happened to the governor's daughter or son his statement about the jury's decision being 'fair and conclusive' would have been different. Injustice breeds violence."

At State College unrest and bitter recrimination threatened to develop into another student-police confrontation. On November 25 about 100 Negro students carrying protest signs and chanting "We're black and we're proud" marched on highway patrol headquarters in Columbia. One sign read, "Just Us for Justice?" and another, "Doesn't Anybody Else Give a Damn?"

Colonel Thompson, the patrol commander, met with two of the leaders, including John Stroman, who had led the demonstrations at the bowling alley, and afterwards told newsmen the students were "well mannered," but had expressed "an attitude of hatred for the white man." He quoted them as saying that they hated all highway patrolmen and that "next time" students would have weapons and patrolmen would die too. Thompson said he told the students that patrolmen were trained that all persons were entitled to the same treatment regardless of race, creed, or color, and he added, "I could say that from the heart because that's the way we try to operate."

The demonstration ended peacefully with the students standing with clenched fists raised in the black power symbol and singing "The Star-Spangled Banner," some of them cheering the closing words, "The land of the free—and the home of the brave."

Students and faculties at black colleges, many other black South Carolinians, and a surprising number of white ones expressed indignation that nothing had been done to make public the facts about the shootings. Maceo Nance, South Carolina State president, told a reporter, "The faculty members and the students have their reputations at stake here and they want to be vindicated in the eyes of the public. They believe an open hearing will do it. The feeling here is that as far as justice is concerned in this case, nothing has been done. There still is a lot of tension and my job is to try to hold off another confrontation—it could be worse next time—and give this matter back to the courts."

On December 4 the South Carolina Christian Action Council, a biracial group of ministers and laymen representing sixteen denominations, adopted a resolution expressing "the concern of many white South Carolinians and of the mass of Negro South Carolinians over the as-yet unresolved Orangeburg situation." The resolution supported an earlier request by the University of South Carolina chapter of the American Association of University Professors that Governor McNair appoint an investigating committee "in order to reestablish confidence in state law enforcement agencies and repair the reputation of the state."

Clark and Pollak maintained an abiding interest in the case, too. Pollak read the transcript of the grand jury testimony and recommended on December 19 that the government bring the nine patrolmen to trial by filing a criminal information. The following day, on Clark's orders, the information was filed in federal court at Columbia. At Clark's request Quaintance and another young civil-rights attorney from Washington, Robert B. Hocutt, signed the information. Normally, it would have been signed by the United States attorney, but Robinson refused to sign it.

Although Pollak had concluded from the transcript that there had been violations of the law, he knew that a jury trial would be especially difficult. For one thing, the case involved the South Carolina state highway patrol, a group not previously involved in major complaints to the Justice Department. However, he felt the department had a responsibility to present the case and he believed that a trial in open court—regardless of the verdict—would have a deterrent effect on police misconduct.

"The United States is learning in the area of police misconduct," he said later, "and if you only brought cases in which you get a jury conviction, you would bring very few cases . . . Laws are enacted to protect people from having police taking the law into their own hands."

The criminal information alleged that on February 8, between 10:30 and 11 P.M., the patrolmen, "acting under color of the laws of the State of South Carolina, did wilfully discharge and shoot firearms into a group of persons on the campus of South Carolina State College . . . thereby killing, injuring and intimidating persons in the said group, with the intent of imposing summary punishment upon those persons and did thereby deprive those persons of the right, secured and protected by the Constitution of the United States, not to be deprived of life or liberty without due process of law."

At the time the offense was a misdemeanor and carried a maximum penalty of a year in prison and a $1,000 fine. Congress subsequently increased the maximum punishment to life imprisonment in cases where the victims die. If a conspiracy had been alleged, the offense would have been a felony with maximum punishment of ten years.

The senior officer charged was Lieutenant Jesse Alfred Spell, who was forty-five at the time of the shooting and who had been a patrolman for more than twenty-one years. Others charged and their ages and years of experience were: Sergeant Henry Morrell Addy, thirty-seven, twenty years; Corporal Norwood F. Bellamy, fifty, almost thirteen years; Patrolman First Class John William Brown, thirty-one, eight years; Corporal Joseph Howard Lanier, thirty-two, almost eleven years; Patrolman First Class Collie Merle Metts, thirty-six, almost eleven years; Patrolman Edward H. Moore, thirty, four years; Patrolman Allen Jerome Russell, twenty-four, one and a half years; and Sergeant Sidney C. Taylor, forty-three, twenty years.

12 : THE TRIAL

IT WOULD take a trial of the nine patrolmen to officially expose the major facts of what really happened at Orangeburg —in contrast to South Carolina's "official version."

Six of the defendants—all except Moore, Taylor, and Russell—testified at a hearing on preliminary motions before United States District Judge J. Robert Martin, Jr., on March 11, 1969, and said they would not have given statements to the FBI if Colonel Thompson had not instructed them to cooperate in the FBI's investigation.

Defense attorneys argued that under the circumstances the statements should be suppressed—a move that would have killed the federal case since the statements were the only evidence identifying which patrolmen fired at the students. The attorneys cited a Supreme Court decision, *Garretty v. New Jersey*, which held that a policeman's statement to the FBI should not have been used against him because his superiors had threatened to fire him if he did not cooperate with the FBI. The threat amounted to coercion, the court said.

In the Orangeburg case, the defense did not contend that the patrolmen had been threatened with being fired, but argued that once they had been instructed to cooperate "they had no free choice to exercise." The attorneys noted that in the Garretty case the Supreme Court said, "Coercion that vitiates a confession under *Chambers v. Florida* and related cases, can be mental as well as physical. 'The blood of the accused is not the only hallmark of the unconstitutional inquisition.' Subtle pressures may be as telling as coarse and vulgar ones. The question is whether the accused was deprived of his free choice to admit, to deny, or to refuse answer."

Judge Martin denied the motion for suppression, ruling that there was no coercion if there was no threat of being fired and that the patrolmen had freely and voluntarily signed the statements after being advised of their constitutional rights and signing a waiver of their rights not to make self-incriminating statements. During the hearing Martin spoke sharply several times to Chad Quaintance, the government's young chief prosecutor in the case—a prelude of what would happen at the trial.

Quaintance, a brilliant Princeton graduate and dedicated civil-rights attorney, had lived so closely with the case, spending weeks in Orangeburg and months poring over the evidence, that he knew it perhaps better than anyone. But he was an inexperienced trial lawyer and his hesitant manner and unfamiliarity with courtroom procedure often tried the patience of the fifty-nine-year-old jurist. Martin, who was chief judge of South Carolina's four-judge district, had been on the federal bench since his appointment by President John F. Kennedy in 1961.

At one point during the preliminary hearing the judge admonished Quaintance for asking an immaterial question and snapped, "You're not playing with a jury . . . When we get through trying this case you and I will communicate very good, we'll understand each other."

Martin, his dark, thinning hair combed straight back, looked his age, but his big-boned, six-foot-two-inch frame carried about 225 pounds—close to his playing weight as a Washington and Lee University tackle forty years earlier. Quaintance, small, dark-haired, and boyish looking, was given to a nervous chuckle during the trial, prompting Martin more than once to freeze him with a stare or a "that's not funny" comment.

The judge was known for being firm with attorneys, but also for impartiality and strict dedication to the law. He had signed most of the district court's orders desegregating schools, hospitals, golf courses, and state parks in South Carolina, and had said privately he thought such unpopular decisions were more palatable if issued by a judge residing within the state.

In 1947 he won national acclaim for his handling of the largest lynching trial the South had ever known. As a South Carolina circuit judge, a post he held for seventeen years, he presided over the trial of twenty-eight defendants, most of them taxi drivers, twenty-one charged with murder and seven with lesser offenses in the lynching of a Negro near Greenville. When a not guilty verdict was returned, Martin told the jurors their services were concluded and their checks were waiting. Without saying even a perfunctory word of thanks to the jury, he strode from the courtroom.

Life magazine concluded that history had been made and added: "It was clear that the South could no longer be considered 100 percent safe for a lynch mob, or at least that lynching could not be kept 100 percent secret." (It was the last lynching in South Carolina.) *Life* said, "The trial might easily have turned into a farce or even a riot. But under the firm hand of Judge Martin the trial was conducted in an atmosphere of dignity and calm."

Martin took extraordinary precautions to see that the trial of the state patrolmen—the nation's first trial of charges of excessive use of police power in controlling unruly campus demonstrations—was held in dignity and calm. He set the case for trial on May 19 in Florence, well removed from the troubled State College campus and from Columbia, home of two other black colleges whose students had been up in arms over the Orangeburg shootings, and of the University of South Carolina where black students, joined by some whites, had demonstrated in protest.

On May 8 Martin issued strict rules governing the conduct of trial participants and the news media. All participants, including lawyers, parties, witnesses, jurors, and court officials, were prohibited from making extrajudicial statements that might divulge prejudicial matter not of public record in the case, and all were instructed to "avoid mingling with or being in the proximity of reporters, photographers, and others in the entrances to and the hallways in the court house building, including the sidewalks adjacent thereto . . ."

The judge barred witnesses from being interviewed during the trial and ordered that no photographs or sketches be made of jurors "within the environs of the court." He shortened the length of the trial considerably by holding pretrial conferences with attorneys for both sides and getting them to agree to written stipulations about basic facts in the case.

The defendants stipulated that three students had been killed and twenty-seven others wounded by patrol gunfire and that the medical records introduced by the government were accurate. The records showed that all but two or three of the students had been shot from the rear or side. The defense stipulated that at the time of the shooting, 127 patrolmen were in Orangeburg, 66 of them at the State College campus, and that 450 National Guardsmen were in town, 45 of them in front of the campus.

Also stipulated was the accuracy of numerous news photographs, including one showing several patrolmen, who could not be identified, firing over the embankment. And the defense agreed that newsreel film taken by CBS-TV cameraman Reginald Smith was an accurate representation of what had happened. (Smith later testified that he began filming the shooting as quickly as he could after it started and that the film depicted 6 ¾ seconds of firing.)

The trial pitted two young government attorneys from Washington—Quaintance and Robert Hocutt—against an experienced array of four attorneys—South Carolina Assistant Attorney General J. C. Coleman, Solicitor Julian Wolfe of Orangeburg, and Frank Taylor and Geddes H. Martin, Jr., both of a Columbia law firm. Martin had formerly served as an assistant United States attorney and had been a law clerk for Judge Martin, but was not related to the judge. Coleman, who lectured regularly at highway patrol training schools on legal aspects of law enforcement, knew most of the defendants personally. The most experienced prosecutor on the attorney general's staff, he moved with ease and confidence in the courtroom.

Quaintance and Hocutt sat by themselves at a large table in front of the jury box. At another table across the room sat Coleman and the other defense attorneys. Behind them and to one side sat the defendants, Chief Strom, Colonel Thompson and other patrol officials, and Orangeburg Police Chief Poston, all dressed in conservative business suits. There could be no question that it was the Federal Government versus the State of South Carolina.

It took less than one and a half hours for the attorneys to select the jury—ten whites and two blacks. Since there were fifteen blacks on the sixty-member venire, it seemed apparent defense attorneys would have to settle for one or more black jurors. Their strategy was to try to make sure any black juror selected had little education, came from a rural area, and belonged to no civil-rights organizations.

Carl N. Edwards, a middle-aged Negro farmer with a ninth-grade education, was the first juror seated. The only other black juror selected was Mrs. Rosa B. Hamer, an elderly farm woman with a fifth-grade education who occasionally dozed during the trial. The government used four of its peremptory challenges, all in striking whites. The defense used only six of its ten peremptory challenges, all in striking blacks.

Other jurors included: Henry A. Spears, a livestock dealer (high school education) who was named foreman; Elizabeth Collins, a piano teacher (college); James T. Hollar, hair stylist (high school); Frederick E. Stephens, food salesman (business college); Sylvia W. Thames, bookkeeper (high school); Marie R. Davis, secretary (college); George K. Floyd, gravel company owner (high school); William C. Jacobs, Jr., industrial engineer (college); Joe L. Bennett, construction employee (tenth grade); and Thomas James Evans, a plumber (high school). Evans was excused during the trial because of illness in his family and his place on the jury was taken by the first alternate, James M. Keisler, white, a chemical plant employee with an eleventh-grade education.

"May it please the court, ladies and gentlemen of the jury," Quaintance drawled in a flat, nasal monotone. "My colleague and I here, Robert Hocutt, he's twenty-seven years old, born in Raleigh, North Carolina, grew up in a small town near Conway, went to school at Wake Forest . . . has been married since last August . . .

"My name is Charles Quaintance. I was born in Johnson City, Tennessee, grew up in Oregon . . . went to school there . . . was in Selma, Alabama, for a couple of years. I'm married, have two children, a girl who will be six two weeks from today and a boy who is three . . . both live in the city of Washington . . ."

Quaintance's folksy, soft-spoken, we're-southerners-too beginning in his opening statement caused the jurors to lean forward and listen intently. The dozen or so newsmen in the front row of the courtroom elbowed each other and suppressed chuckles.

He explained that the statute under which the patrolmen were charged "prohibits public officials from intentionally misusing their authority to punish people" and added, "The statute, of course, applies throughout the country— have had cases recently and have cases now in Illinois, California, New Jersey, Michigan, Mississippi, Missouri, Idaho, and West Virginia, as well as in this state."

Quaintance said evidence would show that at the time of the shooting there were "about as many law enforcement officers as students at the scene, that students had no guns and that the Guardsmen were armed with rifles, with fixed bayonets and the patrolmen with revolvers, riot batons, carbines, and shotguns, and that the students walked toward the patrolmen on the embankment and were still 75 to 100 feet away when the patrol opened fire without warning, striking at least thirty students as they were 'turning, running or crawling away.'" He said the government would prove the shooting lasted ten to fifteen seconds.

Coleman, who looked like television's Lawrence Spivak,

but younger and taller, introduced himself as an assistant attorney general of the state, then pointed to the elderly Julian Wolfe, gray-haired and slightly stooped, wearing spectacles with attached sun shades flipped up, and introduced him as "the dean of South Carolina's solicitors." Coleman emphasized that Taylor and Martin were highly respected attorneys from Columbia. He explained that under South Carolina law any officer accused of committing a crime while performing his duty was entitled to legal representation by the state attorney general's office.

Quaintance was emotionally wrapped up in the prosecution of the case and Coleman was no less engaged in the defense. Coleman told the jury the defense would show that an "extreme emergency existed" in Orangeburg and that the defendants and other patrolmen were only acting "in defense of themselves and the entire population of Orangeburg."

He said evidence would show the shooting was preceded by "a highly dangerous, explosive, riotous situation" for three days, that an outside agitator had caused it, and that at the time the patrol fired "several hundred persons were thundering at them, coming at them, charging, hurling brickbats, hurling pieces of concrete. Our evidence will show that there was shooting at that time from that group." Coleman said the defense would prove the shooting lasted only a "few seconds."

From the outset, then, the strategy of both sides emerged rather clearly. The prosecution hoped to confine most of the evidence to the evening of February 8 and to show through numerous witnesses that the patrolmen, perhaps angered by the wounding of Patrolman Shealy, not only opened fire to punish the students but intentionally continued firing—for at least ten seconds. The defense would weave a story of tension and violence, complete with a bearded black militant and culminated by patrol gunfire that was a last-resort answer to an armed attack by students threatening to burn down the city of Orangeburg.

Testimony by the first witness, Warren H. Koon, a *Charleston Evening Post* reporter, summed up a major part of the prosecution's contention. Some of the pertinent points he swore to were echoed by several defense, as well as numerous prosecution, witnesses.

Koon had watched the confrontation from the grassy triangle across the street from the campus at the intersection of Watson and College Streets and he testified that "a hundred, perhaps up to two hundred students" were involved. He said that he had heard no shooting from the campus "for at least thirty minutes, perhaps forty-five minutes" prior to the patrol gunfire, had not seen any objects being thrown by the students, and had heard no warning to the students before the shooting.

Quaintance brought out that Koon was a Marine combat veteran who had been wounded by gunfire in the Pacific in World War II. The reporter, bespectacled with close-cropped, graying hair, swore he heard nothing and saw nothing that would have led him to believe there might have been shooting by the students.

SLED Chief Strom, testifying briefly and reluctantly as a prosecution witness (he later testified in great detail as a defense witness), acknowledged that the SLED car he had been riding in contained a loudspeaker and a supply of tear gas that no one attempted to use.

"That was available that night?" asked Quaintance.

"It was in the automobile, it wasn't available at the scene."

"Where was the automobile?"

"It was at the scene, but it was—the tear gas was in the trunk of the automobile."

Under defense questioning, Strom then said, "The wind

was blowing directly into the officers' face, into my face, and into the patrolmen's face and it would have been impossible to effectively use any tear gas because it would have come back into the face and eyes of the officers." Quaintance later introduced a photograph showing smoke rising from the bonfire the students had built in the street and drifting back over the college campus.

Charles DeFord, the former agent-in-charge of the Columbia FBI office, testified he had not seen or heard anything that would have prepared him to expect the patrol gunfire. Under cross-examination DeFord said he was standing "very close" to Chief Strom at the time of the shooting. The defense would repeatedly emphasize during the trial the close working relationship between FBI agents on the scene and senior police officers, including FBI participation in strategy conferences with Strom.

FBI agents who took statements from the defendants read them to the court as the jurors listened intently.* Russell and Lanier were the only defendants who referred to the students as "students." Spell, Addy, and Bellamy called them a "mob of people"; Brown, Moore, and Taylor referred to them as "Negroes," and Metts called them "demonstrators." Spell said that shortly after Patrolman Shealy was injured,

> the mob of individuals numbering approximately 200 at this time started moving toward us. I raised both my arms in the air and told them to stop and quit throwing objects at the police. They continued coming at us, throwing rocks, bricks, sticks, and posts from the porch railing. Small-arms fire could be heard coming from the group. They were cursing and making threats verbally toward the officers. Someone from the group threw a firebomb at the back of the

* The texts of the statements appear in the appendix of this book. Any statements attributed to the defendants in this book come from their statements to the FBI.

*house on our right and set it on fire. At this time I realized
the mob of people had to be stopped as they would not
listen to the police and would injure and possibly kill some
of the officers. The mob of people continued to assault us and
small-arms firing could be heard. At this point I ordered my
squad to fire their weapons to stop the mob. I personally fired
two rounds of buckshot from the Model 870 Remington,
12-gauge pump shotgun I was carrying.*

Addy and Taylor said they heard the order "now" given, but the other defendants mentioned no order and said they fired after hearing others fire. Moore said he thought the shooting was "a spontaneous reaction to the situation." (Later, Quaintance, in cross-examining Nelson Phillips, one of two FBI agents called as defense witnesses, was to cast serious doubt on whether Spell actually gave an order or just decided that was the best way to explain the shooting.)

In his statement, Addy said that as "the mob" charged toward the patrolmen, an officer "told them to stop." The officer Addy contended gave the command was his superior, Spell. But the court ordered Spell's name blanked out of Addy's statement before admitting it as evidence. Addy's statement continued:

*They continued to charge toward us, hurling objects
and firing, and ——— again shouted for them to stop. They
didn't stop and continued to charge, hurling these objects
and firing. ——— then told the mob for the third time to
stop and not come any closer. They still charged and
continued to fire and throw these objects. ——— then gave
the command "now," which was the order to shoot. I was
armed with a Model 870 Remington 12-gauge pump shotgun,
which was loaded with sixteen pellet buckshot. I can't
recall how many times I fired, but I think it was about twice.
I fired low and at their feet and legs.*

Bellamy, Brown, and Russell also acknowledged firing their shotguns twice and Lanier said he fired his "several times, exact number unknown." Metts and Taylor said they fired their shotguns only once. Moore acknowledged firing his .38-caliber Colt police special "approximately six times in the direction of the mob."

The defendants' estimates of the number of seconds the gunfire continued—a crucial point in the prosecution's attempt to prove intent to punish—varied greatly. Addy and Taylor estimated two seconds; Spell, two to three; Bellamy, "less than five, maybe three"; Brown, four to five; Metts, five to ten; and Moore, ten. Lanier and Russell estimated "a few seconds."

The prosecution called as witnesses three highway patrolmen and a former patrolman who were on the embankment at the time of the confrontation, but did not fire their weapons.

Patrolman first class Louis B. Judy, Jr., and Patrolman Donald Wayne Crosby, both of Spell's District Six squad, testified they heard no shooting from the campus and saw no objects being thrown after the bannister hit Patrolman Shealy. Judy said the only squad members armed with shotguns were Spell, Addy, and Taylor. He said he was crouched behind a bush by the vacant house when the first shots were fired—"It sounded like a rifle to my left."

"By the way," Coleman asked in cross-examining Judy, "is Sergeant Taylor you referred to then, is he a lieutenant now?"

"Yes, sir."

"Who was in charge of your squad at that time?"

"Lieutenant Spell."

"Captain Spell now?"

"Yes, sir, captain."

Coleman gazed toward the jury for a moment, letting the testimony sink in. Later, he brought out that three other defendants had been promoted since the shooting—Addy from sergeant to lieutenant and Brown and Metts both from patrolman first class to corporal.

Outside the courtroom, Colonel Thompson told newsmen, "This situation had nothing to do with the promotions pro or con. They were promoted on merit just like everybody else in the highway patrol." Inside the courtroom Coleman several times emphasized the promotions for the jury's benefit.

Coleman, who frequently implied that the students might have been expecting the gunfire, asked Judy, "Did it look to you as though they had an understanding, or plan to fall to the ground when the shooting started?"

"I don't know, sir."

"But they did it right together, all seemed to go down?"

"The first shot fired and then the . . . group started falling back towards the campus buildings back behind them."

Judy said he was standing behind a bush near Spell and heard Spell "holler that's far enough," but did not hear anyone shout "now" or anything else that might be taken as a command to fire.

Crosby was a reluctant witness and Quaintance had to occasionally refresh the patrolman's memory with a transcript of testimony he had given to the grand jury.

"Myself and Patrolman Shealy were almost right together," Crosby testified. "He went around me, when he was ahead of me and went around this bush, I was directly behind him. I seen several objects, bottles and bricks and so forth, and I seen two bannisters coming in the air, coming down, like they were falling out of the sky almost, and I ducked and I saw one coming for Patrolman Shealy. It was too late to do anything about it."

Until the trial, the public had been left with the impression that the gunfire was in response to the felling of Shealy, who some patrolmen thought had been shot. That was part of Governor McNair's official version. But defense evidence, as well as prosecution evidence, showed that several minutes— the consensus was about five—passed before the shooting began.

Patrolman Gerald Dobson, also a reluctant witness, testified that shooting from the campus never did "cease completely" before the patrol opened fire. That obviously contradicted testimony he had given to the grand jury and he squirmed uncomfortably as Quaintance showed him a transcript of that testimony and asked if he wanted to reconsider his statement about the gunfire by the students.

"I don't recall, but I'm not saying there wasn't any," he said, "but I don't remember."

Quaintance asked Dobson, who was a member of District Two squad, if anyone in his squad had fired a weapon.

"Well, can I answer that like I did before the grand jury?" Dobson asked.

"Sure," Quaintance said, but Judge Martin, with stern exasperation, interjected, "Just answer it the way the truth is."

"Well, I don't know, sir," Dobson said. "I wasn't down there, but I heard the squad leader after he checked the guns make the statement that they had not been fired."

Arthur Coggins, a young National Guardsman, also squirmed on the witness stand. He seemed to hedge on his grand jury testimony that he had heard no shots from the campus. "It was a lot of commotion and noise and if there were gunshots, I didn't hear them," he testified. "I'm not saying there were not any, or anything like that. I was scared, and it was a lot of noise, and there could have been and there could not have been. I just don't know. . . ."

"What happened, what did you do when the patrol began firing?" Quaintance asked.

"Got under the white line out in Highway 601."

"Got under the white line?"

"Yes, sir."

Coggins was more comfortable answering questions directed by defense attorney Frank Taylor and eagerly told of how frightened he was, a point the defense was emphasizing in trying to depict the scene as dangerous and explosive at the time the patrol fired.

Asked whether he had seen Shealy get hurt, Coggins said, "I tell you the truth I was too scared to try to look around."

"I would have been, too," Taylor said, glancing at the jury. "Now, Mr. Coggins, you knew there was shooting from the campus before you went up to this place. I reckon that helped frighten you a little more, didn't it?"

"Yes, sir."

James R. Powers, of Pinellas Park, Florida, a former highway patrolman who was a member of District Seven squad on the night of the shooting, testified that he was armed with a carbine and a revolver and never took the safety off either one. He said the students were walking "fast" toward the patrolmen when the patrol fired.

"Did anyone make any effort to stop the firing?" Quaintance asked.

"Yes, sir, I did."

"What did you do?"

"After I heard an order of cease fire, I took a whistle out of my pocket and blew it."

Bobby Eaddy, the first of fourteen students to testify, said that just before the shooting he had started toward the embankment and "someone must have started to throw something and . . . you could hear these fellows saying don't throw anything because like these fellows were back in the back and we didn't suspect they could be hurt by anything that could happen." Quaintance asked what happened when the shooting started.

"Well, the majority of the kids started running back towards Lowman Hall and across the street," Eaddy said. "I jumped on the ground as it started . . . I lied on the ground maybe four or five seconds and I was hit. At the time I didn't know what it was, and so I looked back and I saw most of the people were gone, so I decided to get up and I ran behind the tree . . ."

Under cross-examination, Eaddy acknowledged that Cleveland Sellers had attended several student meetings during the week of the crisis, but neither Eaddy nor any other witness testified that Sellers had a significant role in the crisis. FBI agent William J. Danielson was to testify about Sellers agitating students at the bowling alley, but the only evidence the trial developed about Sellers' activities on the night of the shooting concerned his being injured by gunfire. (In an interview later, Attorney General Ramsey Clark said, "In the general student unrest and commotion, Sellers was a provocative factor. In this incident where the shooting took place I never saw anything that indicated that he had anything to do with it except getting shot.")

Government attorneys, concerned that the physical appearance of some of the students might suggest militancy to the jury, cautioned them about wearing dark glasses or African garb at the trial. Although the students generally went along with the idea of trying to look like a black Joe College, some were sensitive about it.

It was too much for Joe Lambright when an attorney who had joined Quaintance and Hocutt in preparing the case suggested that dark glasses might hurt the credibility of

Lambright's testimony. After testifying, Lambright said in an interview, "It got to the breaking point when he touched my glasses like, 'Don't wear 'em now.' I let it go. I said, 'Look, I catered to this when I testified before the grand jury at Columbia, not wearing glasses. These are not shades. I'm not a dittybopper. These are my prescription glasses.' He said, 'Okay, wear 'em.' Just before the grand jury met, he had told me to wear a suit and all that. I started to wear a dashiki. I did wear a sport shirt. I got sick of tailoring to the white man's justice."

The defense was concerned about the appearance of things, too. The state's only two black highway patrolmen (one had been hired since the shooting) showed up in their khaki uniforms, sat where they could be seen by the jury, smiled and waved at the defendants, and during recesses rushed up to talk and backslap with them. It reminded Quaintance of the time in 1957 when former heavyweight boxing champion Joe Louis walked up and put his arm around Jimmy Hoffa in the presence of a biracial jury in Washington, D.C., that ultimately acquitted the teamster boss of a charge of trying to bribe a staff member of a Senate labor-management committee. (Colonel Thompson later remarked, "We had to show the jury we had a couple.")

Joe Lambright, after giving virtually the same account of the shooting as other students, was asked on cross-examination, "Didn't Cleveland Sellers put you in a formation and tell you to charge those patrolmen with every weapon you had?"

"No, I didn't see Cleveland Sellers," Lambright replied.

Three of the students who testified were by now in the Army—Second Lieutenant Nathaniel Jenkins, stationed at Fort Jackson and on orders to Vietnam; Specialist fourth class Thomas Kennerly, who had been given leave by his unit in Vietnam to testify; and Jordan Simmons III, an officer candidate at Fort Benning. All three testified they were on the ground and scrambling to get away when they were shot.

The prosecution rested its case after Simmons completed his testimony. Altogether some thirty-six prosecution witnesses, including students, newsmen, a fireman, three highway patrolmen, two National Guardsmen, and FBI agent DeFord had testified they heard no shooting from the campus immediately prior to the patrol gunfire.

The defense moved for a directed verdict of acquittal on grounds there was insufficient evidence to sustain a conviction. Attorney Geddes Martin argued that among other things the prosecution had produced no evidence showing any specific intent by the defendants to deny the students their constitutional rights.

Judge Martin denied the motion, declaring the government had "made a prima facie showing that the shots were fired in an illegal manner." He said evidence showed that the defendants

> while acting under color of law of the State of South Carolina did wilfully—that means bad motive—without just cause or excuse so to speak, discharge and shoot firearms into this group of persons. Now, if it goes to a jury, of course, the jury would have to determine whether or not in the light of all the testimony, when all the testimony is in, as to whether or not they are satisfied beyond a reasonable doubt that in the light of all the testimony the defense of self-defense is established.

The question of specific intent would also be a matter for the jury to decide, Judge Martin said.

The first defense witness, John Graham Smith, news director of Charleston's WCIV TV, set the stage for the defendants' contention that a dangerous situation had been building up on the State College campus and that Sellers was behind it. He told of going with another newsman to the campus on the afternoon of February 8 to interview Sellers, who had been publicly fingered by police officials as the chief agitator. Some of the students became incensed, apparently because they believed Smith was only interested in interviewing Sellers, not in reporting their grievances. Smith said the first remarks made to him were

> words to the effect "what are you damn honkies doing on campus, you got a lot of nerve coming in here." Well, that sort of set the tempo and it really got from bad to worse the longer we stayed there. I was trying to gracefully back out and get out of there, but the students were complaining about news coverage, that the newsmen had bent over backward to tell the Orangeburg story and had done nothing about telling the students' side of it . . .

The students said they could produce Sellers, but they never did, according to Smith. He said he was leery of picking up the television sound equipment and leaving "because I was afraid it might set them off because it would appear as though we were refusing to cover the students' side of the controversy."

"Do you remember whether or not you had any feeling with regard to your personal safety?" asked Coleman, the state attorney. Smith replied:

> I was scared, to be very frank with you. I was about as scared as I've ever been in my life—they were using a lot of profanity at us, and I just walked up to one student and tried to start a decent conversation with him and I said, "What are you majoring in?" He looked me straight in the eye and said, "I don't have to talk to a Goddamn honky." This was their attitude this time. Then a bunch of them went

over and got around our automobile, the Channel 4 car was
clearly marked with lettering, and got on the automobile and
all around it and one of them reached over and took the gas
cap off of the car, and now whether they were serious—I was
taking them serious. They were laughing and joking and
making a lot of noise around the car and one of them turned
to the other and said, "Let's burn it." Of course, I'm trying
to keep my cool to keep from saying anything to excite the
situation any further and we just kept up a running conversa-
tion. But the more we talked, the more they seemed to
become upset. The leader was a long, tall fellow with a
beard and a goatee, sitting up on the porch, and he . . .

Quaintance interrupted Smith to object that the witness
should not be permitted to engage in hearsay by quoting
something said by someone out of the presence of the
defendants. Judge Martin sustained the objection and Coleman asked Smith to state, without quoting anyone, whether
anybody had made a comment that might have reflected the
feeling of the students. Smith replied:

I think one thing that was said to us would reflect it
. . . the tall fellow with the beard and all was sitting on the
porch and was acting as the spokesman more or less, doing
more talking than anyone else. Of course they were all doing a
lot of talking. They were using us to get a lot off their chest,
because we happened to be the only white people around.
This fellow, he said—it was very clear, he said—we were
talking about the bowling alley operator—he said, "He's
going to die tonight . . ."

Coleman asked Smith if he knew the identity of "the
man to whom you refer as the leader on the campus to whom
you talked."

"Not definitely, no, sir," the newsman replied. "I saw a
picture in the paper of Mr. Cleveland Sellers a few days later
and it looked exactly like the man who was sitting on the

campus doing the talking." Coleman showed Smith a photograph of Sellers, with SLED Chief Strom, snapped after Sellers's arrest, and asked him if he recognized anyone in it. He said he recognized Strom.

"Well, the point is do you recognize the goateed leader of whom you referred in that picture?" Coleman asked, and Smith replied, "This looks like the same man who was sitting on the campus that day." Smith testified that he finally managed to "gracefully" leave the students and return to Charleston for a 6 P.M. news show. Then he returned to Orangeburg, he said.

Asked if he went back for any particular reason, he said, "Yes, sir, because in the news business you have to read the overall situation, and as a result of reading the situation as it was in Orangeburg that afternoon I made the news judgment that here is where we should be tonight because, as we say in the news business, here's where the action is."

In a brief, pointed cross-examination, Robert Hocutt brought out that Smith appeared standing in a news photograph snapped just before the patrol began firing, indicating he had no fear that gunfire was coming from the campus. The following exchange, which concluded his testimony, made Smith sound like a prosecution witness:

Q: *Preceding the firing by the highway patrol, did you hear anything which you took to be, thought might have been shots coming from the campus?*
A: *No, sir.*
Q: *Mr. Smith, you have been in the military?*
A: *Yes, sir.*
Q: *How long were you in the military?*
A: *Nineteen years, seven months and ten days.*
Q: *In World War II?*
A: *Yes, sir.*

Q: *Where did you serve?*

A: *In World War II, I served on Guadalcanal . . .*

Q: *You were in the Marines?*

A: *Yes, sir.*

Q: *Have you been shot at?*

A: *Yes, sir.*

Q: *Mr. Smith, do you remember an interview with me on May 9, 1968?*

A: *I remember an interview with you, the date I don't know.*

Q: *Sometime ago at any rate. Do you recall telling me at that time that if there had been any shooting from the students you would have heard it?*

A: *The statement I made to you at that time was if I had heard any shooting I would have been hitting the ground.*

Q: *Do you recall making the statement?*

A: *Yes, sir, I recall talking to you about it.*

Q: *Well, I was thinking . . .*

A: *If there had been any shooting, yes, I think if there had been any shooting I would have heard it, yes.*

Q: *One last question, just prior to the shooting by the highway patrol, did you see any bottles, sticks, rocks, bricks, anything strike the cement in front of you?*

A: *No, sir.*

The next defense witness, Orangeburg Police Chief Poston, was more helpful to the defendants' cause. He testified that small-caliber gunfire was heard on the campus just before the patrol fired. Quaintance brought out that Poston failed to mention this when FBI agents interviewed him two days after the shooting.

Poston gave a chilling account of events leading up to the gunfire. He detailed student violence at the bowling alley, told of numerous anonymous calls threatening to burn down the shopping center or even all of Orangeburg, and said that owners of businesses that had been damaged "became excited and appeared to be becoming hysterical about the situation and they were more or less expecting their property to be protected, and indicated to us in both what they did physically and what they said verbally that if we couldn't protect their property they could. They were later at another time observed in their places of business with weapons."

Just before the shooting at the campus, Poston said, he heard students hollering "honkies," and "there were profane remarks. There was just a general unruly type situation from the noise and about that time I heard what sounded like three shots, being the same that I had heard earlier for over a period of time there, small-caliber." Cross-examining Poston, Quaintance asked if he had not failed to mention the small-caliber gunfire when interviewed by FBI agents.

"I don't think I denied it either," Poston replied.

Ellis C. MacDougall, who was director of the state Department of Corrections at the time of the shooting and now held the same post in Connecticut, testified he was standing on some steps midway up the campus embankment when an estimated 100 to 200 students "started to charge in the direction of the troopers and myself." He continued:

> At the same time . . . I saw flashes
> and the immediate thought at that time was, my gosh,
> they're throwing firecrackers at us. Then I got hit, and
> about the same time—I had a captain with me—Captain
> Townsend—and I got hit and I turned because I
> thought I had been shot, and as I looked down the
> bank I saw a brick rolling down the hill, about a
> quarter or a half brick, and I realized I had been hit by
> a brick. At that time Captain Townsend
> grabbed my arm and pulled me down, said, "Christ,
> boss, get down, you want to get shot?"

MacDougall said Townsend then pulled him to the bottom of the steps "and it seemed to all happen at one time, bang, bang, bang, and . . . as I looked back up again, I saw the students flattened out on the campus and at this same time the only thing I heard, command I heard, was one officer blew his whistle and said, 'Hold the line,' and everything stopped." He said several patrolmen then rushed up on the campus and "pulled two of the students who had been shot down into the area right at the bottom of the steps. One of them was practically unconscious, didn't make much movement. The other boy was calling for his mother . . ."

Later, during direct examination, MacDougall twice said he could not say that the students were "charging," but that they were "running." Coleman brought out that as a corrections officer MacDougall had been trained in riot-control methods and asked him if he would characterize "the group of persons coming towards you as a mob?"

"I don't think I could answer that fairly, Mr. Coleman," MacDougall replied, "because the type of riot situation we deal with and law enforcement are two different things."

MacDougall, calm and articulate, had won national acclaim for reforming the South Carolina penal system. He was a critical witness for the defense. Although he testified he heard no shots come from the campus immediately before the patrol fired, his testimony about being hit by a brick and thinking he had been shot went to the heart of a major defense contention—that the appearance of things at that time was such that a reasonable man might feel his life was in danger.

Strom returned to the witness stand—this time for the defense. Asked to tell what had happened at the bowling alley on the night of February 6, he turned toward the jury and launched into a long, gesticulating discourse.

"We saw people going into the bowling alley," he said.

"We saw men, women and children." He raised his voice and
cradled his arms, rocking them back and forth, and continued,
"I saw at least one lady, maybe two, with children in their
arms going into this bowling alley. Shortly thereafter a group
of students came to the bowling alley, rushed in, and were not
too disorderly, but we could tell what they had on their
minds." Lowering his voice, Strom continued:

> *I observed them for a little while and I picked*
> *out a man who I took to be the leader, that I later*
> *learned to be a student named Stroman, and I*
> *went to Stroman and I had a conversation with him.*
> *We had a fairly lengthy conversation. I said,*
> *"Stroman, there's not any reason in the world for you*
> *to try to get a bunch of people arrested. If you have a*
> *grievance, I'll tell you how to air it in court."*
> *I told him I attended a conference on the Civil Rights*
> *Act of 1964 in Normandy, Oklahoma, sponsored*
> *by the International Chiefs of Police and I thought I*
> *knew at least a little something about the Civil Rights Act.*
> *That I had had a lot of other dealings with it and we*
> *had gotten along good even down to integrating Clemson*
> *College and so forth and, you know, experiences I've*
> *had and I said, "there's no point in the world in you*
> *having a lot of people arrested here, and if you*
> *have a grievance just get arrested yourself, or*
> *if you don't feel safe with that, take one or two people,*
> *all you want to do is get in court. It's a civil action,*
> *and not a criminal action." And he and I got*
> *along well, and it seemed that he was going to*
> *accept what I was telling him . . .*

Strom continued in lengthy detail, finally saying the
situation at the bowling alley began to deteriorate, especially
when Cleveland Sellers came on the scene.

"Did you know him before then, Chief?" asked attorney
Frank Taylor.

"I knew who he was. I know that he was representing the Atlanta Division of the Student Nonviolent Coordinating Committee hooked up with Rap Brown, Stokely Carmichael, and that crowd. I knew that much about him and we had been keeping up with that group."

Strom said that after the students who were arrested were taken to jail and Sellers came on the scene, "You could hardly realize that you were actually in a civilized country. I didn't believe it. I had been in every situation almost known that I knew anything about, and had been able to talk and deal with people without going to war. But everything we did ... was ineffective ..."

The SLED chief said he talked to some students "without any success whatsoever . . . I mean it was just ineffective. I didn't get to a soul . . . the students at that time were completely out of hand and I don't know if they were responsible for themselves. They were so fired up and under the influence of Cleveland Sellers, who is a trained agitator, they didn't know what they were doing . . . I didn't know whether we were going to survive or not."

On most of the command decisions made later, Strom said, "I conferred with Mr. Charlie DeFord who was in charge of the FBI for South Carolina, and asked him if he had any suggestions and if he felt in his opinion we were doing the right thing . . ." On the night of February 8, just before the patrol opened fire, Strom said, he "heard what I thought to be small firearms fire" and hit the ground.

Cross-examining Strom, Hocutt brought out that at the bowling alley a relatively few officers, without firing a shot, controlled a disorderly crowd much larger than the crowd on the campus the night of February 8. Hocutt was a concise and forceful cross-examiner. This exchange occurred between him and Strom concerning the situation at the bowling alley:

Q: *Approximately how many officers did you have there . . . I guess you didn't have very many?*

A: *We didn't have but very few. Everytime I would see one coming I was glad to see him. That's how short-handed we were.*

Q: *How many would you guess, fifteen?*

A: *I don't know how many was there. We didn't have anything like enough to attempt to handle that wild and unlawful crowd. They didn't have respect for nobody or not even themselves.*

Q: *Then there was this confrontation you talked about. I didn't quite understand what happened at that confrontation.*

A: *When they kicked the door out, we had to move then because we didn't have any choice. We had been using all kind of restraint. We were going to take any kind of verbal abuse, even down to spitting on people, calling them any kind of name, which they had. We were not going to move in until we had enough troops that we thought we could command the situation without seriously injuring someone. When they came in to break into the bowling alley there was no choice.*

Q: *What did you do?*

A: *The patrol had batons and I saw moves like that [Strom pushed both hands forward, fists clinched as though holding a riot baton], I saw students hitting at the patrolmen and city police, deputy sheriffs, just general disorder. Anyway, they took off down Russell Street, breaking out windows, whooping, cursing, hollering.*

Q: *The few officers you had drove away the three or four hundred students?*

A: *I think the only reason that they did leave when they saw this student kick in and break that glass, I think they knew that was so far out of line, the*

> *psychological effect it had on them, the officers*
> *were able to move at that time. I doubt we could have*
> *moved them with that number of officers*
> *without doing a lot of shooting there.*

Q: *I see, they all ran away?*

A: *It was so obvious, you don't just walk up and kick*
the glass out of a door in front of officers. I was
standing in the door.

Q: *I'm not trying to argue.*

A: *It did have a psychological effect on them.*

Q: *I see. They all ran away?*

A: *They didn't run away, no, sir. They charged. After*
the confrontation with the patrol, they took off.

Q: *They charged?*

A: *Yes, sir, to the door.*

Q: *Chief, as I understand it now they ran back to the*
campus?

A: *After, I said after they attempted to break into the*
door . . .

Hocutt also pressed Strom on his direct testimony that he had heard "small-arms" fire just before the patrol's shotguns were fired, and Strom acknowledged "it could have been a .38 pistol—I couldn't tell what caliber as far as I know." Strom estimated the patrol gunfire lasted "a very few seconds" and when the young attorney persisted in asking him to estimate how many seconds, he finally said, "Just bam, bam, and it was all over. I didn't time it, but four or five, six, seven seconds, something like that. Maybe a little longer; maybe a little less."

Strom acknowledged that a speaker that amplifies a voice fifty times was available but was not used, but explained "when they shoot at you, you don't have time to run to the speaker and talk to them." And he acknowledged the availability of tear gas, but said, "You can't use tear gas where people are shooting at you, and it's not very effective anyway

. . . tear gas is not near as effective as you would have people to think it is."

On redirect examination, Strom said the state had always cooperated both in the past and in this case with the FBI. "We furnish them information on robberies, bank robbers and I think agents here will be glad to admit we do that. We did it on this occasion, and we cooperated with everybody until it got to the departmental attorneys to come in to take over from the FBI and we didn't care to cooperate with them and not going to cooperate with them in the future."

Nelson L. Phillips, the FBI agent who had helped train the patrolmen in riot control, followed Strom to the stand. Asked if he had heard any shots from the campus prior to the patrol gunfire, he said, "Yes, sir. I thought I heard some shots just immediately prior to that . . . sounded like small-arms fire to me, .22- or .25-caliber."

Phillips testified that during the FBI investigation a patrolman or a SLED agent gave him "a little vial that you have around a laboratory about three inches in height and about two inches in diameter with a black rubber cork that had a yellow substance in it, and they gave it to us. It was thrown at one of the patrolmen on or near the warehouse area . . . at least that's where I was told it came from, I wasn't there. And we sent it to our lab and the lab report showed it to be highly explosive."

When cross-examined by Quaintance, Phillips said he participated in a crime-scene search after the shooting and found evidence that five or six pellets had been fired into the side of a railroad warehouse across the street from the two colleges. Phillips, who said he was standing beside the warehouse about 9 P.M. on February 8 when he heard bullets strike the building, testified he believed the shots had been fired from the State College campus area where the students confronted the police.

A rebuttal witness, FBI agent Robert N. Zimmers, a firearms expert from Washington, later testified evidence indicated the shots had been fired either from Claflin College campus or from the northern edge of the State College campus, which would have been more than 100 feet from the area where the students were at the time of the confrontation.

Phillips estimated the patrol gunfire lasted three to five seconds.

Delving into the FBI agent's relationship with the defendants, Quaintance found Phillips an evasive witness and implied with his questioning that Phillips had withheld information on the FBI investigation from the civil rights division:

Q: *Mr. Phillips, have you talked to any of the defendants about the case?*

A: *I don't know specifically, sir. I talked to them every day, but not about the case, no, sir. Some of the patrolmen quite often.*

Q: *Do you know the defendants?*

A: *I know most of them, yes, sir.*

Q: *Have you ever—just about this incident though specifically, do you recall having talked to any of them about it?*

A: *Yes, sir, I talked to almost all of them immediately thereafter for one reason or another, sir. Because I had liaison with their departments. I had to set up interviews and things of this nature.*

Q: *Do you recall the first time that we spoke concerning the incident, you and I?*

A: *Yes, sir, May 1968, sir.*

Q: *And at that time did I ask you whether you had talked to any of the patrolmen about the incident?*

A: *Yes, sir, I do.*

Q: *Did you at that time, the first time we talked*
. . . did you tell me that you would not tell me
what they had said?

A: *No, sir, I did not.*

Q: *The first time.*

A: *Yes, sir, but I did not tell you I would not*
tell you.

Q: *At that time you would not tell me, is that correct?*

A: *No, sir, I didn't tell you that I would not tell you.*

Q: *Or that you would—what did you tell me then?*

A: *You asked me for an opinion of somebody's*
feelings and I told you I could not tell you how
somebody feels from my personal opinion.

Q: *Thereafter did you tell me what some of the defendants*
had told you in June?

A: *Yes, sir.*

Q: *Do you recall for example telling me that, that*
Lieutenant Spell told you he had not himself given
an order, but that he was going to tell the agents
that he had because he was afraid that somebody had
misinterpreted what another person had said?

A: *I remember you and I discussing it, yes, sir.*

Q: *Did Lieutenant Spell say something like that?*

A: *We discussed some stuff, yes, sir. We discussed the*
fact of authority, who was in charge of that squad,
and all that was discussed, yes, sir. As to the exact word-
ing, I don't recall, Mr. Quaintance.

The next witness, FBI agent William J. Danielson, also could not recall some facts when cross-examined by Quaintance, but in direct testimony he strengthened the defense's contentions about the shooting and the trouble earlier at the bowling alley. Asked by defense attorney Geddes Martin if he had observed anyone attempting to incite the students at the bowling alley, Danielson said:

> *Well . . . I don't know whether you can say it*
> *was actually incite. I saw an individual who was known*
> *to me as Cleveland Sellers walking around, I never*
> *heard him say one word because there was a lot of*
> *noise . . . but he was talking to groups; and from*
> *my observations he talked to a small group of*
> *eight or ten and he would walk away, and as soon as he*
> *left they would start yelling and jeering and hollering*
> *and just raising cain . . ."*

Danielson testified that when the patrol opened fire on the students two nights later he was standing behind a boxcar across the street for protection because he "believed there were shots being fired" from the campus. On cross-examination, Quaintance asked Danielson if he saw patrolmen swinging batons at the students at the bowling alley. This exchange followed:

A: *I saw batons, yes, sir.*
Q: *Were they being used, swinging to move the*
   crowd?
A: *I saw, I believe they were used to probe them back,*
   and most of the students did leave.
Q: *I believe you told me that you saw some swinging,*
   is that correct?
A: *Well, I didn't finish. I did see most of them leave*
   and some of them refused to leave, and when the
   officers attempted to get them to leave they struggled,
   and at this time there was small scuffles.

Quaintance bore down on Danielson's testimony about believing there had been shots fired from the campus at the time the patrol fired and asked the agent if he had heard any shots after Patrolman Shealy was injured.

"I don't know," Danielson said. "I do not know. I know I heard small-arms fire, and I know I heard it during the time the highway patrolmen were moving up, but I just do not know whether the small-arms fire was in evidence as far as I can remember after Patrolman Shealy . . . was knocked down." Danielson acknowledged he knew when Shealy was injured and said, "I saw him go down."

Supporting their contention that the patrolmen were only returning fire from the students, defense attorneys put on seven more witnesses who testified they heard or "thought" they heard shooting from the campus—Orangeburg County Sheriff Robert F. Dukes, Deputy Sheriff Fox Hill, Patrol Captain Carl Fairey, Patrol Lieutenant Earl Bennett, television newsman George E. Terry, and SLED Lieutenants Carl B. Stokes and J. Leon Gasque.

In cross-examining Sheriff Dukes, Quaintance showed him a transcript of testimony he had given in the case to the grand jury and asked if he had not testified that no shots had come from the campus for four minutes prior to the patrol gunfire. "If that is what is on there, it is, yes, sir," Dukes acknowledged.

Quaintance also asked Lieutanant Bennett why he failed to mention the campus gunfire in a signed statement he had given to FBI agents eight days after the shooting. "Well," Bennett said, "there's quite a few things after something like that you don't think about, at least I didn't. Several things came to my mind since . . ."

Although Spell, Addy, and Bellamy had noted in their statements to the FBI that they might be called upon to testify to the contents of the statements in a court of law and that they would be willing to do so, the defense rested without putting any of the defendants on the stand.

And another major figure in the case—Cleveland Sellers—did not testify because neither side subpoenaed him. The overriding reason the government attorneys failed to call him was that they thought chances were good his attorney would have advised him to take the Fifth Amendment be-

cause of the state charges still pending against him in Orangeburg. Moreover, government attorneys were not sure he was
a credible witness. After interviewing him, they concluded—
rightly or wrongly—that he would be inclined to exaggerate
the size of the crowd of students and the number of objects
they were throwing in order to help the defense secure an
acquittal, thereby showing blacks that the nation's system of
courts did not work for black people.

The defense, on the other hand, failed to call Sellers
apparently because he could contradict some of the defense
testimony about his activities at Orangeburg. Defense attorneys had not interviewed Sellers and had no way of knowing
how the articulate SNCC organizer might testify.

In the government's opening argument to the jury,
Quaintance dramatically, but dispassionately, summarized
prosecution evidence and acknowledged that there might be
a question about the guilt of three defendants—Metts and
Taylor because they admitted firing only one round of buckshot, and Bellamy because he said he was not sure whether
he fired buckshot or the less deadly birdshot. Quaintance told
the jury:

> *Undisputed facts require verdicts of guilty at*
> *least as to the patrolmen who fired bullets or buckshot*
> *more than once into the crowd. Now that's Edward*
> *Moore, six bullets; Jesse Spell, two buckshot rounds;*
> *Henry Addy, two, possibly three buckshot rounds; Lanier,*
> *he said several, he didn't know how many; Allen Russell,*
> *two; John Brown, two. As to the other three defendants*
> *. . . your verdict must depend on what you believe*
> *as to the surrounding circumstances, and whether*
> *the shooting was justified under those circumstances . . .*

Quaintance argued that repeated shooting was an
offensive act, rather than a defensive one, and declared that

to acquit all the defendants "would be to say when the going gets rough, the enforcers of the law are permitted to act beyond the law; and that those who are sworn to uphold the law may disregard the law."

In an emotional opening for the defense, Coleman, the state assistant attorney general, declared that students were not to blame for what had happened at Orangeburg, that the trouble had been caused "by a professional agitator . . . whose only purpose . . . was to stir up trouble and get these students in a frenzy." He said the students who were shot were "victims of one Cleveland Sellers and the irresponsible burn, kill, power group that must some way, at some time, be stopped, or we will have anarchy in the United States." Coleman said the patrolmen fired as a last resort to prevent frenzied students from "getting out into the city of Orangeburg, burning, doing God knows what!"

Taylor also expounded on the "outside agitator" theme in a defense argument and called for a not-guilty verdict

> to show our disapproval of militants coming into
> South Carolina and inciting students . . . The same
> thing could happen at Clemson College, University of
> South Carolina . . . Citadel, anywhere else. We want to
> put a stop to it . . . taxpayers sending our students
> and children to school, we want them to learn, we
> want them to know right from wrong, want them to
> respect law and order. If you convict anybody in this
> case, how would you ever get a highway patrolman,
> deputy sheriff, city policeman or anybody to serve if the
> state didn't back them up? It's your duty to back up these
> men . . .

The nine defendants themselves were "the most important bit of evidence" in the case, Taylor said, and he asked them to stand and they did.

"Now, ladies and gentlemen, I do that because I want

you especially to look at them," said Taylor, pointing to the neatly dressed defendants, several smiling faintly, the others gazing without emotion. "In your own mind put yourself in church on Sunday, or in your bridge group, or in the club, any group you're connected with in your profession," Taylor continued. "In your own mind, picture—could you find nine nicer looking southern gentlemen?"

Taylor called the shooting "a sad event in the history of this state, something that shouldn't have happened," but added, "it's not any fault of the highway patrol. They did what any man with any firmness and courage would have done under similar circumstances."

During a brief closing argument, Quaintance said, "Policemen in this country and every country have a difficult job. They need more support from the public. But is it support to write a blank check in difficult circumstances?" Quaintance told the jurors he knew that the circumstances of the case and the fact that the defendants were police officers made it difficult for them to view the evidence dispassionately. But he pleaded for a verdict that "stands squarely and honestly with the hard facts of this case."

In his charge to the jury, Judge Martin said that the crux of the case boiled down to two essential elements—did the defendants believe they were in imminent danger when they opened fire and would a person of "ordinary prudence, firmness, and courage" have believed himself to be in imminent danger under similar circumstances? If the answer to both questions was affirmative, then the defense had made out a defense of self-defense, the judge said. A negative finding as to either question would negate the self-defense argument, he explained.

The jurors filed out of a side door of the courtroom, just to the rear of the jury box, and retired to a nearby room to deliberate. One hour and forty-two minutes later a bailiff led the jurors back into the courtroom. Judge Martin, looking over the small courtroom, which contained a dozen newsmen and about twice as many spectators, warned that "regardless of what the verdict is, there will be no demonstrations in this courtroom, or outside . . . you can go home and cry or celebrate, either way you want, but not here. Keep your seats after the verdict is announced until I get the jury out of here." The clerk read the same verdict for each defendant: "Not guilty."

13 : EPILOGUE

IN THE jury room only the two Negro jurors had questioned whether the patrolmen fired in self-defense. There had been no question in the minds of the ten white jurors. In the words of James T. Hollar of Columbia, a hair stylist, they thought "it was clearly a case of self-defense . . . most of the patrolmen thought Shealy had been shot and really felt in danger." Hollar explained in an interview, "It was just too evident that the men's lives were in danger with so many students approaching and they thought they had been fired on."

It had not taken long to convince the two Negro jurors. "They seemed to understand when we explained," said Hollar. "At first they didn't believe the patrolmen should have used the method they did, but it was a dangerous situation, we all thought, and something had to be done."

The jurors had briefly discussed the possibility that tear

gas could have been used, but remembered Strom's testimony about the wind blowing in the wrong direction. "We concluded it would have done more harm than good," Hollar said. The jury had reached its decision in less than half an hour, but Hollar said the court "asked us to stay in longer, rather than walk out so quickly."

No one had really expected a guilty verdict—not even the prosecutors. So why had the Justice Department brought charges, especially after the grand jury failed to indict the patrolmen?

The probability of getting a conviction was not a determining factor in the mind of Attorney General Ramsey Clark. He knew chances of a conviction were remote. After the patrolmen had been acquitted, he told the authors of this book:

> I think we should not be affected by what may be the probabilities of conviction arising from local attitudes or emotions at the moment. If you let those things control enforcement policies, you would never have a government of law because every time the situation would be really critical the government would do nothing. The very law we're talking about presupposes a set of circumstances in which local law enforcement is corrupted or paralyzed or so emotionally involved that it cannot act. This is a time when it is imperative that the government act and the federal government has an obligation to go ahead. What it means when you prosecute and there is an acquittal is subject to various interpretations. Some would say it shows what the truth is and the defendants were innocent. From a law enforcement standpoint, I would say that it would have a sobering, stabilizing effect on law enforcement. Law enforcement would be careful because you don't invite prosecutions against yourself. At the very best it's unpleasant and time-consuming and presents some hazard, too.

In arguing the case to the jury, the defense had said that perhaps the trial was a good thing for the patrolmen, so their names could be cleared. And in some respects each of them was as much a scapegoat as Cleveland Sellers, for they were not responsible for loading their shotguns with deadly buckshot, nor were they primarily responsible for some of the other mistakes, such as inadequate training (Colonel Thompson had testified that in riot training there had been no emphasis on indiscriminate firing into a crowd), the apparent lack of a tactical plan, and the failure of any police official to have command of the situation.

Clark and other Justice Department officials involved in the Orangeburg case viewed it as a classic example of excessive police force used by ill-prepared and undisciplined officers who were without adequate leadership and who panicked when the going got rough. The Attorney General said:

> The men were conditioned in entirely the wrong way and they could not have been more poorly equipped to contain and handle a confrontation they had been aware of for days and working on for days. You know just the idea that you've got shotguns with double-ought buckshot for a confrontation situation like that is horrible. It's an instrument that you should never use in a situation like that.
>
> Law enforcement hasn't had a long experience in riot control and shotguns haven't been used much in riot control. The basic purpose of a shotgun is close-range defense against someone who is armed. You don't have to take quite as careful aim and you shoot quick and knock some guy out if he's assulting you with a pistol or if there are two or three guys. But to use double-ought buckshot—it's a killer shot, you use it when you're trying to kill somebody. To think that law enforcement had to try to kill somebody to contain those students is to think wrongly. That cannot be true.
>
> The contrast that I always come to concerns what hap-

pened when riots broke out at Ole Miss when James Meredith was admitted, compared to what happened at South Carolina State. At Ole Miss we had deputy United States marshals, prison guards, border patrolmen, and a handful of lawyers come into a town that they didn't know—with very few exceptions—and a state they really didn't know, an environment that was intensely hostile to their presence, many coming in at dusk or evening when you couldn't even see where you were or get a general feel for where you were and many not even ever having an opportunity to get the feel because they were taken from an airport by car or truck through a town that they had not seen. They couldn't even case the place to see what it was. The deputy marshals were not trained; the prison guards were not trained; the border patrolmen had no really relevant training, although they had higher level of general enforcement training. But these officers had never worked together; they had never been coordinated together. They were confronted with an extremely hostile crowd that was throwing and firing at them and there are chips all over the front of the Administration Building to this day where that was going on. They were older men, not enforcement men, from all over the country. They didn't even know each other.

There was a crowd that must have been over a thousand and there were two people known to them to be dead [a French newsman shot from behind at close range and a local jukebox repairman who was killed by a stray bullet as he watched the confrontation]. And the officers were under siege, a real siege, no other way to describe it. And not one of them ever drew or fired a gun as far as we know to this day. There were three or four instances when permission was asked. I was handling the Department post and Burke Marshall and Bob Kennedy were at the White House. Nick Katzenbach was primary communicator. We had an open line and we were talking all the time and there were several occasions when they asked me, "Can we draw guns?" and I would pick up the other phone and ask Burke and he would ask Bob and we never gave them the authority.

Now they weren't really disciplined, professional law enforcement people, but they were under strict orders not to fire without permission. And it shows how easy it is to contain a crowd like that. Now the officers used a lot of gas, a tremendous amount of gas, but they didn't even draw their guns. Of course, they didn't have shotguns. Now at Orangeburg you had professional people that lived in law enforcement, that were involved in making arrests and pursuing felons, that worked with each other constantly over a period of years, and that were in a general environment that overwhelmingly supported them—I mean they weren't in a foreign land that they didn't know late at night where you could be frightened. They had been there for several days. They'd watched the students. They had every opportunity to be prepared to handle any situation with minimum force—gas or whatever might be indicated. And under those circumstances, look what happened. The cases of Ole Miss and Orangeburg are irreconcilable. It just shows two entirely different purposes. One was to use force and the other was to accomplish your mission with minimum force.

Once the Justice Department's investigation at Orangeburg was completed, Clark never seriously questioned whether the government was obligated to prosecute. But he viewed the Orangeburg incident as a case that went far beyond the specific legal question of whether excessive force had been used. He stated:

In a generalized sense, the fault at Orangeburg was the fault of the nation and the people—our failure to right grievous wrongs, permitting conditions to arise and continue where tens of thousands of black Americans were deprived of constitutional and statutory rights—and really their opportunity for personal fulfillment in our society. In a specific sense, the shooting was a failure of discipline and professionalism in law enforcement and leadership attitudes. I think people in charge of law enforcement contingents that are working in these highly volatile areas must recognize their responsibility to realize that the men will be under a lot of pressure and the risks of their shooting people are real and present.

The federal government's handling of the Orangeburg crisis—before and after the shooting—reflected serious deficiencies that long have existed in its civil-rights enforcement program. For one thing, the FBI has never been as committed to civil-rights investigations as to other types of criminal investigations. Moreover, there is an inherent weakness in a situation where agents are charged with the responsibility of investigating officers with whom they have long been associated in other cases. Although agents have often worked closely with the Justice Department's civil rights division, Orangeburg was an example of cases where aspects of the FBI's performance were little short of disgraceful. Such cases are difficult to document and persons who know of them are reluctant to incur the ire of the FBI by speaking out publicly, but the facts are well known to attorneys of the civil rights division. After Stephen Pollak resigned as head of the division to enter private law practice, he said in an interview,

> *Sometimes you get fantastic performances out of the*
> *Bureau and sometimes you get bad performances and it has*
> *a lot to do with personnel and it has a lot to do with*
> *reaction of personnel to the particular kind of law violation.*
> *The toughest kind is the kind you had at Orangeburg. The*
> *FBI likes criminal cases that are clear-cut. It does not*
> *like civil-rights cases with their strong, conflicting emotions.*

Ever since Dr. Martin Luther King, Jr., initiated the nonviolent direct-action era of the civil-rights movement with a bus boycott in 1955, many civil-rights figures have viewed the FBI in the South as little more than an extension of the all-white state and local police apparatus. In fact, the local FBI offices invariably have been all-white, too.

The close working relationship between FBI agents and police, coupled with the attitudes of its long-time director, J. Edgar Hoover, has fortified that view despite the fact that FBI investigations and the presence of agents at demonstrations have had a deterrent effect against anti-Negro violence. Civil-rights figures, seeing that relationship in force, and hearing Hoover refer to Dr. King as "the most notorious liar in the country," as he once did, and talk of the movement as being infiltrated by communists, as he sometimes did, could hardly be expected to come to any other conclusion.

The FBI's image as a top law enforcement agency with rock-ribbed integrity has been so vividly implanted in the American mind, however, that many Negroes have been reluctant to see it in any other light. Dean Oscar Butler of South Carolina State College said, "I had a lot of respect for the FBI right up until the trial of the Orangeburg case. Then I could understand why there was a breach between the FBI and the civil rights division—those agents are caught up in socialization."

Civil-rights attorneys long have discussed the need for reforming the FBI's role in civil-rights enforcement. Some have suggested that perhaps the FBI should have a special civil-rights section so that agents working on such cases would not be working with state and local police on other matters. Others have suggested the establishment of a civil-rights investigative agency separate from the FBI, similar to the Narcotics Bureau.

By 1970, there was a growing feeling among many Americans that the FBI could stand more scrutiny, perhaps from Congress. Evidence of increasing use of wiretapping in areas beyond national security and organized crime, such as eavesdropping on civil-rights figures, created concern, especially among liberals. Some critics also questioned the extent of the FBI's collaboration with local police in violent crackdowns on militant Black Panthers, in which young blacks and sometimes police were killed. Under Hoover, the FBI had enjoyed virtual immunity from congressional scrutiny, however, and most critics despaired of reform of the FBI under his autocratic directorship.

Another deficiency in the government's civil-rights enforcement program underscored by the Orangeburg case was the critical shortage of manpower in the Justice Department's civil rights division.

Ramsey Clark, discussing the Justice Department's failure to initiate legal action against Harry Floyd's bowling alley until after the shooting, said:

> That's a matter of very great concern to me. Basically we felt that public accommodations could not be the highest priority in our civil-rights enforcement and we had a very, very limited enforcement capability because of manpower— just a fraction of what we needed. For example, we had created priorities in employment cases. In public accommodations we wanted to be as close as possible to the ones that were the most provocative, the ones most likely to cause an accumulation of problems. Part of the mission in law enforcement where you've only got capability to do, say, 5 percent of what you ought to be doing and maybe less than that is to prevent escalation of emotions and a sense of injustice. By hindsight we wished very much we had moved earlier in Orangeburg. After Orangeburg we established a policy of taking some initiative on public accommodations around black colleges as a matter of high priority.

In South Carolina after the trial, there remained no official acknowledgment that mistakes had been made. On the contrary, most white South Carolinians felt the jury verdict exonerated the state as well as the patrolmen.

Colonel Thompson said he planned no changes in riot-control tactics for the highway patrol. He said firearms are used by the police only as a last resort, "and if it's necessary to shoot at someone, you want to be able to stop them." However, General Robert McCready of the South Carolina National Guard, who commanded the Guardsmen at Orangeburg, said his men would use birdshot of the smallest kind if forced to fire into a mob, but would also have buckshot available. "We would like to think no one is going to be so wild as to keep coming when they're being fired on," he said.

When Governor McNair turned down a request for an interview for this book, he conceded mistakes were made at Orangeburg—something he had never acknowledged publicly. He commented that when law enforcement officers, "whose lives are placed at risk," make mistakes, there is a proper time and place for correcting them, but not publicly.

McNair shares the feeling of most politicians about the political importance of supporting law enforcement officers. He has commented privately that as a politician he would rather have the support of law enforcement officers than any other group. This helps explain the great reluctance of elected officials everywhere ever to criticize police misconduct. One of the dangerous implications of this political deference is that law enforcement practices generally reflect the will of the highest authority. Failure to correct mistakes thus sanctions them.

The promotion of the highway patrolmen was a source of consternation among South Carolina blacks. "Those that shot got promoted . . . I guess this is southern justice," Dean Butler remarked after the trial.

The use of buckshot had been suggested by FBI instructors who trained the patrolmen, according to Colonel Thompson. He added that no changes had been recommended by the FBI.

The authors wrote to FBI Director Hoover and asked what recommendations the FBI makes in training law officers in crowd control, specifically in regard to use of firearms, the type (size) of shotgun ammunition, when ammunition should be issued and weapons loaded, and what type of instructions should be issued to policemen—who should be responsible for making decisions to shoot firearms and what criteria should be used in making the decision. Hoover replied:

> The basic rule, when applying force, is to use only the minimum force necessary to effectively control the situation. The degree and order of the application of force must be decided by officials of the agency involved and should be part of its overall planning. All officers participating in a riot control situation should be aware of these degrees and should know when each is to be applied and by whose authority.
>
> The FBI does not make "recommendations" in connection with the implementation of these plans—such is the prerogative of the administrative officials of the agency whose personnel are being trained.

Hoover stated that at FBI-conducted police training schools on riot control, strong emphasis "is first placed on planning for their prevention." Such planning, however, apparently does not include special training on handling racial matters. A Civil Rights Commission interviewer, who asked Colonel Thompson about training of patrolmen in handling matters related to race, reported, "He appeared to be taken aback by the question."

Although the FBI manual discusses extensively the use of riot-control equipment, it nowhere mentions riot guns, short-barreled shotguns which by dictionary definition are "used to disperse rioters rather than to inflict serious injury or death." The failure to recommend how firearms should be used when force is required to control disorder results in no national standards whatever on this most crucial element.

The President's Commission on Civil Disorders (the Kerner Commission) in its comprehensive 1968 report recommended that chemical agents be used before the use of deadly weapons and that only seasoned commanders in the field make major decisions on use of force. At Orangeburg, individual patrolmen were issued buckshot and authorized to decide for themselves whether their lives were sufficiently threatened to shoot. Under former Governors Donald Russell and Ernest F. Hollings, who preceded Governor McNair in office, only Chief Strom was authorized to give a command to shoot in racial confrontations.

The FBI manual states that chemical agents "are the most effective and most humane means of achieving temporary neutralization of a mob with a minimum of personal injury." The Kerner Commission report points out that the United States Army relies heavily on the use of CS, a chemical agent for controlling riots: "The Army has found it to be both much more effective and safer than the more traditional tear gas, CN. The use of CS is prescribed in the standard military sequence of force prior to the employment of any lethal firearms."

The after-action report of the South Carolina National Guard on Orangeburg states, "The CS grenades as well as canisters were available in addition to the portable gas equipment. However, they were not utilized. We considered using gas against the campus mob on Thursday night, but were prevented from doing so by the fact that the wind was blowing against our positions and because at that stage the highway patrolmen did not have gas masks."

The report was written by General McCready, who was stationed more than a mile from the campus at a National Guard armory at the time of the shooting. In an interview, General McCready said he did not know highway patrolmen on the scene were equipped with gas masks until he later saw photographs showing the gas masks. He was unaware of the photograph introduced by Quaintance at the trial that showed smoke from the bonfire drifting in the direction of the campus before the shooting. The information in the National Guard report on tear gas came from Chief Strom and others on the scene, General McCready said.

He expressed concern in the report that live ammunition had not been issued the National Guardsmen, who had been instructed not to load or shoot without orders. He wrote, "I am not an advocate of a casual approach to the problem, but feel very strongly that we should reconsider our general approach to the use of live ammunition. I cannot reconcile a man being called on to put his life on the line—and that's what we are asking when we deal with these Communist-trained black power advocates—without a positive means of self-protection."

The failure of the state to hold an inquest was explained in part by Attorney General Daniel McLeod, who said he persuaded Governor McNair against it after the grand jury failed to indict the patrolmen. When interviewed, McLeod said, "I felt that having a coroner's inquest would be such a weak investigation into the thing that it would do nothing but present a basis for someone to say, 'This is a whitewash.' I didn't think it would be effective. I don't think it would have helped the situation one way or the other."

McLeod had agreed with the governor that the FBI should investigate because they were on the scene and because of their reputation as an investigative agency. The fallacy, McLeod said, was that there would be no FBI report unless charges were made. McNair called Ramsey Clark several times—once more than a month after the shooting—asking that the FBI report be issued. Clark, who felt that the governor was hoping the report would vindicate the state, told McNair consistently that such reports are never released. "There was something about this thing that it became almost a point of honor with the state," Clark said later. "It was as if the state itself was involved." He viewed McNair's public statements as "terribly unfortunate and for the large part unfounded in fact."

In February 1970 McNair demonstrated that he had learned something from the pain and tragedy of Orangeburg. He was called for the second time in less than a year to deal with a student uprising, this time at Voorhees College, a predominantly black institution owned and operated by the predominantly white Episcopal Church in South Carolina. Students were boycotting classes to protest the firing of professors they considered black-oriented, and the college asked McNair to send National Guardsmen in force to remove the students from the campus. School officials, remembering a display of guns the year before, expressed fear of violence.

This time, McNair refused to rely entirely on "official" sources as he had at Orangeburg. He called in two young black leaders who visited the college and reported little militancy or mood of violence among the boycotting students. McNair refrained from evicting boycotting students from the campus with force until after the college administration had formally closed the school and secured a court order requiring all persons to leave the campus. Then, he directed that announcements be made throughout the next day to inform all students they had to leave. When National Guardsmen finally were brought in, they cleared the campus with only two arrests. There were no injuries.

The change in approach was striking to Terrell Glenn,

the former United States attorney, who now represented the Voorhees administration. As U.S. attorney, he had found McNair inflexible and insensitive. After the 1970 confrontation at Voorhees, Glenn said, "I was impressed by his restraint and caution and personal control . . . if there was one word, it was restraint."

However, McNair showed three months later he had learned only a limited lesson from Orangeburg. Less than two weeks after the killing of four Kent State University students by National Guardsmen, hundreds of University of South Carolina students were routed with tear gas after a small group ransacked the ground floor of the administration building.* McNair imposed a 9 P.M. campus curfew.

But again he sent in highway patrolmen with shotguns loaded with killer buckshot. Again they were authorized to shoot individually if they believed their lives endangered. There was no shooting, but the same elements were present that brought tragedy at Orangeburg.

Despite the limited and sometimes distorted news accounts of what happened at Orangeburg, the case had a significant impact on black America. Ramsey Clark felt it

> had a tremendous impact on thousands of people—you can't read about college kids being wounded—three killed—on their campus by police using shotguns without having that indelibly impressed on your memory. And you wonder if this had been Clemson or Amherst or Princeton or some place like that, what the public reaction would have been. To hundreds of people who were directly and personally involved in the sense they were family members, or they were there at the time and know what happened, or they identify with the college, I would say this would be a dominant factor in their lives for several generations and through them a dominant factor in the lives and attitudes of hundreds of other people.

* See Appendix B for comparison of Orangeburg and Kent State.

Allard Allston III, assistant director of the South Carolina Council on Human Relations, who had been president of the first Afro-American group at Yale University in the mid-1960s, commented after the trial:

> Orangeburg made the black middle class in South Carolina question what had happened. There had been high expectations, but now they feel there have been no basic changes. There became an awareness that when the patrolmen fired indiscriminately, even "good Negroes" would be killed, and that the patrolmen fired with little fear of prosecution. There was the realization that whatever your credentials, anyone on the field that night would have been treated as "just another nigger."

The Reverend I. DeQuincey Newman, the veteran state NAACP field secretary, declared:

> The fact that such a thing could happen and did happen is an indication that despite all that might be considered progress in terms of interracial cooperation, beneath the surface South Carolina is just about in the same boat as Alabama and Mississippi. The perpetrators of the tragedy and those who have covered up for them have rendered a great disservice to sometimes heroic efforts that have been made in the area of race relations and interracial cooperation.

The Orangeburg case caused the wounded students to seriously question the American system of justice, although they generally retained a surprising dedication to the system.

Thomas Kennerly, who was given leave by his Army unit in Vietnam to testify at the trial, said that despite the acquittal of the patrolmen, "the trial served a purpose because it made people aware that this kind of thing still goes on—just out-and-out killing. It was a massacre. I would think most people thought this thing should have been done away with a long time ago." Kennerly said:

I discussed Orangeburg with my black brothers in Vietnam and they already knew about it. There's a lot of bitterness and in Vietnam you can definitely see the parallel with this thing happening in Orangeburg and our brothers getting shot and killed in Vietnam. It has an effect upon you. It had on me especially because I was exposed to it in Orangeburg and then going to Vietnam and seeing it all over again. The big question is, what am I doing here? What am I fighting for? These things just naturally come to mind and I can't seem to find the answers.

Another of the wounded students, Joe Lambright, the first Negro to enter the Marine Reserves, in Charleston, said,

Speaking for myself, after four years of college, I can't say I'm going to give up and say the democratic process won't work because if it doesn't where you going? Russia? There's nothing there. Africa? Like they say, "Go back home"? How? I was born here in the United States, my father and grandfather and great-grandfather, too.

You know I was out on bivouac with my Marine unit after the shooting and I had a talk with my company commander and he said, "I know you feel bitterness toward every white man you know." I said—for once I wasn't looking at the captain bars—I was thinking I was going to tell it like it is—and I said, "I do hate every white man there is because of what happened to me. I wasn't doing nothing; if I was out there throwing or shooting, what can I say, I have to suffer the consequences, but I'm out there and I got shot down for no reason at all."

And my company commander is from Alabama. Whenever I hear the word "Alabama" it makes my skin crawl because I figure that people from down there got it in their minds that black people are supposed to be subordinate, and ain't anything they can do, doesn't matter what achievement they make, they'll never be on a level where they can be considered a human being. But my company commander said,

"You shouldn't carry this bitterness in your heart because there are some people doing an injustice. I don't know what happened at Orangeburg, but I'm taking your word as to what you say happened." For some strange reason he changed my mind about pure bitterness because if I kept the bitterness, how could I function? I'm going to stay here in America. I'm going to be here.

APPENDIX A

FOLLOWING are the statements made by the nine defendant highway patrolmen to the FBI.

Lieutenant Spell's statement is printed in its entirety. Portions of other statements referring to activities before Thursday and after the shooting have been deleted. All of the statements were introduced as evidence at the trial. Some words and sentences were deleted by the court to conform with rules of evidence.

Lieutenant Jesse Alfred Spell was interviewed after being shown a rights and waiver form by Special Agent Ivan D. Lee, which form he executed. He furnished the following signed statement:

239

February 14, 1968
Orangeburg, S.C.

I, Jesse Alfred Spell, voluntarily furnish the following signed statement to Creton G. Samellas and Ivan D. Lee, who have identified themselves to me as Special Agents of the Federal Bureau of Investigation.

I realize I may be called upon to testify to the contents of this statement in a court of law and I am willing to do so.

I am a Lieutenant in the South Carolina Highway Patrol assigned to district #6, Charleston, S.C. I reside 1106 Smithfield Place, Hanahan, S.C.

On Tuesday evening at approximately 7:45 P.M., (2–6–68), I was notified that I should proceed to Orangeburg, S.C., with the other members of my riot squad and report to Captain Fairey. I arrived at the A&P shopping center, where the All Star Bowling Lanes is located, at approximately 9:30 P.M.

At the time of my arrival at the shopping center I noted that the area was almost clear of people and everything was quiet. I remained on duty with my squad at the shopping center until approximately 2:00 A.M. February 7, 1968.

After leaving the shopping center we went to the motel where we remained on standby until late Wednesday afternoon, February 7, 1968. I received instructions to take my squad to the Claflin College end of Highway 601 (College Street) to divert the traffic on Highway 601 from traveling past the Claflin and South Carolina State campuses as the group of students on the campus had littered the highway with rocks, bricks, pipes, sticks, bottles, and glass as the students were throwing the above objects at passing vehicles and endangering the lives of the occupants of these vehicles.

Just after we had placed our road block two automobiles, containing women and children, came from the direction of campus on Highway 601. Their cars had been hit by a barrage of the objects thrown by the group of individuals on the campus. Evidently the two cars came by the campus on U.S. Highway 601 prior to the police blocking that end of the road.

We were located near the intersection of Goff Street and U.S. Highway 601 and remained at this location for 15 to 20 minutes at which time the group of individuals on Claflin campus spotted us and started cursing us and using profane language. They also started throwing rocks, bricks and bottles at us. To avoid injury to the officers and damage to the automobiles, I had the men move back about 100 feet. The objects continued to be thrown at us so I ordered my squad to move back to the corner of Sifly Street and U.S. Highway 601. During the time we were being cursed and assaulted by thrown objects we did not say anything to the mob of people and ignored their remarks. Prior to moving from our first location a Pepsi Cola bottle hit the street between my feet. I also heard the noise of impact from other objects being thrown at my squad. After moving out of range of their thrown objects the group of individuals moved to the adjacent campus of South Carolina State College. My squad had no further contact with the group of individuals that evening.

At approximately 1:00 A.M., Thursday morning, February 8, 1968, we helped clean up the rocks, bricks, bottles, glass and sticks from U.S. Highway 601 in front of the campus. After clearing the highway we went to the motel where we remained on standby in case of further trouble.

My squad remained at the motel on Thursday until a few minutes after 8:00 P.M., at which time we received a radio call to report immediately to U.S. Highway 601 and Russell Street as a report had been received that a group of students were getting ready to march off the campus. Upon arrival I was told to take my squad to the corner of Watson and Russell Streets to block Watson Street in the event they attempted to leave the campus and march in our direction. It was feared that they would do considerable damage to property and possibly citizens.

Shortly after arriving at this location I heard the noise of small arms being fired from the direction of the campus. Subsequently I heard on our radio that two squads of South Carolina Highway Patrolmen, located across U.S. Highway 601 at a warehouse, were being fired at by small-arm weapons.

I heard someone give orders to the two squads to stay behind the warehouse for protection. During this period of time I looked down Watson Street, toward the campus, and observed a firebomb go off along the wall of the Livingston Warehouse and the building appeared to be burning. I left my post and ran a short distance down Russell Street to U.S. Highway 601 to inform the officers at that location of the fire and possibly call a fire truck. I then noticed the fire had gone out so I returned to my post. I continually observed individuals darting out on the highway and throwing objects at the police officers stationed across U.S. Highway 601 from the campus.

Subsequently the group started a bonfire on Watson Street near a point where Watson Street intersects U.S. Highway 601 and the entrance to the campus of South Carolina State College. As the fire grew larger the group commenced tearing down traffic control signs and placing them on the fire. I observed them tearing objects off the house, located next to the campus entrance, screen door, shutters and porch railings, placing these items on the fire. I observed some individuals come out of the house carrying furniture which they placed on the fire. I observed the members, tearing the porch railing from the house, take the posts and throw them back on the campus instead of placing them on the fire. I went to the intersection of U.S. Highway 601 and Russell Street and furnished this information to my superiors. Shortly after returning to my post, I received instructions to move my squad forward to the campus to protect the firemen who had been called to put out the fire and protect the house from further damage.

My squad arrived at the edge of the campus near the vacant house and took a position to protect the firemen. Just prior to arriving at our location the group of individuals started throwing rocks, bricks, bottles, sticks at us. I took my squad up the embankment as the group on campus, which was probably made up of 200 or more persons, retreated back into the campus area. I had to have my squad go to the top of the embankment to observe the mob and protect the fireman from the thrown objects. During this movement intermittent gun fire could be heard.

At this time one of my men was hit in the face and fell to the ground. I ran to where Patrolman Shealy was laying unconscious on the ground with blood all over his face. I told two of the men to take him to the rear and I ran back to a point in front of my squad. We stopped at this point near the corner of the vacant house and the entrance to the campus. The mob of individuals numbering approximately 200 at this time started moving toward us. I raised both my arms in the air and told them to stop and quit throwing objects at the police. They continued coming at us, throwing rocks, bricks, sticks and posts from the porch railing. Small-arms fire could be heard coming from the group. They were cursing and making threats verbally toward the officers. Someone, from the group, threw a firebomb at the back of the house on our right and set it on fire. At this time I realized the mob of people had to be stopped as they would not listen to the police and would injure and possibly kill some of the officers. The mob of people continued to assault us and small-arms firing could be heard. At this point I ordered my squad to fire their weapons to stop the mob. I personally fired two rounds of buckshot from the model 870 Remington 12-gauge pump shotgun I was carrying. I immediately ordered my squad to cease firing. The shooting was over within two or three seconds as the group of individuals had started to turn and retreat back into the campus. I am positive we could not have stopped the group if we had not fired our shotguns. I fired my gun in front of them and had no intention of killing any of the group as I fired low. I am positive that if we had raised our weapons to a level position we would have killed a large number of the group.

I had the two wounded Negro males removed to an ambulance and taken to the hospital. I instructed the men to return to the sidewalk to have protection of the embankment. Later I told the squad to cross U.S. Highway 601 and take cover behind the embankment between the highway and the railroad tracks.

At that time, and at the present, I am of the opinion that I would have had officers seriously injured and possibly killed if we hadn't stopped them. The group of individuals would not listen to instructions and was attempting to injure the police officers. I have read this eleven-page statement and it is true.

(signed) *Jesse Alfred Spell*
Lt., S.C. Highway Patrol

WITNESSED:

(signed) *Creton G. Samellas, Special Agent,*
FBI, Columbia, S.C., 2/15/68

(signed) *Ivan D. Lee, Special Agent,*
FBI, Columbia, S.C., 2/15/68."

STATEMENT BY HENRY MORRELL ADDY:

I . . . remained in my room on standby duty until 8:00 P.M. Thursday evening, 2/8/68. At this time I received a radio call that the students at South Carolina State College were moving off the campus armed with sticks. Our squad was instructed to report to Captain Fairey at the corner of Russell Street and U.S. Highway 601. I proceeded to this location with the rest of the squad. When we arrived we were assigned to take up a position at the intersection of Watson and Russell Streets. We walked to this position and our orders were to prevent the students from the campus from coming up Watson Street and spilling out over the rest of the city. This was done to prevent them from destroying the rest of the city and to protect the lives of the Orangeburg citizens. We held this position for about two hours.

While holding this position I heard sporadic small-arms fire coming from the direction of the S.C. State College campus. This continued off and on throughout the evening. At one point I heard about 6 shots fired in rapid succession. From this location I observed, during numerous intervals, individuals, one and two at a time, coming off the campus and out onto the highway. They remained on the highway for a few seconds and would then return to the campus. In my opinion their purpose for doing this was to scout the area and to determine how many policemen were in the area and to see what they were doing. They did this for about 30 minutes.

I could also hear hollering and shouting coming from an area on campus near U.S. Highway 601. When the hollering and shouting started a firebomb was thrown from the campus onto Watson Street, which immediately burned out. Another was thrown, and almost went out. Several individuals then came off the campus and poured out onto Watson Street. They fanned the fire to keep it going, and it began to blaze. Sporadic small-arms fire was continuing to come from the direction of the campus. As this fire burned, the people on campus began throwing boards, planks and anything else that would burn on the fire. The fire raged and the flames rose to about six feet. They were shouting and hollering all the time.

I could hear what sounded like boards being pulled from a house on the campus, located by Watson Street. They began piling larger objects on the fire. Boards were thrown from the campus area out onto Watson Street, and those individuals in the street would pile them on the fire. Some of the wood being thrown out on the street was thrown back on campus by those individuals in the street. I learned later that what they were throwing back on campus were posts from the porch railing coming from the house on campus. Those posts were about three feet long. I then saw them place a screen door and two window screens on this fire. They also tore down a stop sign located on Watson Street and I saw them throw this on the fire. They also crossed U.S. Highway 601, to get some other traffic signs to throw on the fire. I also saw them throw, what appeared to be, pieces of furniture coming from small tables and chairs, on the fire. The shooting continued and the fire blazed even more.

. . . Our purpose for moving up the street was to clear the street, and to protect the property in the house on campus, and see if anyone was inside the house, and to furnish protection for the fire department which had been dispatched from the Fire Station. We moved from our position on foot and headed in the direction of the fire. We were about 150 feet from the fire, being bombarded, before the fire engine arrived. About this time we were bombarded with rocks, bottles, bricks, and I continued to hear small-arms fire. This bombardment and shooting continued until we reached the fire. Most of the individuals moved from the street and returned to the campus near the house. But some remained out front and continued to hurl "missiles." We moved from Watson Street up the bank and onto the campus near the house. Larger objects were then hurled as we moved up onto the campus. I moved up the bank and took a position between the large tree and the edge of the house on the campus. As I reached the cover of this house, Patrolman Shealy, a member of our squad, who was directly in front of me, about four feet away, fell to the ground. As Patrolman Shealy fell to the ground a baluster was hurled and hit at his feet. After Shealy hit the ground a firebomb was hurled and hit the rear of the house, setting it on fire. During this time I continued to hear small-arms fire and didn't know whether Patrolman Shealy had been hit by this gunfire. I stopped to look at Shealy and saw that he was bleeding profusely about the face and observed him to be unconscious, and his entire body was jerking rapidly. I assumed he had been shot by gunfire in the face. I looked towards the crowd on the campus in front of me, and saw there were 250 to 300 individuals in this group. I saw them hurling balusters, iron pipe, pieces of brick and other objects at us. I heard [deleted] tell two men from our squad to take care of Shealy. I saw Shealy moved to the street. I stayed in my position and saw them still bombarding us with debris, and I continued to hear small-arms fire still coming from their direction. The mob appeared to be retreating while firing and hurling these objects, and they fell back about 200 feet towards the campus college buildings. I remained in my position. I saw them regroup, and saw them charge in our direction hurling balusters, bottles, bricks, rocks, and heard gunfire coming from the direction of this mob. As they continued their charge [deleted] who was about two feet to my left, as they got closer to our position told them to stop. They continued to charge towards us, hurling objects and firing, and [deleted] again shouted for them to stop. They didn't stop and continued to charge hurling these objects and firing. [deleted] then told the mob for the third time to stop and not come any closer. They still charged and continued to fire and throw these objects. [deleted] then gave the command now, which was the order to shoot. I was armed with a model 870 Remington 12-gauge pump shotgun, which was loaded with 16 pellet buckshot. I can't recall how many times I fired, but I think it was about twice. I fired low and at their feet and legs. When the firing began several of the individuals in this mob in front of our squad fell to the ground. As these individuals hit the ground [deleted] gave the order to cease fire. All the firing ceased and it only lasted for about two seconds. After the command to cease fire was given there was no further shooting by either side, and the students retreated back towards the campus buildings.

STATEMENT BY NORWOOD F. BELLAMY:

On Thursday evening, February 8, 1968, shortly after dark, our squad was assembled and proceeded to the intersection of U.S. Highway 601 and Russell Street. We were ordered to block off the road to prevent vehicle traffic from traveling past the two campuses on U.S. Highway 601. At this time I could hear the noise of small-arms fire coming from the direction of the campuses. The group on the campuses could be heard yelling and I observed them again throwing objects out on the highway.

I was assigned to take a position between our squad and the campus entrance to stop traffic coming from the direction of the campus. Sometime after we were at our location I observed that the mob on campus had started a bonfire on Watson Street, near the point where it intersects with U.S. Highway 601. I observed members of the group tear down traffic signs and place them on the fire. Throwing of objects onto the highway and sporadic small-arms fire continued. I saw a member of the group on campus throw a firebomb in the grass area between the railroad tracks and U.S. 601, starting a grass fire.

At approximately this time, a Negro male, driving an automobile with the wording "Jet Magazine" roughly printed on the car, came to our location from the direction of the campus. A short time later he was allowed to return to the campus of South Carolina State College. As he neared the entrance he honked his horn several times and cut his lights off and on several times. He was allowed to enter the campus without being bombarded with missiles. I also recall that one of the coaches, from one of the two schools, came to our post stating that he couldn't do a thing with the students and that they had gone wild. He is described as a light yellow complexion, 5'10" and weighing 180–185 lbs.

Members of the group tore down another traffic sign and placed it on the fire and carried objects from the house located on Watson Street next to the campus of South Carolina State College and placed them on the fire.

My squad moved down the street to where I was located indicating to me that we were moving down to the fire areas to protect the firemen and the fire truck while they put out the fire. We continued down U.S. Highway 601 and crossed Watson Street walking toward the campus. On our right I observed that another squad had come down Watson Street and went up the embankment near the house, adjacent to the campus.

I believe we had arrived at the bottom of the embankment, about half way between the entrance to the campus and the house located adjacent to the South Carolina State College campus, when I heard someone yell that an officer had been hurt. I looked to my right and observed an officer lying on the ground. I immediately ran to his location and observed his face was covered with blood and his gasping giving appearance of a man who was dying. Some officers carried him back to Watson Street and I returned to my place in our squad which was a position on the right side of the squad. I do not know if a squad was located to the left of our squad or not. Most of the time I was so busy watching for and dodging objects such as bricks, rocks and wooden sticks that I did not observe what was going on to either direction to the side or to the rear. During the time that the officer was down and injured the mob had moved back into the campus area and were gathered around the car labeled "Jet Magazine." At this time they started to advance in our direction. I would estimate that the group was approximately 200 or more members by now. I could hear them cursing us and yelling. They were carrying pieces of 2 $\times$ 4s approximately four feet long and balusters from a porch. They were throwing these items at us including rocks, bricks and other objects. A brick, thrown by a member of the group, hit the ground approximately three feet in front of me. I was yelling at them to stop and quit throwing at us. They continued marching in our direction. I observed the flash and noise of the shots coming from the group to the right front of my location.

At this time we opened fire on the group, shooting low to stop their assault on us. The firing by the patrolmen lasted less than five seconds, maybe three seconds. The mob either fell to the ground or turned to run back into the campus. The ones that fell jumped up and ran back into the campus. Shortly thereafter I observed some officers bring a Negro male down the embankment and place him in an ambulance.

I was carrying a model 870 Remington 12-gauge pump shotgun and fired two rounds. The first round I believe was birdshot load and the second round was either birdshot or buckshot. During their advance, and assaulting us, I yelled at them to stop and go back but they refused to listen. It is my opinion that only the force necessary to stop the mob was used. I am positive that with the number of shots fired we could have killed a large number of the group if we had this in mind.

STATEMENT BY JOHN WILLIAM BROWN:

At approximately 8:30 P.M., February 8, 1968, I met with other members of the S.C. Highway Patrol at the intersection of Highway 601 and Russell Street. My group or District 5 formed a line across Highway 601 for the purpose of preventing traffic from going into the area of the State College and Claflin College campuses. We remained in that position for approximately two hours during which time I observed bottles, rocks and other objects being thrown from the campus of State College onto College Street and were striking cars as they traveled down College Street. During this time I saw a Ford Falcon station wagon with its left rear side broken out, although I did not see any object strike this window. At approximately 10:00 P.M. or 10:15 P.M., I observed some Negroes build a bonfire on Watson Street feeding this fire with boards taken from a house located just off Watson Street near the vicinity of the State College entrance. At this time I also observed several Negroes tear down at least two highway department signs and throw them on the fire. During the entire two-hour period I could hear sporadic small-arms fire which sounded as though it were coming from the college campuses. All the while the Negroes were hollering and shouting obscenities at the patrolmen. Too, at this time I recall seeing a flaming object hurled across College Street in the direction of some buildings located on College Street. At that time I saw a group of Negroes in the vicinity of the fire; however, at that time I did not know the number of Negroes involved.

The next thing I recall was seeing the fire truck approach the bonfire, remain there a few seconds, and then leave the scene without extinguishing the fire. Almost immediately after the fire truck departed or at approximately 10:30 P.M., District 5 group proceeded down College Street toward the group of Negroes in the immediate vicinity of the fire. As we approached the fire near the State College entrance I heard someone shout, "A man has been hit." Just prior to that, I heard what I thought to be small-arms fire coming from the State College campus. I then observed 2 or 3 patrolmen carry the injured party to a waiting vehicle located either on Watson Street or College Street. Although I only got a glimpse of the injured person and could not state the extent of his injuries, it was my impression that he had been shot. By this time I had positioned myself behind an incline on the edge of State College campus on Watson Street. At about this time, the group of Negroes approached us at a rapid pace throwing wood, bricks, bottles and what appeared to be white wood posts. At this time I again heard what appeared to be shots coming from the group of Negroes and observed flashes of gunfire mingled in the group. In this regard, the flashes of gunfire appeared to be coming from one limited area located almost directly in front of me. At this time, the patrolmen and other police opened fire on the group of Negroes. To the best of my knowledge, District 5 group was armed with 4 shotguns, and each patrolman had his service revolver which is a .38-caliber weapon.

I was armed with a shotgun when the firing commenced and I fired this weapon twice at the group which now was located at approximately 25–50 feet away. I do not recall a command to fire being given and I fired when an object flew past me and I saw what appeared to be gunfire coming from the group of Negroes directly in front of me. At this time other persons, in all probability patrolmen, were firing. The firing lasted for approximately 4–5 seconds at which time I heard other patrolmen shouting, "Stop firing." At no time before or after the shooting did I hear a trumpet, bugle, whistle or anything of this nature. To my knowledge there was no pre-set signal to fire. When the patrolmen returned the fire, the Negro group fell to the ground. When the firing ceased the Negroes regained their feet and retreated back onto campus away from Watson Street. I do not recall seeing any of the Negro group left on the ground.

STATEMENT BY JOSEPH HOWARD LANIER, JR.:

On Thursday night, 2/8/68, I worked with the same riot squad, District 5. Starting somewhere around 8:00 P.M. and 9:00 P.M. we formed a roadblock at the same intersection of Highway 601 and Main Street. After being at this location for awhile, a Ford station wagon, either a Falcon or a Fairlane, came up to the roadblock on Highway 601 from the opposite direction. A white male and young boy were in this car, and it was noticed that the left rear window of the car was broken out. They said that as they passed by the entrance to S.C. State College, a bottle containing gasoline was thrown from the campus through the window but the bottle did not ignite. I observed that there was a broken bottle in the car, and there was the smell of gasoline in the car. This man, name unrecalled, made a full report of the incident to Chief Poston of the Orangeburg Police Department. Several other cars with white occupants also came up to the roadblock from the opposite direction on Highway 601, and these cars would have passed by the two campuses. It was noted that these cars had dents in the

side as if having been hit by some type of missile. Capt. Carl Fairey
of the Highway Patrol then dispatched other Highway Patrol cars
to seal off the other end of Highway 601 so that no cars would be
able to travel on 601 by the campuses.

Sometime around 10:00 P.M. on 2/8/68, I observed a fire on
Watson Street near the entrance to State College. At that time,
Sgt. McDonald instructed me to move up closer to determine what
was happening. I then moved to the entrance of East End Motors
used car lot, between Watson and College Streets. At this point, I
was between 100 and 150 yards from the location of the fire in the
middle of Watson Street. There were a lot of Negroes standing
around the fire, and they were coming down the hill from the
campus. I saw the Negroes feeding the fire. I saw them throw a
large screen door, a chair, a table, and several highway road
signs, onto the fire. I saw some students bringing some objects
from an old house, just off campus, and placing them on the fire.
I also saw several Negroes come from the campus and cross College Street and throw flaming objects at a warehouse by the railroad tracks.

. . . The Negroes also started a small fire in the grass by the
railroad track. There were possibly 150 to 200 students in the
vicinity of the fire and the campus. The students were shouting,
yelling, cursing, and saying, "Come on up here whitey." I then
went back to the roadblock and reported what I had observed to
Lt. Sullivan and Sgt. McDonald. By that time, a fire truck had
arrived at the scene of the fire, and my squad was ordered to proceed to the scene of the fire to protect the fire truck. By the time
my squad arrived at the scene, another squad of highway patrolmen
had already arrived at the fire, having come down Watson Street.
The other squad was on the other side of the fire on Watson
Street. My squad extended from the fire on Watson Street to the
intersection of the entrance to State College. I was at the extreme
left flank of my squad at the entrance to State College. It was about
that time that someone from the other squad yelled that one of
their men had been hurt. I did not see the patrolman from the other
squad get hurt. Both squads then moved up the hill onto the cam-

pus at the same time. The students began retreating back onto the campus. I moved up the hill a short distance onto the campus by a bush, and I have marked my location on a map which is attached to this statement, and I have initialed the map. At this time I heard what sounded like three shots coming in rapid succession from the direction of the students on the campus. The students then turned and began running towards the two squads of highway patrolmen. There were approximately 30 highway patrolmen in the two squads, and there were well over 100 screaming, yelling students who were coming at us. The students had large boards, bricks, and possibly other objects in their hands, and they began throwing these objects at the highway patrolmen. One brick landed right in front of me. I did not hear any command to fire or any whistle being blown. But shortly thereafter as the students advanced toward us, I heard gunfire from my right, apparently from the ranks of the highway patrolmen, and at that time I fired several times, exact number unknown at the oncoming students. I was firing double-ought buckshot. I do not know whether or not I hit any student. At the firing from the highway patrolmen, the students then hit the ground, and some highway patrolmen yelled for everyone to cease firing. The firing immediately ceased. I would estimate that the firing lasted only a few seconds. The students then got up off the ground and ran back in the direction of the campus. There were no more shots fired after the students got up and started running back towards the campus. I do not know which of the other highway patrolmen did any shooting. Everything happened so fast, it was over within a few seconds. We were then ordered off the hill to take up position across College Street on the railroad track. From there, I noticed some cars leaving the campus, and they were apparently taking some wounded students to the hospital. I did not recognize any of the students who were involved in the demonstration Thursday night. For the remainder of the night everything was quiet. I remained in my position on the railroad track until about 4:00 A.M. the following morning.

I would like to state that I fired at the students on the night of 2/8/68 only to protect myself and my fellow officers. There were only four men in my squad who were assigned shotguns. The other men in my squad were equipped with night sticks and side arms. Lt. Sullivan and Sgt. McDonald were equipped with carbines. I do not know what weapons the members of the other highway patrol squad had. It was a bad situation, and we were greatly outnumbered. I had heard what I thought were shots coming from the students, just prior to the time the students began their charge at the highway patrolmen, and the students were throwing bricks and other objects at us. I feel that had we not taken the action we did, that the students would have overrun us and there would have been a number of highway patrolmen either injured or killed.

I would like to say that Lt. Sullivan had previously instructed us not to fire unless the lives of ourselves or our fellow officers were endangered.

STATEMENT BY COLIE MERLE METTS:

On Thursday, I was on duty at Orangeburg, S.C. At approximately 8:30 P.M. I was stationed at the East End Motors Company, Orangeburg, with other officers from district 5. The officers in charge were Sgt. C. C. McDonald, and Lt. Sullivan. During the period from approximately 8:30 P.M. until 10:30 P.M. I observed a large group of Negro demonstrators on the campus of the S.C. State College. These demonstrators numbered approximately 150–200, and were located in the vicinity of the corner of Watson and State Streets. During this same period I observed these demonstrators build a bonfire in the middle of Watson Street near the corner of State Street. I also observed several demonstrators take a door from a private residence located on Watson Street next to the college campus and place this door on the bonfire. I watched these demonstrators take several other parts from this residence and place on the bonfire. A demonstrator also threw a bottle through the rear window of a white Ford Falcon station wagon. I stopped the driver of this station wagon and inspected the inside of his vehicle. When I inspected the inside of the vehicle I found the interior of the vehicle to be wet and it smelled of gasoline. During this same two hour period I could hear reports from small caliber weapons being fired from the vicinity of the demonstrators. Also during this same period, someone set the private residence on Watson Street next to the campus on fire.

When this residence started burning a fire truck and fire chief car drove past my duty station at East End Motors and proceeded down College Street to the fire at the residence on Watson Street and the bonfire. Shortly after the fire truck arrived at Watson Street someone called for help. Lt. Sullivan and Sgt. C. C. McDonald then led me and the other officers from District 5 down College Street to Watson Street and the immediate area of the bonfire. At the same time a squad of highway patrolmen, which I believe was District 6, proceeded down Watson Street and went up the embankment in front of the private residence next to the campus on Watson Street. When I arrived at the immediate area of the bonfire with the other officers of District 5, the demonstrators began throwing bricks, bottles, large pieces of wood and were shooting at me and the other officers. The shooting was coming from the area of the demonstrators and I could hear bullets singing as they passed near me. During this same time I saw something go into the private residence and observed the inside of the house flame up and then go out. At about the same time I observed Patrolman Shealy on the ground in front of the private residence and I started towards him to help him. As I was moving towards Patrolman Shealy, 4 other patrolmen picked up Shealy and I called for a police car and the four patrolmen placed Shealy in the police car. When Patrolman Shealy went down and was being carried away, someone hollered that Shealy had been shot and was badly hurt. At this time the crowd of demonstrators moved back a few feet and then started rushing at me and the other patrolmen. As the demonstrators were coming at us they were throwing debris and shooting, and I could again hear bullets singing as they passed me. Someone hollered for the demonstrators to halt, but they kept coming and a few seconds later the demonstrators were fired upon by the patrolmen. When the patrolmen began firing I was armed with my service revolver and a shotgun loaded with buckshot. I fired one shot from the shotgun into the onrushing demonstrators. Approximately 5 or 10 seconds after the patrolmen began returning the demonstrators' fire, someone yelled cease fire and the shooting stopped. I did not hear a command given to fire, but there was a lot of noise and a command could have been given which I did not hear. When I fired, I only fired one shot and I fired this shot after other patrolmen began shooting. When I fired, I fired because I felt that my life was in jeopardy. After the shooting the demonstrators ran back to the S.C. State College campus taking the wounded with them . . .

While at Orangeburg, at a conference sometime prior to the evening of 2/8/68, I was instructed along with the other patrolmen of District 5 not to get hurt and not to fire unless necessary to protect myself. These instructions came from either Sgt. C. C. McDonald or Lt. Sullivan.

STATEMENT BY EDWARD H. MOORE:

On February 8, 1968, between 8:00 P.M.–8:30 P.M., I assembled with the rest of my group of S.C. Highway Patrolmen at Russell Street and Highway 601. We formed a blockade across Highway 601 on College Street and remained in that position until approximately 10:30 or 10:43 P.M. Shortly after we arrived, or around 9:00 P.M. I observed a firebomb or Molotov cocktail being thrown from the area of the State College campus onto Watson Street. After this occurred, a group of Negroes stacked up boards on the street where the firebomb had ignited. After the fire was burning good, I observed some Negroes carry a door, possibly a screen door, from the area of a house located just off Watson Street approximately 50 yards from the State College campus entrance, and throw this too on the fire. I also observed a Negro take a burning board from the fire and throw it at a building which I believe was the depot located across the street from the college campus. At about this time I also saw some Negroes break down two traffic signs from the vicinity of the State College campus entrance and place these on the fire. I also heard some shouting coming from the vicinity of the fire and some objects were hurled or thrown in the direction of Russell Street and Highway 601 or toward where I was standing. Also, I observed a 1965 Pontiac pelted with objects coming from the campus grounds. During this same time, I heard what appeared to be gunfire coming from the vicinity of the college campuses. I could hear the bullets striking something, however, I do not know whether they struck the car or whether it hit a building.

At approximately 10:30 P.M. my group of patrolmen, including myself, proceeded down College Street followed by a firetruck which had arrived on the scene to extinguish the fire. Our orders were to protect the firemen. As we approached the area of the fire, the group of Negroes, now numbering approximately 150, moved back away from the fire to a position approximately 15 yards off Watson onto a grassy area located between the college entrance and the previously mentioned house. As we approached the fire, I heard what sounded to me like a shot following which I observed that a patrolman had been injured and was lying on the ground. Subsequently, patrolmen picked up the injured patrolman and carried him to a police cruiser located at the corner of Watson and College Streets.

At this time I observed that the patrolman's face was bloody. After the cruiser carrying the injured patrolman left the area, my group stationed itself around the College entrance and on Watson Street. Immediately after arriving at that position, the group of Negroes ran at us from an area located approximately 25 yards off Watson Street on the campus. During this charge by the Negroes, they were throwing bottles, boards and other objects toward the patrolmen. I was not struck with any object and to my knowledge no other patrolmen were struck at this time. During this advance by the Negroes I also again heard what appeared to be small-arms fire coming from the area of the Negro group. At this time the patrolmen who were armed with 4 shotguns, 1 carbine, caliber unknown, and their service revolvers, returned the fire. The above weapons apply only to my group. No command was given to fire so far as I know and I heard no trumpet, whistle or bugle. The firing was done, in my opinion, as a spontaneous reaction to the situation. I drew my service revolver which is a .38-caliber Colt police special which fired approximately 6 times in the direction of the mob. The firing continued for approximately 10 seconds and had ceased when an order to cease fire was given. It is noted that prior to the Negroes advancing on the patrolmen, I heard no order for them to stay where they were or for them to stop. This is not to say that such an order had not been given, but if it was given I did not hear it.

As soon as the patrolmen and other police opened fire, the group of Negroes fell to the ground and upon cessation of the firing, the group regained their feet and retreated away from Watson Street and back toward the center of the college campus. There were two Negroes left lying on the ground when the mob retreated and they were immediately picked up by patrolmen and carried to the Orangeburg Rescue Wagon located at intersection of College and Watson Streets.

STATEMENT BY ALLEN JEROME RUSSELL:

On Thursday, Patrolman C. J. Lawson and I patroled the Orangeburg area during the day and no incidents were observed. On Thursday night between 8:00 P.M. and 8:30 P.M., Lawson and I stopped at the intersection of Russell Street and Boulevard where we conversed with two highway patrolmen, whose names I do not know. We remained at this intersection about 1 1/2 or 2 hours. Off and on during this period, I heard shots which appeared to be coming from the direction of the State College campus. It was dark and I did not see any students on campus, but I know students were outside on campus as I could hear their voices. Lawson and I each had a shotgun which was issued to us by the highway patrol. The only instructions I was given was to protect life and property and enforce the law.

After remaining at the above intersection for 1 1/2 or 2 hours, I saw a fire in the middle of Watson Street, near the intersection of State Street and College Street, near the State College campus. I could see Negroes putting wood on the fire, and the fire kept getting larger. I saw some Negroes remove a traffic sign near the intersection and place this on the fire. A short time later, I saw a fire truck arrive at the scene of the fire. Lawson and I then walked over to the area of the fire. When we arrived, there were other highway patrolmen and possibly other officers in the vicinity of the fire.

I noticed a large number of students congregated on the hill, on the campus side, near the fire. Lawson and I went up the hill, near the top of some steps, to help move the students back on campus as they had begun to move down towards the fire. I have marked the spot on an attached map where Lawson and I went. Other officers also moved up the bank at this time, to help move the students back. The students began to move back up on campus as the officers approached them. The firemen were busy putting out the fire on Watson Street.

When the students began moving back, Lawson and I moved back down towards the fire. I would estimate that there were 250 to 300 students in the area. All of a sudden, the students started coming back down the bank towards the fire. Lawson and I then moved back up the bank to the point which I previously mentioned. I noticed that some of the students had large pieces of wood in their hands. The students began throwing the pieces of wood at the officers. One of the officers apparently was hit with a piece of wood as I saw him being helped into a police car.

I did not notice any students with guns in their hands. Shortly after the students began coming in the direction of the fire the second time, and when they began throwing some pieces of wood, I heard gun shots in the immediate area. I do not know whether the shots were being fired by the officers or students, or both, as everything seemed to happen so fast. I do not know if Lawson fired at the students. I was busy myself, and everything was breaking fast, and I did not actually observe any other officer fire at the students. But as Lawson and I began moving up the bank the second time, I had to dodge to keep from getting hit by the pieces of wood thrown by the students. After seeing the wood thrown by the students, and hearing some shots fired, I fired my shotgun two times in the direction of the students. I do not know whether or not I hit anyone when I fired. The shooting lasted only what seemed like a few seconds.

I do not know any of the students. I do not know of any other officers or students who fired weapons, however, I know that some shots were fired prior to the time I fired my shotgun twice. When the firing began, the students began running back up the hill towards the campus. Shortly after the shooting, I saw two students, who apparently had been wounded, being brought down the hill on stretchers and placed in an emergency vehicle for transportation to the hospital.

I would like to state that I only fired my weapon when it appeared to me that my life and the lives of my fellow officers were in danger.

STATEMENT BY SIDNEY C. TAYLOR:

I was on standby status at the Edisto Motel, Orangeburg, on Thursday, February 8. About 8:30–9:00 P.M. I received orders to report to the intersection of Watson and Russell Streets . . . I was with [deleted] the District 6 riot squad. I arrived at the intersection and with the squad took up position across Watson Street. At this time I could see a group of people on a lawn of the State College campus at the intersection of Watson and College Streets. Some of these people were piling wood in Watson Street, some of these people appeared to be ripping boards from a house which adjoins the campus and piling these in the street also. Soon, I saw a man, a Negro throw a bottle onto the pile, this bottle bounced off and was picked up by the Negro who went back into the crowd, which I could tell appeared to be Negro males. Another Negro then approached the pile of boards in the street, threw a bottle on the pile which broke and the boards started burning. I then saw Negro males taking furniture; I could see window screens from the house being thrown onto the fire. The Negroes also had taken bannisters from the house, the spokes were thrown on the State College campus, the rails were being thrown on the fire. During all this time I could hear what sounded like small-arms fire, probably .22-caliber coming from the State College campus. I also saw a Negro from the group go across the street from the fire and throw a bottle at a warehouse which broke and started a blaze which died down. I also saw Negroes take burning boards from the fire and throw them across the street into the grass, trying to start a fire.

. . . soon thereafter Lt. Pace of District 7 came to our group and told us a fire truck was being sent to put out the fire in the street. Pace told [deleted] to move the District 6 riot squad up so as to protect the fire truck. By this time it was about 10:30 P.M. I moved up the street with the squad and I took a position near the house adjoining the State College campus. As we arrived a group of Negroes on the lawn of the campus started throwing bricks, bottles, rocks, etc., also bannisters at us.

I could also hear shots from this group. Patrolman David Shealy who was slightly behind me to the left hit the ground and I heard a patrolman yell, "Shealy's been shot." I went back over to him and I rolled him over on his back. He was bleeding profusely around the mouth and nose. I yelled to get a car and then helped carry Shealy to a city police car which had pulled up nearby. The Negroes at this time had pulled further back up on the campus. I then went back to the bank area facing the lawn of the campus just to the left of some steps. I could see that the group of Negroes had reassembled and had started coming toward me and other patrolmen on the bank. Some of these Negroes were armed with bricks and bannisters. [deleted] went to the top of the bank and yelled to the Negroes to stop and not come any closer; he told them to stop three times and that if they didn't stop we would have to shoot. The Negroes kept coming. I also heard a small caliber weapon being fired from what seemed the rear of the group of Negroes. I yelled to [deleted] to get down behind the embankment and he stepped back, halfway down the embankment. At this time the Negroes were about 25 yards from us and were throwing things at us. Some of the patrolmen were shouting, "now?" "now?" and someone answered, "now!" At this point the highway patrolmen opened fire. I was armed with a 12-gauge riot gun and fired one round at the legs and feet of the group. I then heard someone yell, "hold your fire!" I repeated this myself two or three times. I also heard a whistle blow to my left. The shooting by the patrolmen lasted maybe 2 seconds. I could see the group of Negroes hit the ground when the firing started, after the firing ceased the group arose and ran back toward the campus. I could see two Negroes lying on the ground. They were carried down the hill by the highway patrol, placed in an ambulance and taken to the hospital.

APPENDIX B : ORANGEBURG to KENT STATE

Kent, Ohio

"Yesterday marked the second anniversary of the deaths of three Orangeburg students—shot by policemen," *The Gamecock*, the University of South Carolina's student newspaper, editorialized on Feb. 9, 1970.

"We know that nothing like that will ever happen to us because we are white, we are middle-class, we are cautious liberals and we are at the big university and not at State. But when one or 28 get shot in the night, can others, even though popular or safe at the time, be safe for long?"

Now it has happened at a predominantly white, middle-class university—Kent State University in Ohio. And the similarities between the two incidents are uncanny—except that Kent State already is a national *cause célèbre*. South Carolina State caused

by Jack Nelson in the *Los Angeles Times*, May 1970

little more than a ripple outside the black community and had been all but forgotten until the Kent State incident.

The real tragedy is that there were lessons to be learned from the Orangeburg incident: lessons in how not to exacerbate a situation of mounting student tension and frustration and in how not to handle student demonstrations. Ohio officials learned nothing from the South Carolina experience.

On Feb. 7, 1968, during a lull in student demonstrations and violence at South Carolina State, Gov. Robert E. McNair issued a tough statement, warning that outside agitators were stirring up the students and that "we have no intention of letting things get out of hand." The next day demonstrating students hurled rocks at state highway patrolmen and the patrolmen retaliated by firing indiscriminately into the crowd. Three students fell mortally wounded and 27 others were injured.

On May 3, 1970, during a lull in student demontrations and violence at Kent State, Gov. James Rhodes issued a tough statement, warning that outside agitators "worse than the Brown Shirts and the Communist element" were stirring up the students and that "we're going to employ every force of law that we have under our authority." The next day demonstrating students hurled rocks at national guardsmen and the guardsmen retaliated by firing indiscriminately into the crowd. Four students fell mortally wounded and 10 others were injured.

About 15 South Carolina highway patrolmen fired their weapons (shotguns, rifles and a pistol), most of them into the crowd but several into the air. Some of the students who were struck were spectators—one was hit while standing on a dormitory porch more than 400 feet away. All but two or three of the students were shot from the rear or side.

The first reports out of Orangeburg erroneously listed a patrolman as having been shot to death. The first reports out of Kent erroneously listed two guardsmen as having been shot to death.

The parallels don't end there—either in the way campus trouble mounted and exploded into violence and counterviolence or in the manner in which state officials reacted to the situations.

In both cases, tension and frustrations mounted for two days, erupting into violence initially in the towns outside the campuses. At Orangeburg, students smashed windows in downtown stores, protesting a bowling alley's racist policies. At Kent, students smashed windows in downtown stores, protesting the nation's war policies.

On the third day in both cases the governors issued hardline statements and the protesting students seemed further frustrated.

On the fourth day the Orangeburg students tried to let off steam by building a bonfire in front of the campus on a street blocked off by highway patrolmen. Firemen rushed in and extinguished the fire. The shooting occurred several minutes later.

On the fourth day the Kent students held a protest meeting on the campus commons. National guardsmen rushed in to break up the meeting. The shooting occurred several minutes later.

Both South Carolina State and Kent State students later said that at first they could not believe live ammunition was being fired at them. They felt that either blanks were being used or the shots were being fired overhead.

Unarmed students were fired upon without warning. In both cases there was strong evidence that no order to fire was given, that tension and confusion swept through the ranks of the armed forces and that when one of them fired, others opened up spontaneously.

In both instances a senior state official was on the scene and ostensibly in command—Chief J. P. Strom of the State Law Enforcement Division at Orangeburg and Asst. Adj. Gen. Robert Canterbury at Kent State—but neither had control of the situation. Both Strom and Canterbury defended their men's actions as necessary to protect their own lives and both said they were afraid their men would have been overrun by the students if they had not fired.

Both officials said they heard shots fired from the campuses away from the ranks of their men just before their forces opened fire. But most witnesses in both cases say all of the gunfire came from the direction of the lawmen.

South Carolina officials blamed the Orangeburg trouble on snipers and outside agitators. They never produced a sniper and there was overwhelming evidence that the patrolmen were not fired upon immediately before opening fire. (There was evidence that there had been firing on the Orangeburg campus earlier in the evening.) No patrolmen were struck by gunfire.

The only "outside agitator" the state produced was Cleveland Sellers, a black militant who was injured in the gunfire and who was later arrested on riot charges, although he has never been tried.

Ohio officials blamed the Kent State trouble on snipers and outside agitators. So far they have produced no snipers or any substantial evidence that there were any. No guardsmen were struck by gunfire. No "outside agitators" have been arrested—yet.

The U.S. Department of Justice, after a lengthy investigation and failure to get an indictment against nine South Carolina highway patrolmen, filed criminal informations against them in December, 1968, charging the patrolmen violated the students' civil rights.

A jury acquitted the patrolmen, but the trial raised many questions similar to those raised by the Kent State incident.

Why did the state, instead of encouraging a dialogue with students, respond with tough talk and a massive show of force? If officials found the situation so potentially explosive that they felt massive force was necessary, why did they wait until after the shootings to close the institutions?

Why were alternative methods of crowd control not used? At Kent State, guardsmen did use tear gas first (South Carolina patrolmen did not), but later explained they ran out. If so, why? If the guardsmen were worried about being outnumbered, as Gen. Canterbury indicated, why did he not call for reinforcements? He had several hundred other troops in the vicinity at the time.

Why were students given no warning before the gunfire? Why were lethal weapons and ammunition used when shotguns loaded with birdshot could have been used to wound, but not kill? (At Orangeburg most patrolmen who fired shotguns used heavy loads of buckshot.)

There were a few significant differences between the South Carolina State and Kent State incidents, too. For one thing, there was no hint of a racial angle at Kent—black students had disassociated themselves from the demonstrations.

The Orangeburg shooting occurred at night while the shooting at Kent occurred at noon under a bright sky. Most of the South Carolina highway patrolmen were veterans who had undergone riot control training with FBI assistance. Most of the Ohio guardsmen were young men who had little experience and who had undergone no riot control training. Most, like their commander, Gen. Canterbury, had had no combat experience.

At Orangeburg a group of about 150 students confronted an armed force of about the same number. At Kent State the confrontation involved several hundred students and about 50 guardsmen, although there were about 750 other guardsmen in the vicinity.

Another vital difference, of course, was that the Orangeburg victims were black. If they had been white, perhaps the nation would have learned something from "The Orangeburg Massacre."

INDEX

Abernathy, Reverend Ralph David, 146, 178
Abraham, Nathaniel, 73, 79–80
Addy, Henry Morrell, 78, 82, 84, 177, 184, 185, 194–97, 217, 218, 244–47
Allen, Samuel W., 22–23
Allston, Allard, III, 236
American Association of University Professors, 7, 108–9, 120, 182
American Bowling Congress, 21–22, 25, 28
American Civil Liberties Union, 142
American Friends Service Committee, 145
American Party, 10
Arrants, J. Clator, 123
Associated Press, xii, 99–100, 104

BACC Speaks, 12
Bankhead, Sarah, 13
Barnett, Ross, xiii
Bass, Jack, xii, xiii–xv
Bellamy, Norwood F., 56, 76, 84, 184, 185, 196, 217, 218, 247–49
Bennett, Earl, 217
Bennett, Joe L., 190
Bethea, A. W. Red, 16
Bibson, Louis, 134
Black, Hugo, 145–46
Black Awareness Coordinating Committee (BACC), 9, 12, 24, 28, 48, 62, 67, 72, 118–21, 142, 155
  primary aim of, 12–13
Black Power, 7, 11, 24, 63, 71, 139, 233
Black studies, 11
Blackwell, Gordon, 8, 66
Blatt, Sol, 151
Bledsoe, David, 64
Bogert, John, 135–37
Boller, Herman, Jr., 88
Bookhart, Johnny, 84
Braddy, Thompson, 86
Brown, H. Rap, 11, 13, 64, 106–8, 194, 196, 197, 210
Brown, John William, 76, 84, 90, 184, 185, 218, 249–51
Brownlee, Nelson, 134
Brunson, Mrs. Jenny, 58, 64
Bryant, Farris, 158

Burton, Bobby K., 44, 86, 127
Butler, Oscar, 21, 23–25, 27, 28, 35–37, 44, 48, 68, 73, 128–29, 172, 228, 230

Calhoun, John C., 3, 14
Campbell, George, 55, 65–66
Campbell, Dr. Roy C., 94, 97
Carmichael, Stokely, 11, 13, 55, 62, 64, 106–8, 139, 210
Carson, Ernest Raymond, 89
Carson, John, 93–94
Carson, Willie, 93, 94
Cauthen, John K., 7, 8, 66, 79
Cawley, Louise Kelly, 72, 90–91, 96
Center for Democratic Institutions, 143
Chambers v. Florida, 186
Charleston Evening Post, 193
Charlotte Observer, The, xii, 12, 110, 153, 154, 160
Chicago Daily News, 157
Civil Rights Act of 1964, 20–22, 26; 30, 31, 34, 41, 51–53, 116, 209
Civil Rights Commission, 178, 231
Claflin, Lee, 3
Clark, Ramsey, 101, 103, 110, 113, 164–71, 174, 176, 179–83, 200, 223–29, 234, 235
Clay, Cassius, 146
Clemson, Thomas, 3
Coggins, Arthur, 198–99
Coleman, J. C., 189, 191–92, 196–97, 203–5, 209, 219
Collegian, The, 181
Collins, Elizabeth, 190
Collins, Leroy, 21
Columbia Journalism Review, 104
Columbia Record, 54
Columbia State, 63–64, 106
Communism, 10, 107, 108, 233
Community Relations Service, 21–25, 65
Concerned Citizens' Conference, 173
Connally, John, 158
Cotton, 14–15
Crosby, Donald Wayne, 75, 196, 197
Curtis, Wayne, 48, 119–20, 155

Dabbs, James McBride, 14, 15
Daniel, Price, 158